The Humanist Ethics of Li Zehou

SUNY series, Translating China

Roger T. Ames and Paul J. D'Ambrosio, editors

The Humanist Ethics
of Li Zehou

LI ZEHOU

Edited and Translated by
ROBERT A. CARLEO III

Published by State University of New York Press, Albany

© 2023 State University of New York

All rights reserved

Printed in the United States of America

No part of this book may be used or reproduced in any manner whatsoever without written permission. No part of this book may be stored in a retrieval system or transmitted in any form or by any means including electronic, electrostatic, magnetic tape, mechanical, photocopying, recording, or otherwise without the prior permission in writing of the publisher.

For information, contact State University of New York Press, Albany, NY
www.sunypress.edu

Library of Congress Cataloging-in-Publication Data

Names: Li, Zehou, 1930– author. | Carleo, Robert A., III, editor, translator.
Title: The humanist ethics of Li Zehou / Li Zehou ; edited and translated
   by Robert A. Carleo III.
Description: Albany : State University of New York Press, 2023. | Series:
   SUNY series, Translating China | Includes bibliographical references and
   index.
Identifiers: LCCN 2022021047 | ISBN 9781438491431 (hardcover : alk. paper) |
   ISBN 9781438491455 (ebook)
Subjects: LCSH: Ethics. | Ethics—China. | Humanistic ethics. | Neo-Confucianism.
Classification: LCC BJ1012 .L489 2023 | DDC 170—dc23/eng/20221024
LC record available at https://lccn.loc.gov/2022021047

10 9 8 7 6 5 4 3 2 1

Contents

Acknowledgments	vii
Introduction: A Particular Sort of Rationalist Humanism *Robert A. Carleo III*	1
On Ethics	21
Further Comments on Ethics	59
History, Ethics, and Metaphysics	75
Appendix: A Response to Michael Sandel and Other Matters	119
Notes	221
Bibliography	249
Index	255

Acknowledgments

The work that follows draws from many sources, and two require special mention. An earlier version of the Appendix appeared as Li Zehou, "A Response to Michael Sandel and Other Matters," translated by Paul J. D'Ambrosio and Robert A. Carleo III, in *Philosophy East and West* 66, no. 4 (2016): 1068–1147, and a long passage on "The Deep Structures of Confucianism" is reproduced from Li Zehou, *The Origins of Chinese Thought: From Shamanism to Ritual Regulations and Humaneness*, translated by Robert A. Carleo III (Leiden: Brill, 2018), 215–20. I hope it is a credit to both *PEW* and Brill that those publications are given further life here.

This book would not have been possible without the tremendous encouragement and support of Deng Delong and Jenny Zhang over many years. Deng zong's passion for Professor Li's philosophy is of a rare caliber and has pushed many of us to become much better scholars of it. Exceptional gratitude is owed also to both academic editors of this book series, Roger T. Ames and Paul J. D'Ambrosio, for introducing me to Li Zehou's thought, for supporting this project, and for their myriad vital contributions to translating Li's philosophy more broadly. Jana S. Rošker deserves extra-special mention for her selfless assistance on this project. Perhaps most importantly, all these wonderful people—along with Andrew Lambert and Jia Jinhua too—have invaluably contributed to my understanding of Li's philosophy, through both many conversations and their insightful, prolific scholarship. Finally, this translation was above all else motivated and enriched by Professor Li's generous, devoted personal guidance. Li laoshi, your extraordinary energy, warmth, magnanimity, humor, and patience will be missed. Thank you for sharing your prodigious intellect with us.

R. A. Carleo III, translator

Introduction

A Particular Sort of Rationalist Humanism

ROBERT A. CARLEO III

The works collected and translated here culminate a prodigious effort—the effort with which Li Zehou met our third millennium. In them, and especially in the concluding essay on "History, Ethics, and Metaphysics," Li gives the final word on his "ethics." This ethics, as I understand it, is an ultimately humanist project: Li affirms actual living humans to be the fundamental source of morality and insists we take into account the specific, empirical conditions of human life in deciding what principles to live by. So rather than a didactic or exhortatory argument promoting humanist ideals or principles, Li argues for a comprehensive view of morality that is humanist in its structure and orientation.

Below I draw in broad strokes some basic elements of these ideas as put forth in the writings that follow. Many were first elaborated in the foundational essays of Li's *Ethics*, originally published 1999–2004. The dedication he thereafter poured into elaborating these views and their implications shows how dear they were to his heart, as well as the urgent philosophical and social import he assigned to them. Those original statements of Li's moral philosophy were collected alongside subsequent explication as his *Ethics* (*Lunlixue gangyao*) in 2010,[1] which became part of Li's larger *Outline of a Philosophy* (*Zhexue gangyao*), published the following year.[2] Therein, Li prioritized *Ethics* in presenting his overall philosophy, placing it first in *Outline*'s tripartite organization of Ethics,

1

2 | The Humanist Ethics of Li Zehou

Ontology, and Epistemology in both the original and later expanded editions.[3] That grander philosophy offers much beyond Li's moral theory, but is also deeply integrated with it. Even a basic understanding of Li's ethics intertwines with his broader views on human existence and understanding. But there and across much of his published work, Li's ethics takes pride of place. Most importantly, elaboration of these views, and especially their uniquely rationalist and humanist dimensions, poured forth in recent years through Li's ever-impressive industry.[4]

The texts in this volume were originally published 2014–2019 and culminate that prolific rush. As with the foundational essays on ethics, these recent works bear less on specific questions of ethical conduct (substantive rules for how we should or should not act) and more on how to understand and approach those questions in the first place. In them, Li pushes us to see that our vision of human values and morals, of ethical acts and moral principles, occurs through a lens of human psychology that is shaped by culture and history. Li guides us to critically examine that lens itself rather than just the moral landscape we see through it, and he induces us to adjust the lens to a more humanist tint.

Li Zehou spearheaded these later writings by elaborating his ethics as "A Response to Michael Sandel," included as the appendix to this volume. But there Sandel, a major contemporary moral philosopher, functions mostly to offer a thin comparative framework for re-presenting and contextualizing Li's own views, and less as a true object of criticism. Why Michael Sandel? For one thing, Li tells us below that addressing "questions like those Sandel puts forth" is the "true task of philosophy"—a task largely lost in the more specialized inquiry that dominates the academic discipline today (*Response* §1.2). This makes Sandel a model philosopher, and also one of the relatively few scholars who engage in the same kind of discussion as Li. It probably doesn't hurt either that Sandel has risen to astronomical heights of popularity in Mainland China, not simply academic but among the broader public—and so matches Li Zehou here as well.[5] But most important, I expect, is that like the main thrust of Li's *Response*, Sandel's work forms a robust and sustained attack on modern liberal philosophies of individualism and rationalism. Their outlooks and agendas overlap. So what is Li responding to, exactly?[6]

Li insists we shift our basic approach to ethical questions and bid farewell to the typically modern search for abstract principles by which to reliably, rightly guide moral choice. Sandel's works of public philosophy—his bestsellers *Justice: What's the Right Thing to Do?* and *What*

Money Can't Buy in particular—largely rehearse the familiar ways that modern philosophers have attempted to answer moral questions: Should we sacrifice the fat man to stop a trolley about to kill five people? Or is there a proscription from harming him that means the trolley should run its brutal, murderous course? Especially in *Justice*, Sandel uses this approach as a heuristic to examine the strengths and weaknesses of predominant moral philosophies, and in doing so he illustrates that none of the familiar lines of philosophical reasoning seem broadly successful. This dramatically, if unintentionally, illustrates part of Li's main point: that sort of purely rational, abstract, universalizing approach to moral reasoning fails us. We need to move beyond asking simply what principles—deontological or utilitarian—better guide our choices and which better align with moral intuition. Sandel gives us a bunch of ethical lenses to try out. Li wants us to consider where the lenses come from and why.

This is one important reason to have centered his discussion on Sandel. Another is to more precisely frame his true targets of criticism and praise. Sandel offers arguments that, like "communitarians" generally, criticize liberalism while remaining to some extent philosophical bedfellows with it. Li intends to do the opposite. He affirms rather than rebukes liberal principles and liberal tradition: though hardly infallible, the tenets of liberalism are of tremendous value and should be broadly implemented, affirmed, and prioritized. But he wants to graft these onto a new philosophical foundation, one based in concrete human life, its situated history, and its emotional relations. Here Li is often much closer to Sandel than he lets on.[7] Both fundamentally reject the individualist Kantian conception of the self. But Li wants us to turn our sights further, and perhaps even in a different direction, than Sandel—toward the classical Confucian outlook of an "emotional cosmology," "emotion as substance," and the integration of emotion and reason in Chinese virtue ethics. The contrast with Sandel's turn toward republican and Aristotelean conceptions of virtue, which remain relatively individualist and tend to oppose the passions to reason, helps more sharply distinguish and precisely delineate the finer points of Li's arguments.

Li's refined elaborations of these views in "On Ethics" and "Further Comments on Ethics" were published following a series of symposiums held in 2014 (the year *Response* was published) in which Li deployed the ideas of *Response* in the style of Sandel himself, as public philosophy. At open forums with students and professors in Shanghai, Li discussed Sandel's examples within the framework of his own philosophy.

4 | The Humanist Ethics of Li Zehou

His published comments, translated below, bring out Li's insights, concerns, and clarifications in reflecting on those discussions so as to better elucidate ideas central to his *Ethics*: the nature of moral psychology, the Confucian conception of the self, the distinctively Chinese tradition of virtue ethics, the pervasive but implicit influence of Xunzi's philosophy in Confucian tradition, the contemporary importance of classical Confucianism, the shortcomings of sociobiologist explanations of morality, and other themes broached in *Response*. Li is relatively systematic in these comments compared with the freer dialogic style of the rest of this volume, and in this more organized manner he develops select points of his ethics—those of particular importance and continuing relevance—in novel and illuminating ways.

The crown jewel of these short texts on ethics is "History, Ethics, and Metaphysics." In many ways it presents a distillation of the core points of *Response* and *Ethics*—their ultimate maturation and refinement. The dialogue—this time with an actual, real-life interlocutor, Liu Yuedi 劉 悅笛 (in *Response* Li poses the questions to himself)—is informal and loosely structured. It is itself the maturation of public, published discussion between Li and Liu that has been ongoing for years.[8] Here the ethical role of "emotion" so highly emphasized in *Response*, although still crucial, takes a backseat to Li's rationalism and concrete historicism. The dialogue centers on his argument that "metaphysics" and the "*a priori*" are constructions of human reason that arise historically through lived human culture. In elaborating this, Li brings forth new dimensions of his theory. For one, he adds emphasis on Mencius's "tremendous contribution" to his affirmation of traditional Chinese "emotional cosmology." Having long celebrated the thought of Xunzi, a main philosophical rival of Mencius, Li here "tops off" his philosophy by lauding core dimensions of Mencius's moral teachings. He also renounces the label "Marxist," which he has long given himself. For those familiar with Li's oeuvre, this is a dialogue of fireworks. It has depth, color, and excitement to boot.

The texts below thus have a particular chronology to them, and their interconnections trace the path and crescendo of Li Zehou's culminating work on ethics. The later texts give increasingly refined expression of the arguments of the former. They are also richly informed by the former and fully grasped only in light of them. At the conclusion of the final dialogue, Li expresses that he is content to leave it all at this: he has said what he has to say on the issues. We have here a tremendous finale.

As a testament to the fruitfulness and import of these ideas, Li's ethical philosophy is steadily receiving increased international attention among scholars of philosophy. The most recent scholarship on his thought bends more toward discussion of Li's ethics than previous Anglophone collections—consider the articles in Roger T. Ames and Jinhua Jia's edited volume on *Li Zehou and Confucian Philosophy* and in the recent special issue of *Asian Studies*.[9] The most recent monograph on Li Zehou, Jana S. Rošker's *Becoming Human: Li Zehou's Ethics* (Brill, 2020), devotes itself to his ethics.

For scholarly biography and overviews of the broader academic work on Prof. Li, readers will do well to look to (in no particular order) Roger Ames and Jinhua Jia's Introduction to *Li Zehou and Confucian Philosophy*, Jana Rošker's "Li Zehou and His Time" in *Following His Own Path: Li Zehou and Contemporary Chinese Philosophy* and "Li Zehou, His Life and Work" in *Becoming Human*, Andrew Lambert's Philosophical Introduction to *A History of Classical Chinese Thought*, my own introduction to Li's *The Origins of Chinese Thought*, and the entry on Li Zehou in the *Biographical Dictionary of the People's Republic of China*, among the other great resources available.[10]

Now to outline and briefly contextualize some defining components of Li's ethics. I will focus in particular on those he gave special attention in recent years and those that bear most importantly on the discussions collected here. Beginning with the unique bent of his rationalism, and sketching the moral psychology and the theory of the constitution of morality that support it, I go on to review how Li thereby affirms both the relativity and the absoluteness of moral norms, and then the humanism foundational to all of this.

Rationalism

Li is an ethical rationalist, but in a manner very different from the sort predominant today. Preeminent contemporary theorists like Derek Parfit, T. M. Scanlon, and Thomas Nagel offer rationalist accounts of morality that adjudicate moral questions through weighing "reasons," that is, through cognitive assessment of "reason-giving properties or facts" of the world.[11] Li sees morality as a matter of exercising reason in a different manner, one more traditionally Kantian.[12] For Kant and Li, the exercise of

6 | The Humanist Ethics of Li Zehou

moral reason is a matter of choosing which maxims to act on. Practical reason operates in the will choosing to act on maxims one sees as universally legislative, making *moral* acts exclusively and distinctively driven by reason. Li is in this way a proper rationalist in the manner of Kant: morality occurs exclusively in the acts of a universally legislative rational will, a will that sees itself acting on maxims valid for all.[13]

But Li also revises Kant's conception of reason with several unique twists. These revisions are part of the broader theory of moral psychology and the constitution of morality that Li brings up often in the essays in this volume. In his moral psychology, emotion and reason interrelate in various complex ways. The texts in this collection often mention the "three elements of morality"—ideas, emotions, and the will, or the cognitive, affective, and conative—which Li's ethics shares with traditional Chinese moral philosophy. Li emphasizes that the three are never fully separable from one another.

> I continue to happily follow the classical way of putting this, primarily in terms of the three elements of *zhi* 知, *qing* 情, and *yi* 意, associated with ideas, emotions, and the will, respectively. Each of these three, moreover, itself has conceptual, emotional, and willful aspects, and the three are also mutually interpenetrating. Knowledge consists primarily in ideas, aesthetics primarily in emotions, and morality primarily in the will. These consist in diverse connections, structures, modes, and schema that are formed by diverse neural pathways, networks, and signals, all of which operate in a variety of ways on a variety of levels. (*Further Comments*, Comment 6)

This integrated complex of thought, feeling, and action make up what Li refers to summarily as the "emotio-rational structure," emphasizing the integration of emotional with rational elements that constitute the human mind and moral psychology.

As far as I can tell, we can say that while emotion is one of the three elements of morality, reason is a matter of the other two. Li distinguishes the "content" of reason from the "form" and "force" of reason. The *form* and *force* of reason are conative, a matter of governing action through the will. How the will is exercised is determined by the *content* of reason, made up of ideas, especially ideas about good and bad. These tell reason how to direct the will. The thing is, under this view, reason itself is sufficient for morality, leaving one of the "three elements of morality" seemingly nonessential: Since morality just is when reason exercises control over the will, when the will is effectively directed by our ideas about good and bad, why then does Li include emotion as one of the elements of morality?

One reason is this: Emotions are part of morality in that morality involves rational governance of them. But also, among the more important ways in which the elements of moral psychology interrelate is that the rational elements shape emotions in a uniquely human way, so that the kind of naturalistic feelings and impulses that predominantly drive the amoral behavior of other animals become rationalized, so to speak, in humans. These moral emotions can then provide "ancillary" motivation for moral action, alongside the rational force of the will. (Note how this diverges from Kant, for whom the only *moral* emotion is reverence for the rational moral law.) In this view, then, reason primarily and directly drives moral action through the will, but it may also indirectly motivate moral action through shaping our emotions. In any case, we can say that since the moral human mind includes emotions, they make up one of the elements of morality—despite being nonessential to moral action.

Endorsing the complex integration of affect and reason also allows Li to make further powerful and prescient moves as a moral theorist, for example, in response to intuitionist challenges to rationalism. Intuitionists argue that moral truths cannot be rationally explained. Rather, they reveal themselves through intuited judgments: we just know that murder is wrong. We do not (and do not need to) reason to this conclusion; and we do not have to (and in fact cannot) give adequate reasons why. This challenge is prevalent in Confucian philosophy, both traditionally and today. The Neo-Confucian teachings of Lu Xiangshan 陸象山 (1139–1193) and Wang Yangming 王陽明 (1472–1529) argue for intuitive access to the good through each person's inherent capacity of moral conscience, challenging the influential doctrine of Zhu Xi 朱熹 that we should seek moral truth through "investigation of things" (*ge wu* 格物). A similar view is adopted also in the modern New Confucianism of Mou Zongsan 牟宗三 and others. The modern New Confucian views thrive in philosophy departments today, especially in Hong Kong and Taiwan, and their followers maintain substantively Neo-Confucian lines of argument in attempting to criticize Li on this and other fronts. Intuitionism has also recently risen to prominence in the field of moral psychology, led most of all by Jonathan Haidt's demonstrations of moral dumbfounding.[14] These experiments seem to show that

8 | The Humanist Ethics of Li Zehou

reason is not in fact the source of people's moral judgments: we rely on moral intuitions, which rational justifications generally chase—when we bother to come up with such justifications at all. If reason neither determines our moral views nor adequately explains them, as these theorists hold, then moral rationalism has little ground left to stand on.

In the psychology literature, a powerful response to this has gained increasing traction. It argues that our intuitions themselves are internalizations of rational norms. Terry Horgan and Mark Timmons's "morphological rationalism" accepts the intuitionist debunking of traditional psychological rationalism: our judgments most often do not result directly from moral reasoning. But it questions the assumption that moral intuitions in no way rely on moral reasoning or principles. Horgan and Timmons affirm "an important and perhaps ineliminable role for moral principles in people's moral judgments" in that rational principles become "morphologically embodied" in our cognition and thereby "operate automatically" as intuitions.[15] This is precisely the view on moral intuitions Li Zehou has given for several decades, sometimes in response to New Confucian intuitionist challengers—and which he gives again in the articles below. When we act on intuitions, Li tells us, we are in fact acting on rational maxims. It is just that they have been internalized in ways that shape our intuitive responses. This accords with common moral experience, and the psychologists show it may have serious scientific legs.

It also has important implications for moral philosophy. This offers a novel form of rationalism that works in tandem with intuitions as well as emotions in driving moral behavior. But while emotions and intuitions have these valuable moral functions, Li maintains that only reason—as the will acting on rational maxims—makes us moral. Thus Li also stands opposite other more radical advocacy of the moral importance of emotion, such as Michael Slote's sentimentalism, which argues for direct and constitutive roles of empathy in moral determination (and against viewing morality as a matter of reason—although Slote is mostly concerned with the weighing-reasons version of rationalism). Yet like Slote, Li draws us strongly toward a more inclusive and affective view of the human psychology that houses morality's maxim-based reason, one in which emotions, the will, and ideas interpermeate. Li himself states that this affirmation of "the complex relations of emotions and reason" intends to "avoid simply collapsing the source and motivation for ethics and morals into either reason or emotions" (*Response* §3.5). Li's description of moral psychology not only precedes a now increasingly important theory in psychology; it also furrows new ground between rationalist and anti-rationalist moral philosophy, doubling down on reason's centrality to morality while also drawing moral emotions and intuitions into the picture.

But the relatively robust role Li depicts of emotions and intuitions in moral psychology is not, after all, the only or even the most important way in which he incorporates emotion into morality. There is another, greater role for emotion, one that more fully demonstrates the depth to which he sees emotion and reason as interrelated and mutually constitutive: reason is ultimately based in emotion. While reason shapes and governs emotions within moral psychology, it also originates from and has its grounds in the sensible, concrete experience of human life. Since this life is made up of emotion—of felt experience shared among human beings—the broader interrelations of reason and emotion occur also on a second level.

The Basic Schema of Li's Ethics

Li diagrams the basic ways emotion relates to reason in a general schema of his ethical theory. Figure I.1 is a simplified early formulation of that schema, which he fittingly calls a diagram of four arrows.

At the middle of this diagram is a reciprocal relation between "ritual regulations" and reason. "Ritual regulations" refer mainly to the "external social norms" and "ethics" Li discusses much in the dialogues below, and the arrow from it to "reason" depicts what Li below calls the movement from external to internal and the movement from ethics to morality. It is also where "history enters metaphysics" and ideas generated through human culture are taken to be *a priori* in individual psychology. Li has explained:

> The second arrow moves from ritual to reason . . . as the transformation of external ethical norms, customs, order, institutions, and standards into concepts of right and wrong and good and evil within the individual. This involves rational, cognitive knowledge. In this process, religious leaders and philosophers often elevate reason from the empirical to the

Emotionality ⟶ Ritual Regulations ⇄ Reason ⟶ Emotion

Figure I.1.

10 | The Humanist Ethics of Li Zehou

> *a priori* and transcendent in the form of orders or principles from God, innate conscience, pure reason, the true nature of the cosmos, and so on. (*Response* §3.5)

This relation has primary emphasis in Li's philosophy, and readers will encounter it often in the texts collected here.

We should note the arrow in the opposite direction, as well, which indicates that the "reason" of individual humans also influences shared social norms: reason can and does tell us how to structure society and treat one another, and communicating and enacting our personal thinking publicly shapes our shared "external" ethics. This arrow is obviously important: it includes most of our moral and political theories, in that they take reason as our starting point in telling us how to live. This arrow is thus also obviously very well attended to, and Li wants to call our attention to the less recognized flow of determination in the opposite direction, from social conditions to how we reason. While celebrating the important role of our reason in guiding action and social institutions, the model pushes us to keep in mind the broader conditions from which those ideas, values, and principles arise and in which they function meaningfully and positively (or not).

To do this, Li emphasizes the rightward direction of movement not only in this middle relation from social norms to reasoning. He also dramatically widens its scope, adding "emotion" (*qing*) on either side. Because "emotion" has two different meanings on the two sides, the general schema translates it as emotionality on the left and emotions on the right. Li succinctly but summarily states the entire left to right movement in the schema as follows.

> I continually emphasize the importance of history and education throughout my work. Ritual regulations are produced through the historical lived existence of emotionality and instilled into individuals as reason (concepts of good and evil) through education, which allows the free will to govern emotions. (*Response* §3.5)

Actual, historically situated human life gives rise to the patterns and order of social life. The regulations of that order are then internalized in individual psychology as reason, and that reason governs emotions in the individual. So it all starts from "the historical living existence of emotionality." Li famously calls this, among other things, a theory of "emotion as substance" (*qing benti* 情本體).

But how exactly are we to understand "emotionality"?

> "Emotionality" (*qing* 情) here includes human emotions and desires, but is not limited to these. It refers more broadly to the circumstance (*qingjing* 情境) of the living existence of the entire community, which is interrelated with individual emotions and desires. (*Response* §3.5)

> "Emotionality" here refers to the circumstances and conditions of life for humans (both individuals and communities). It is situation and context (*qingjing* 情境) as well as emotions and desires (*qinggan* 情感, *qingyu* 情欲). Emotions and desires are inseparable from actual life situations, and these situations are likewise inseparable from the human emotions and desires present in them (primary among these being the desire for life itself). (*Response* §2.1)

Human life is historical and composed of living, breathing, acting, feeling humans. "Emotion" as "emotionality" refers to the relational fabric of this life, composed of sensible experience.

The felt experience of social life, of interaction with the environment and with one another, is the original substance in and through which the patterns, order, standards, and norms of human life arise. Those patterns and norms in turn constitute the source and grounds of knowledge, reason, and morality. This is an idea Li identifies in early Confucianism, often citing recently unearthed bamboo texts that tell us "rituals are generated from emotionality" and "the Way begins in emotionality." The communicable patterns and norms of actual, historical, situated human existence are internalized in individual psychology and shape the way we live, and at the far-right side of the model they govern how we feel. And of course, the ways we each individually live and feel partly constitute the collective relational fabric, and thus in more elaborate diagrams Li draws a light dotted line all the way back from emotion on the right side, as "individual emotions and desires," to emotionality on the left side, as shared sensible existence (*Response* §3.5; see the General Schema of Ethics in *Response* §2.2).

In this we also see that the model of four arrows emphasizes that emotion and reason are deeply social in their constitution.

12 | The Humanist Ethics of Li Zehou

> Individual psychology is thus formed through cultivation by social norms. When children learn language, they are really learning behavioral norms of social life, or the "rules of the game." This is why Wittgenstein rejects psychologism and individualism. In terms of ethics, this is my model of "four arrows." Both "emotionality" as interconnected emotional circumstance and the individual's personal experience of cultivated "emotions" have essentially social aspects. (*Response* §3.7)

Li also calls his theory one of "relationism" (*guanxi zhuyi* 關係主義), and here we see his "relationism" is closely integrated with conceiving of "emotion as substance." Li aims to draw our attention to the foundational importance of the actual felt experiences and interrelations of human lives and their shared forms of life.

Li in these ways emphasizes our situated sociality and emotions and places them in positions of fundamental importance. He does so without opposing this situatedness and emotionality to rational individualism—an opposition common in contemporary moral and political philosophy. In fact, rationalism and individualism both take a front seat in Li's ethics, while the ground on which he affirms their value is precisely the relational and emotional nature of human life. Reason serves this life. It drives morality and is our greatest tool for increasing human flourishing. The morality of modern individualism, moreover, provides "content" for reason that is especially conducive to the flourishing of that life. This is also one of the central arguments of Li's ethics: the affirmation of modern liberal individualism as a set of morals promoting collective human flourishing. The model of four arrows presents a framework for endorsing those morals that is quite different from the modern liberal theories through which they arose and continue to be debated. In Li's philosophy, we cannot ask which is more important: emotions and relations or reason and individuality. The model of four arrows, in its movement left to right, helps establish that reason and individuality are valuable precisely through the more fundamental importance of emotions and relations in constituting human life.

History, Ethics, and Humanism

Li endorses the core Kantian notion that we ought to treat "humans as ends." But he does so in a novel way, one that breaks from Kant on deep

Introduction | 13

levels. The principle of humans as ends does not constitute a universal and timeless moral law, but rather is merely a core premise of "modern social morals." These morals and their view of humans as ends are objectively good in modern society, but not necessarily beyond that. This is because moral principles are, Li argues, products of history. They become normatively valid within particular social conditions, and the conditions of our particular era validate the basic principles of liberal individualism. How is this, you ask? Their objective goodness is grounded in the fact that, given the circumstances of modern life, these modern moral principles serve human flourishing.

This leaves our morals with no further grounding beyond human life itself. And since human life is historical—lived in particular times and places, through particular cultures and technologies—shifts in the conditions of human life affect morality. Li writes, "Ethics is attendant on history" (*lunli congshuyu lishi* 倫理從屬於歷史).[16] Of course, ethics also shapes, creates, and constitutes history in turn. Our shared and particular ethical beliefs and practices form our ways of life and thinking. So history and ethics are mutually constitutive. They also shift together across place and time, from culture to culture.

Li in this way affirms moral relativity in the sense that ideas about right and wrong, the "ethical content" of reason, may be affirmed in certain times and cultures and conditions and not in others. No moral principle applies uniformly across all human conditions. "Even Kant's idea that people should be treated as ends in themselves cannot be affirmed as a universal law or ethical principle in some circumstances."[17] Li sometimes gives examples of exigent circumstances,[18] but the thrust of his ethics regards larger shifts in cultural institutions, technologies, material conditions, and most importantly, shared morals. We see this where he writes, "within a long-established slave society, the manner in which a slave lives as a means is in line with the historical conditions of that particular society's understanding of morality."[19] Now one may want to object: "On the surface of it this may be true, as far as it goes, but it does not go very far. That a bunch of people somewhere, somewhen, agreed that slavery, or murder, or torturing babies is okay does nothing to show that these things were in fact okay. Such a society's understanding of morality could have been—and from the standpoint of modern morals certainly was—simply wrong." Li has something more in mind, however: "Compared with tribal warfare in primitive societies, where enemies were simply killed, the ancient use of slaves was less cruel. This was a major historical advancement, and in this way can be seen as just" (*Response*

14 | The Humanist Ethics of Li Zehou

§2.1). Li sees humanity as historical, and reason and morality serve the advancement of that history. Would it have been better if there was never any slavery? Yes. But history is a process by which actual humans under difficult and often tragic conditions have together developed and deployed their capacities to improve their lot. Those conditions have varied dramatically across time and place, and therein ethics and morality have played important roles in navigating as well as reshaping the conditions of human life. Since this and only this provides the context in which moral norms are meaningful, we should move away from seeing standards of good and bad or right and wrong as uniformly applicable across different cultures and eras, or even across different situations within a single culture and era. We understand and evaluate them better with an eye to historical circumstance.

As we see from the passages above (and in the works that follow), human reason has developed to address matters of situated human life, and the advancement of morality is a main component of our attempts to remedy problems and overcome concrete challenges. Despite occasional failures, the overall thrust of reason and morality is toward improving human life. It is fitting, then, that the broad trend of historical change in our morals has been one of progress—of life getting better.

> The ruins of ancient Rome show areas where people battled and were often eaten by animals. At first the masses found great pleasure in watching the mauling of early Christians. Later, when Christianity became the state religion, the same stands were filled with cheering Christians who supposedly held a doctrine of love. Would this be possible today? (*Response* §3.9)

It is here that Li's relativism most fully kicks in, and also where it gives way:

> Ideas of good and bad differ across times, cultures, and religions, and these changes possess historical particularity and cultural relativity. However, through the long processes of history, the various cultures, religions, and societies of humankind also gradually accumulate universal and absolute ethical ideas from within these relative and particular concepts of good and bad. For example, we have progressed away from murder and exile of the elderly in primeval tribes and away from murder of cap-

Introduction | 15

tives, women, and children in war. Female infants are no longer drowned and female feet no longer bound. This shows that not only does internal will possess absoluteness, but external ethics also accumulate absoluteness. (*Further Comments*, Comment 5)

There has been scientific advancement and improvement in the material conditions of human life. And there has also been progress in the content of moral reason, the ideas of good and bad by which we navigate and structure our relations. These advances can be affirmed in so far as they overall serve to advance human wellbeing and flourishing.

Such progress is not linear. Sometimes there is digression, and sometimes advances in the overall human lot come at a regrettable cost. Li describes this in terms of an "antinomy between history and ethics," telling us, "Humans will get many things wrong. When we make these mistakes we gain experience and strive to correct things. This is precisely the pursuit of the 'Way of heaven' within history" (*History, Ethics, and Metaphysics*, "Philosophy with Humans"). As Li likes to say, "History proceeds in the midst of tragedy." (He deploys both these conceptions of antinomy and tragedy often below, sometimes together.) Or more dramatically, "History always takes evil as leverage, progressing on a winding path through filth and blood."[20] But overall we see overwhelming evidence that our collective wellbeing and happiness have advanced through the muss, distress, sorrows, and regrets of history.

Li mentions two forms of moral absoluteness, that internal to individual psychology and that of shared social ethics. I understand these to be matters of the two components of moral reason, the "formal force" of the will and the "content" of ideas of good and bad. The formal capacity of the will takes its content, ideas of good and evil, categorically. When the will deems something right, it deems it absolutely right, which gives it motivating force: deeming it absolutely necessary, the will acts on it. This accords with moral experience, and it gives an account that neatly distinguishes the motivational force of the rational will from emotions (even moral emotions) and desires. It also explains the special overriding force we attribute to moral judgments relative to other judgments of good and bad. The internal will possesses absoluteness in that ideas of right and wrong become absolute for the individuals who hold them.

Internal absoluteness is simply the nature of morality, or moral psychology. Thus Li says that terrorists also "possess morality." But their morality, so to speak, is mistaken. This is because their ideas about good

16 | The Humanist Ethics of Li Zehou

and bad are bad. Their notions of right and wrong are wrong. Li is a relativist, but not in the "anything goes" sense. In what follows, Li writes:

> The particular social and communal norms that individuals abide by in their various times (represented as the solid line from ritual regulations (*li* 禮) to rational principle (*li* 理) on the general table of my ethical theory) along with their divergence from and opposition to these norms (the table's dotted line running back from rational principle to ritual regulations) are what regulate the course of history. One cannot judge the past me by reference to the present me. . . . The problem is, within the broader recognition of such moral relativity is a type of "unrestricted moral relativism" that sees various incommensurable ethical norms as entirely equal in essence and value. This precludes evaluative distinction as to what is superior and inferior, better and worse, advanced and backward, and makes drawing such distinctions politically incorrect. It thereby also rejects the accumulative nature of history and its affirmation of historical progress, including that of morality and ethics. Such progress is especially clear when it comes to women. Whether or not women have a right to education or can work outside the home or freely marry or choose abortion are all examples. (*On Ethics*, Kant, Ethical Relativism, and Virtue Ethics)

Li derides "postmodernists" in particular for failing to see that ideas about right and wrong "possess absoluteness" in this external sense. Such anti-Enlightenment opponents fail to see that absoluteness is "accumulated" within and through the concrete conditions of relative morals.

So, relying on the existential value of morality to actual humans, Li affirms the absolute value of particular morals for particular circumstances. Insofar as shared morals contribute positively to the conditions of human life, we can affirm diverse and even mutually opposed morals when applied in different circumstances. Importantly, we can also reject certain morals for those circumstances, if they do not contribute to human flourishing. So even when certain morals become absolute for particular subjects or groups, that does not mean they are good. We can still ("absolutely") judge those morals to be wrong, misguided, bad, evil. Li's examples of genocide, suicide bombers, self-immolating activism, and traditions of foot-binding fit here. So even within his thorough affirmation of cultural relativity, morality is understood both as absolute for the individual and as having an objective external standard.

The theory of accumulated absoluteness affirms that uneven but cumulative historical improvements in the conditions of human life evidence progress toward greater flourishing. Historical shifts in people's moral values and standards, Li argues, are part and parcel of this improvement. This evidences moral progress. The modern social morals of Enlightenment humanism are objectively right because they support conditions of modern life in which human wellbeing thrives. We should uphold these morals and extend them to those realms of life where humanist values remain all too absent: "the modern social moral of 'humans as ends' is, in regard to the entirety of humankind, still far from fully realized" (*On Ethics*, Kant, Ethical Relativism, and Virtue Ethics). But this is not the end of history, and the values and principles of modern social morals are not the last word. Li insists on nuance and a pragmatic outlook: There are so many factors to navigate as technology and social change advance—bioengineering, artificial intelligence, big data, and surveillance—that it is uncertain how far the outlook of liberal individualism, and specifically its manner of conceiving and valuing our selfhood, will hold going forward (see *On Ethics*, The Self).

The value or end I call "flourishing" Li himself most often refers to as the "continuous extension of the living existence of the totality of humankind" (*renlei zongti de shengcun yanxu* 人類總體的生存延續). I find the extremely literal rendering of "continuous extension of living existence" most accurate—more accurate, anyway, than the more comfortable option of "survival," because this extension is much more than survival. It is historical and cultural expansion: the inheritance and development, enlargement and enrichment of human life in its social, cultural, and psychological dimensions rather than in a merely biological sense. It reflects Li's openness to change in the conditions of human life and values. There is not one aim or good to human life, because that good shifts with progressive changes in the conditions of human life. And this is part of the reason there can be no universal, eternal content to the categorical imperative. "According to my anthropological historical ontology, 'categorical imperatives' are based in the empirical living extension of the totality of humankind, and not in 'heavenly principle,' 'God,' or 'pure reason.'"[21] And Li's "totality of humankind" is not an abstract notion of "humanity": "What I call the 'totality of humankind' is inseparable from the specific ages, societies, and communal groups of particular times and places."[22] It

18 | The Humanist Ethics of Li Zehou

refers always to the concrete living existence of humankind as such, *in toto*. This precludes notions of organismic unity or holism common to other ethical visions, including other versions of Confucian humanism. One does not and cannot see oneself as holistically interconnected with this whole. Instead, Li explains, one sees individual members of this totality as "good" and to be valued in their contribution to—as components of—its "continuous extension."

Professor Li himself offered a model of the human flourishing his ethics promotes for all. Let me thank him here for all he accomplished, for his ideas and insights, and for the inimitable diligence and patience with which he shared with us those insights. Thank you, Professor Li, for your outsized contribution to our human totality. I end my comments here, and let Li speak for himself in the rest of this volume.

References

Ames, Roger T., and Jinhua Jia, eds. 2015. *Li Zehou and Confucian Philosophy*. Honolulu: University of Hawai'i Press.

Carleo, Robert A. III. 2016. Review of *Huiying Sangdeer ji qita*. *Philosophy East and West* 66 (3): 1027–29.

———. 2020. "Is Free Will Confucian? Li Zehou's Confucian Revision of the Kantian Will." *Philosophy East and West* 70 (1): 63–83.

Chong, Woei Lien. 1999. "History as the Realization of Beauty: Li Zehou's Aesthetic Marxism." *Contemporary Chinese Thought* 31 (2): 3–19.

D'Ambrosio, Paul J. 2016. "Approaches to Global Ethics: Michael Sandel's Justice and Li Zehou's Harmony." *Philosophy East and West* 66 (3): 720–38.

———. 2020. "Li Zehou's 'Harmony Is Higher Than Justice': Context and a Collaborative Future." *Asian Studies* 8 (1): 127–46.

Ding, John Zijiang. 2002. "Li Zehou: Chinese Aesthetics from a Post-Marxist and Confucian Perspective." In *Contemporary Chinese Philosophy*, ed. Chung-Ying Cheng and Nicholas Bunnin, 246–59. Malden, MA: Blackwell.

Haidt, Jonathan. 2001. "The Emotional Dog and Its Rational Tail: A Social Intuitionist Approach to Moral Judgment." *Psychological Review* 108: 814–34.

Horgan, Terry, and Mark Timmons. 2007. "Morphological Rationalism and the Psychology of Moral Judgment." *Ethical Theory and Moral Practice* 10: 279–95.

Li Zehou 李澤厚. 1994. *The Path of Beauty*. Trans. Gong Lizeng. Hong Kong: Oxford University Press,

———. 2006. *Four Essays on Aesthetics*. Trans. Zehou Li and Jane Cauvel. Lanham, MD: Lexington Books.

———. 2010a. *The Chinese Aesthetic Tradition*. Trans. Maija Bell Samei. Honolulu: University of Hawai'i Press.

———. 2010b. *Lunlixue gangyao* 倫理學綱要 (Ethics). Beijing: Renmin Ribao chubanshe.

———. 2011. *Zhexue gangyao* 哲學綱要 (Outline of a philosophy). Beijing: Peking University Press.

———. 2016. *Renleixue lishi bentilun* 人類學歷史本體論 (A theory of anthropo-historical ontology). Qingdao: Qingdao Publishing.

———. 2017. *Lunlixue gangyao xupian* 倫理學綱要續篇 (Further discussions of ethics). Beijing: SDX Joint Publishing.

———. 2018. *The Origins of Chinese Thought: From Shamanism to Ritual Regulations and Humaneness*. Trans. Robert A Carleo III. Leiden: Brill.

———. 2019a. *Renleixue lishi bentilun* 人類學歷史本體論 (The anthropo-historical ontology: An outline of my philosophy). Beijing: Renmin wenxue chubanshe.

———. 2019b. *Lunlixue xinshuo shuyao* 倫理學新說述要 (A new sketch of ethics). Beijing: World Publishing.

———. 2020. *A History of Classical Chinese Thought*. Trans. Andrew Lambert. New York: Routledge.

Li Zehou 李澤厚 and Liu Yuedi 劉悅笛. 2014a. "Cong 'qing benti' fansi zhengzhi zhexue" 從「情本體」反思政治哲學 (Reflecting on political philosophy from 'emotion as substance'). *Kaifang shidai* (4): 194–215.

———. 2014b. "'Qing benti' shi shijiede" 「情本體」是世界的 ('Emotion as substance' belongs to the world). *Tansuo yu zhengming* (4): 4–9.

———. 2014c. "Guanyu 'qing benti' de Zhongguo zhexue duihua lu" 關於「情本體」中國哲學對話錄 (Dialogue on Chinese philosophy's "emotion as substance"). *Wen shi zhe* (3): 18–29.

———. 2017. "Li Zehou, Liu Yuedi 2017 nian zhexue duitan lu" 李澤厚、劉悅笛2017年哲學對談錄 (Li Zehou and Liu Yuedi's 2017 philosophical dialogue). *Shehui kexuejia* (7): 39–48.

———. 2018. "Lunlixue zatan: Li Zehou, Liu Yuedi 2018 nian duitan lu" 倫理學雜談——李澤厚、劉悅笛2018年對談錄 (Thought rambling on ethics: A dialogue between Li Zehou and Liu Yuedi). *Hunan shifan daxue shehui kexue xuebao* (5): 1–17.

Parfit, Derek. 2002. "What We Could Rationally Will." The Tanner Lectures on Human Values. Available at tannerlectures.utah.edu/_documents/a-to-z/p/parfit_2002.pdf.

Rošker, Jana S. 2019. *Following His Own Path: Li Zehou and Contemporary Chinese Philosophy*. Albany: State University of New York Press.

———. 2020a. *Becoming Human: Li Zehou's Ethics*. Leiden: Brill.

———, ed. 2020b. *Ethics and the Beauty of Human Becoming—Special Issue Dedicated to Li Zehou on His 90th Birthday. Asian Studies* 8 (1).

20 | The Humanist Ethics of Li Zehou

Sandel, Michael J. 1998. *Liberalism and the Limits of Justice*, rev. ed. Cambridge: Cambridge University Press.

Scanlon, Thomas M. 2011. "How I Am Not a Kantian." In Derek Parfit, *On What Matters*, vol. 2, ed. Samuel Scheffler, 116–39. Oxford: Oxford University Press.

———. 2014. *Being Realistic about Reasons*. Oxford: Oxford University Press.

Song, Yuwu, ed. 2013. *Biographical Dictionary of the People's Republic of China*. London: McFarland & Company.

Wawrytko, Sandra A. 2013. "Sedimentation in Chinese Aesthetics and Epistemology: A Buddhist Expansion of Confucian Philosophy." *Journal of Chinese Philosophy* 40 (3/4): 473–92.

On Ethics

Science + Poetry

It is often said that the elderly love to repeat themselves, and it seems my essays may have come to acquire this characteristic. Many criticize me for continuing to say the same old thing. My defense is: First, some things benefit from being repeated. It reinforces their impact. And second, when viewed more closely, I might not be merely repeating myself. My work in recent years has put forth various ethical views covering a wide range of issues. Yet despite continuing to propose new ideas, I have so far hardly succeeded in fully communicating what I have to say. I feel this especially to be the case with the symposium discussions held at East China Normal University in 2014.[1] Nevertheless, sitting down to write today, I indeed feel again like I am retreading old ground. We'll just have to start from here and see where it goes.

I remember in the early '80s I described philosophy as science plus poetry. What I meant by that was that philosophy involves abstract, general speculation on contemporary reality and modern science along with more nebulous aspirations and emotional commitments oriented toward the future. To various extents and in diverse ways, past philosophies seem to integrate, mingle, and vacillate between the two. This is perhaps what Wang Guowei 王國維 identified as the problem of being believable (*kexin* 可信) and lovable (*keai* 可愛). Many philosophies are both unbelievable and unlovable. Very few are both believable and lovable. In the twentieth century, Heidegger and Wittgenstein pushed each to its extreme (philosophy as poetic thought and philosophy as correct linguistic expression, respectively). Following this, it is very unclear what direction philosophy will move toward. Epistemology ranges from analytic philosophy to philosophy of mind; ethical theories extend from meta-ethics to liberalism and communitarianism; and aesthetic philosophy reaches from the aesthetics of museums ("the art world" and "institutional theory") to the aesthetics of everyday life (*shenghuo meixue* 生活美學) and environmental aesthetics. Philosophy in some practices seems to be moving toward positivistic or empirical surface-level description while in other aspects it is turning into a highly specialized and abstruse use of language. Heidegger and Wittgenstein were already quite displeased with this trend toward intense specialization of discourse, yet they found themselves unable to avoid it. These days philosophical discussions may remain impassioned, dynamic, and popular among philosophers, but they have become inaccessible to the uninitiated. How many people are able—and willing—to read contemporary papers on philosophy of mind, phenomenology, or postmodernism?

In the preface to my work *Historical Ontology* (*Lishi bentilun* 歷史本體論),[2] I wrote that I do not want my own philosophy to have this characteristic. Regardless of particular content and form, I want to walk the path of a philosophy of common sense (*changshi zhexue* 常識哲學) and popular philosophy (*dazhong zhexue* 大眾哲學). I have done so over recent years, which may be related to my increasing intolerance for Heidegger. The ideas I have put forward—"sedimentation," "the fundamentality of proper measure," "historicism," "the emotio-rational structure," and so on—are all common to daily language. For example, I propose "the emotio-rational structure," yet I have not expounded on the exact nature of this structure and the precise relations among emotion, reason, and desire therein. In fact, I cannot do so. If one were to insist on borrowing Aristotle's "theory of four causes," we could call reason a formal cause, emotion and desire material causes, practice an efficient cause, and continued human survival a final cause. But this would not help explain anything. We can explain the emotio-rational structure another way, seeing morality as the "solidification of reason," cognition as the internal structure of reason, aesthetics as the "melting of reason into emotion," and so on. But the distinctions and connections established therein again remain unexplained. None of this would tell us how these aspects of human psychology are generated, develop, and transform, or how their universal and particular aspects are related. Likewise, the idea of "proper measure" I put forth, and which I leave substantively undetermined, requires people themselves strive to define and integrate "proper measure" in their actions. This is due to the manner in which the behavioral commands given by the external community gradually become categorical imperatives of individual psychology— the movement by which ethics becomes morality[3] and by which we have practical reason. Through sedimentation this reason further comes to constitute universally necessary, inviolable structures of human thought and knowledge: formal logic, mathematics, and notions of cause and effect. The nature of the relations, forms, and structures of emotion and reason herein, along with similar issues, are important matters interrelated with a variety of intractable questions of psychology, education, and other areas of study. I believe the kinds of investigation they require fall under the domains of the empirical sciences, and especially that of brain science. Even though I closely follow the present discussions of philosophy of science as well as the trends and fate of humankind, nevertheless, the philosophy I am able to provide remains merely the formulation of basic concepts and ideas from ordinary everyday language. I propose my views in this way and no more. This is the first clarification I would like to add.

Language and Method

The second thing I would like to mention, and something I discovered during our discussions at East China Normal University, is the problematic generalization of the term "morality." Various very different sorts of moral behavior and psychology are all referred to as "morality." The Confucian teaching of sacrificing oneself for virtue and moral principle is called morality, while stopping at red lights and not cutting in line are also called morality. The choice of death over unrighteousness is moral, rich people donating to charity is moral, and not littering or spitting in public is moral. While all of these behaviors and psychological states more or less possess the property of morality, the differences between them are very large. The principal mark of morality that arises in the ability to sacrifice one's life is completely drowned out in this generalization of the term's usage. This makes discussion of the question "what is morality"[4] even more confused. Because of this, I feel this phenomenon of everyday language deserves special attention. Analytic philosophy here can prove very helpful, emphasizing the need to focus on the fact that the term "morality" possesses greatly divergent content and connotations in its concrete application. We cannot discuss morality effectively without

24 | The Humanist Ethics of Li Zehou

differentiating the various entirely different moral behaviors and psychologies to which the term refers.

This connects with my advocacy of a historicist methodology. In the symposium discussions held at East China Normal University we focused especially on "concrete issues and concrete analysis." This is the Marxist methodology we are familiar with from the 1950s, and I believe to this day it is correct. For example, neither the utilitarian principle of "the greatest benefit for the greatest number" nor the liberal principle of "humans as ends" is wrong. However, how to correctly apply them within specific contexts and conditions can vary greatly. Therefore, neither can be said to be *generally* right or wrong, nor applied directly and fully in all circumstances. As was stated in the East China Normal University discussions, the famous trolley car problem (whether it is permissible to kill one to save five), the cannibalism at sea case (whether it is criminal to eat a shipmate when starving and stranded at sea), and instances of price gouging during disaster relief (a choice between market principles and moral principles) are all cases to which we are unable to directly and fully and exclusively apply either utilitarian or liberal principles.[5] Rather, we must take into account particular context and conditions so as to judge and manage these cases concretely. In disaster relief and war, individuals and groups must sometimes be sacrificed and utilitarian principles ought sometimes be adopted over liberal principles. Yet if faced with the trolley car scenario, even if we may permit killing one to save five, an onlooker cannot push someone onto the track to stop the car, as people's intuitions generally agree. This endorses liberal principles rather than utilitarian ones. The methodology of historicism I advocate is precisely this. It emphasizes the historical particularity of things.

Historicism also possesses—in addition to concrete particularity—accumulativeness and contingency. I refer to these as "the three qualities of history." Accumulativeness can also be called progress, as I believe that the material culture, daily life, and spiritual life (including ethical norms and moral psychology) of humankind all exhibit progress. This runs contrary to anti-Enlightenment and postmodern positions, and it is a historical methodology as well as ontology.

The Terminological Distinction between Ethics and Morality

The third remark I would like to add reiterates the importance of distinguishing between the terms ethics (from *ethikos*) and morality (from *moralis*). The communal norms of ethics and the individual acts of morality are indeed originally closely connected and difficult to separate. Communal norms are expressed in the moral acts and psychological states of the individual, but generally speaking an individual's moral acts and psychological states are not necessarily manifestations of communal norms. The two are always closely related, and yet I stress the need to differentiate between them. Why? Firstly, I believe this distinction helps elucidate many difficult ethical issues. Secondly, it helps clearly express a basic view of my ethical theory, which is the movement from external to internal and from ethics to morality. This can also be understood in terms of the movement from cultural and social history to personal education, which is an important part of my theory of the historical sedimentation of human psychology.

Other forms of this distinction have been made in the past. For example, one such formulation sees common and non-self-consciously practiced customs and conventions as belonging to morality, whereas ethics involves conscious and systematic rational self-restriction. This and similar views, however, actually continue to conflate the two notions that my formulation distinguishes. That conflation runs throughout historical use of the two terms, one coming from Greece and the other from Rome. They each originally include both internal and external. Because of this, and considering their long and often synonymous usage, insisting that the Greek-derived term "ethic" refers exclusively to the external and the Latin-derived term "moral" refers exclusively to the internal might be inconvenient and unconventional.[6] The terms in Chinese do not have this problem. It is quite natural and coherent to see the Chinese term for "ethics," *lunli* 倫理, as referring exclusively to external social norms and the term for "morality," *daode* 道德, as referring exclusively to individual behavior and psychology. I draw out the different emphases inherent in the Chinese terms to help distinguish between internal and external and to thereby highlight the way demands of communal society relate with individual moral action and external norms relate with internal psychology. (These are equivalent to the distinction between internal and external, and between the self and community.) This helps to more effectively approach a variety of issues that have resulted from or been exacerbated by conflating the two.

My use of the term "ethics" is broadly inclusive, referring to communal human society, and extends from narrow primeval communities to the public morals of all of contemporary humankind. It ranges successively

26 | The Humanist Ethics of Li Zehou

from totems, taboos, shamanistic ritual ceremony, superstitious imperatives, and religious doctrines to later legal regulations and state religions.
It even includes various customs and conventions. These all fall within the
range of what I call "ethical norms." Basically, ethical norms are demands,
commands, restrictions, controls, and the jurisdiction of the community
over individual action. They are various, myriad, and complex.

My use of the term "morality" refers to the personal cultivation and
internalization of the demands of communal norms through history and
education (in the broad sense) into the conscientious acts and psychological states of the individual, and then from such self-conscious con-
scientiousness to unconscious intuitions. Thus, morality does not consist
in instinctual desires and impulses, but rather involves the integration of
emotion and reason in a type of emotio-rational structure. It is also characterized by reason's governance of emotion, desire, and instinct. Reason
here is, moreover, divided into its conceptual content and the form of
the will. It is also differentiated from other aspects of the emotio-rational structure, including knowledge (rational internal structures, which do
not directly govern behavior) and aesthetic appreciation (the melting of
reason into emotion, which also does not govern behavior).

Through the individual's self-consciousness and the concepts of her
moral psychology, the external ethical norms of the community govern
her moral action. Therefore, morality cannot be merely concepts. Morality cannot be merely the idea of the good, but rather must also be good
action—that is, the practice, fulfillment, and realization of this idea (concept) of the good. This can rely only on the long-term cultivation and
training of the rational will.

I have stated before that the primary word of Christian ethics is
generally "faith"—faith in God. The primary word of Chinese Confucian
ethics is probably "learning" (xue 學)—learning to be human. Both of
these, faith and learning, are matters of rational ideas, not animalistic instincts or biological desires. They are thus principally expressed
in the self-conscious choice of the individual. Human moral acts are
in this way distinct from the behavior of animals, even if they seem on
the surface similar—for example, when animals sacrifice themselves for
the benefit of their group. During the symposium discussions at East
China Normal University, we debated whether animals possess morality.
The basic theme of that discussion, although it was not fully developed,
was clear: opposition to sociobiological views of morality, which have
become extremely popular. Sociobiological theories see animals as pos-

sessing morality. They say morality originates from natural instincts that were developed through competition for survival among biological species. They assert as evidence for this position that some animals exhibit individual sacrifice for the preservation of their group, which allows that species to be victorious in its competition for survival. I believe, however, that if morality lies in instincts and desires evolved naturally in animal species, then this sort of morality comes to possess absoluteness of universal necessity for individual members of that species, leaving no freedom of individual choice. Human morality, in contrast, exists precisely within the context of individual free choice, and in the conscientious choice to self-sacrifice. The preservation of one's own life is an instinct and desire possessed across biological species and humankind is no exception. Humans respect, revere, and celebrate those exceptional and resolute figures who sacrifice their lives for virtue precisely because these figures self-consciously carry out moral actions of which the majority of people are incapable. Why are most people incapable of these acts? Because of the powerful animalistic instinct to preserve their own life. Why is this moral minority, then, capable of such action? Because they use more powerful rational ideas and the will to repress this strong instinct. Here we see morality expressed as free will, personal choice, decisiveness, and overcoming considerations of individual survival and other selfish interests so as to carry out what one simply believes one ought to do. It is also precisely due to this minority's capacity to act in opposition to biological instinct and natural desire, as well as their guiding influence as models on the future of the community, that differentiates the continuous extension of the existence of humankind from the survival of other animals. I believe this is the ethics promoted by Chinese tradition as well as by Kant. Only this type of ethical theory truly captures the essence of human moral behavior and psychology, and because of this we must distinguish carefully among the broad-ranging uses of the term morality mentioned above.

Of course, some will ask how I can be sure that animals do not possess such an ability for self-choice. How do we know animals do not have free will? I am no specialist in this area. I am merely questioning whether governance by naturally evolved biological instincts ought to be applied in understanding the psychology and actions of all members of our species. I also do not understand why sociobiological theory has so much support and yet there is such extremely little, or even no, discussion of this issue.

From External to Internal

Not long ago I read the Chinese translation of an interesting book, *Moral Origins: The Evolution of Virtue, Altruism, and Shame*.[7] Its author, Christopher Boehm, is an erudite professor who has spent decades observing and researching the activity of primates and primeval human communities, and his book adopts an evolutionary sociobiological perspective in interpreting their morality. But what is extremely interesting is that Boehm's conclusion can be summarized as stating that morality originates in demands of the external community (including those of primates and primeval humans) on the individual to be "self-regulating" within the interspecies competition and continuous extension of existence of that species. Morality is the individual's biological mechanism for "self-regulating." Boehm explicitly emphasizes that "gaining a self-regulating conscience was the first milepost in human moral evolution" and "the imposition of at least a few 'rules' on individuals by sizable *groups* was already under way with the Common Ancestor and even more so with its successor."[8] While the book is full of presumptions that I believe lack adequate foundation,[9] nevertheless, Boehm invokes an important, rich pool of evidence to support the proposition that the internal psychological mechanisms for "self-regulating," which fundamentally characterize human morality, originate from external communal regulations. This shows that individual moral psychological states and acts have their source in the coercive norms of external community. Therein Boehm describes instances in which individuals were murdered, punished, or exiled (which was equivalent to death) for not adhering to communal regulations. He mentions "capital punishment" in the animal kingdom several times. At the same time, he also emphasizes that the production of morality was a long historical process, that "moral origins took place gradually, over thousands of generations."[10] The book focuses on discussion of the problem of "conscience," arguing that animals also exhibit self-restraint based in fear of social sanctions, but that truly powerful moral conscience came into existence only 250,000 years ago.[11] This happened when primeval human communities began cooperatively hunting large hooved animals such as zebras and antelope. Boehm focuses "specifically on the conscience and how this uniquely self-conscious agency came into being as a result of a punitive social environment."[12] He believes that the process of choosing social sanctions produced shame of conscience, and that conscience "internalizes rules that favor cooperation."[13] Isn't all of this precisely what

I emphasize as the movement from ethics to morality, the production of moral psychology internal to the individual from external communal norms and demands? People's "internal humanization of nature"?

However, I believe that Chinese Confucianism is still entirely correct in emphasizing the distinction of human from animal. This goes directly against the equivalence, drawn by sociobiologists, between human and animal morality. As I see it, the significance of such research is its proposal of the theory that even in the animal world, individual "moral" behavior still consists in self-restraint produced through the reception of communal "regulations." This is hugely important. I believe also that animals exhibit forms of self-restraint that do not involve internalizing communal norms. For example, the patience and discipline exerted in capturing prey is instinctual for many species of animal. This is the more primeval biological foundation for the possibility of imparting communal norms to the individual.

In my *Critique of Critical Philosophy: A New Approach to Kant* (*Pipan zhexue de pipan: Kangde shuping* 批判哲學的批判：康德述評) (1979),[14] I stressed—and thereafter often continued to point out—that individual human morality begins in encountering "no" in childhood: no, you cannot take other people's food; no, you cannot harm others. The "Qu li" 曲禮 chapter of the *Record of Ritual* (*Li ji* 禮記) records a great many such proscriptions. Such strict normative regulations, from childhood to adulthood, on behavior, activities, speech, bearing, appearance, and so on shows that ethical norms involve precisely the shaping of individual behavior and psychology that makes one human, which the *Analects* refer to as "establishing oneself through ritual" (*li yu li* 立於禮).[15] I believe that the similar behavior Boehm identifies in other primates merely clarifies that the movement from external to internal that marks human morality is made possible by biological potential inherited from our animal ancestors. Yet it is only humans that actualize this—through "transformative creation"—as "ritual regulations" (ethics) and "virtue" (morality). Isn't the period Boehm refers to, when we hunted large animals 250,000 years ago, precisely the period in which primeval communities manufactured and used tools on a large scale, which required closely cooperative division of labor, thereby producing society and reason? Boehm also discusses the manufacture and use of tools, but does not see the pivotal, tremendous significance of this crucial step in producing humanity.

As I explain in my epistemology, humankind produced reason in the social practices of cooperative division of labor and coordination in warfare, through the processes of continuous refinement in the manufacture and use of tools. Only then was this reason transformatively created into the practical reason of the human subject, which has been communicated and preserved through the semantics of language from generation to generation. Communal demands and practical experience formed the external norms of society. The individual's internal morality and knowledge sprouted, formed, solidified, and developed from this. What is reason? Reason consists in the patterns, regulations, order, and norms produced in the practices described above and which serve the continuous extension of existence of human communities. It is often referred to as a manner of according with regulations, wherein "proper measure" plays a fundamental role. First, society was formed through practical reason, which was concurrently applied to objects, creating cognitive reason, which is also speculative reason. As it continuously developed and expanded within practice, reason produced a fundamental turn in the continuous extension of human existence that gradually moved humans beyond the animal realm.

Boehm completely fails to discuss these points, but his theory of morality originating in the movement from external to internal—including his emphasis on conscience, self-consciousness, shame, and so forth all originating from communal norms—aligns with my views. His research, moreover, further challenges the opposing theories of morality, namely theories that ascribe to humans an intuitive and innate moral conscience bestowed by Heaven or lying in *a priori* reason. From Christian predestination and Kantian pure practical reason to China's Neo-Confucian conceptions of principle and their contemporary iterations, such theories have held predominance from ancient to modern thought, both within China and globally. Boehm's work as a sociobiologist helps expose the trouble with these views, helping us more accurately see morality's origins in the structure of human practices.

Especially worth pointing out here is that the movement from external to internal and from ethics to morality has at times involved severe coercion. In terms of natural biology, such individual self-regulation did not come easily. As Boehm describes, morals formed gradually only through severe punishments, including capital punishment, meted out by the community over very long periods of time. In terms of Chinese tradition, a similar point has been largely overlooked by scholars: By the time of the three ancient dynasties, shamanistic ritual ceremony was directly interrelated with severe punishment. This is also true of ritual ceremony in the Zhou dynasty. Lacking filial piety or failing to associate with others in a proper friendly or allied manner both were strictly and harshly punished. What are called "rule by virtue" and "rule of ritual" were in their early stages established on the severe punishments of conventional laws. Later generations, and especially people today, mistakenly take "ritual regulations" to have been warm and emotionally rich standards of etiquette. In actuality, precisely the opposite is true. The *Analects* records a discussion of ritual sacrifice that states, "The men of Zhou used the chestnut, saying that it made the common people tremble."[16] It was not until the time of the decline of ritual and collapse of music during the Spring and Autumn period, following Confucius's rooting of ritual in humaneness, that the theory of ritual regulations arising from humane love of the inner heart-mind was created. Confucius responds to the issue of the Zhou "making the common people tremble" with the statement, "One does not explain away what is already done, one does not advise against what is already accomplished, and one does not condemn what has already gone by."[17] The idea that we should not dwell on mistakes of the past lies at the core of the prodigious contribution of Confucius's rooting of ritual regulations in humaneness. We can see then that internal moral conscience comes originally from strict and severe ethical commands of external community. To this day, the moral education of children, from family to school, cannot avoid a certain element of coercion. I believe this is necessary and important to recognize.

Herein, moreover, the significance of my distinction between the terms "morality" and "ethics" also becomes quite clear. It equips us to better resolve many difficulties and problems brought on by failing to make this distinction.

Some may ask, since I referred to the views of natural evolutionary theory above, whether I fully agree with Darwin's theory. The clear answer is: No. Darwin did not adequately recognize that humans are not merely naturally evolved animals, but also at the same time and even more importantly manufacturers and users of tools and therefore animals that produced reason and society. Because of this, many of Darwin's conclusions resemble the one quoted by Boehm: "Any animal whatever, endowed with well-marked social instincts, the parental and filial affections being here included, would inevitably acquire a moral sense or conscience as soon as its intellectual powers had become as well developed, or nearly as well developed, as in man."[18] Millions of years of history prove that this is not the case. Not only are important terms here, including "intellectual

32 | The Humanist Ethics of Li Zehou

powers" and "development" of "moral sense or conscience," extremely ambiguous, many primates have also been evolving for millions of years but to this day remain unable to create an airplane or cellphone. Nor do they have practically regulative concepts of parental love and filial piety, fraternal and sororal esteem, liberal equality, individual rights, and so on.

Intuition and Inherent Goodness in Mencius and Xunzi

Originally, Confucian teachings included the movement from external to internal and from ethics to morality. However, a theory of movement from morality to ethics has maintained predominance for a very long time, especially in China. Although the West has intuitionism, it is not prominent. In China, on the other hand, the theory of inherent goodness has been central and influential. The didactic moral text of the *Three Character Classic* (*Sanzi jing* 三字經) opens with the line, "For humans in the beginning, their nature is fundamentally good" (*ren zhi chu, xing ben shan* 人之初, 性本善). Why is this the case? This requires additional clarification. I believe there are two important reasons for it. One is that this type of ethical outlook fits relatively well with people's day-to-day moral behavior. Also in line with this is the idea proposed in the ECNU symposium discussions, where some argued that morality moves both from the empirical to the *a priori* and from the *a priori* to the empirical.

In fact, the notion of "movement from the empirical to the *a priori*" involves external ethical norms (the empirical) entering individual psychology and becoming seemingly *a priori* emotions and will (the *a priori*). This bears on fundamental questions of the origins of morality. "Movement from the *a priori* to the empirical" involves the commonplace empirical dimensions of individual moral behavior and psychology (the empirical) being seemingly generated by intuitive innate moral conscience (the *a priori*). The two are issues of entirely different levels. The latter is seen in the famous classical Confucian idea of the "compassionate heart-mind" (*ceyin zhi xin* 惻隱之心) seemingly possessed by all. Mencius states, "Humaneness, righteousness, ritual propriety, and wisdom are not welded to us externally. We inherently have them."[19] In the many examples of generalization of the term "morality" discussed above, we see that these virtues or moral powers indeed seem to be universal phenomena. Yet viewed anthropologically or through research on human development and education, these are just products of long-term cultivation and edification. They come from coercion and learning, first transforming into self-conscious regulations and then into subconscious and unconscious ones, thereby seemingly produced without reflective thought or studied effort. Just like the skills of swimming and riding a bike, morality also enters into an unconscious state through training and cultivation. In fact, feral children and other persons who go uneducated will lack these intuitions.

Thus, the moral psychology that Mencius refers to as innate—the possession of four virtues (humaneness, righteousness, ritual propriety, and wisdom)—is not necessarily so. Mencius believes that rulers having "a heart sensitive to the suffering of others" (*burenren zhi xin* 不忍人之心)[20] are thereby capable of carrying out "government that is sensitive to the suffering of others" (*burenren zhi zheng* 不忍人之政),[21] and therefore can preserve all within the four seas and under heaven. This presents a political philosophy that moves from morality (internal psychology) to ethics (external political policy and institutions). It is also, of course, not necessarily so. Later Song-Ming Neo-Confucianism similarly tells us that grasping the heart-mind of the virtuous ruler will bring stability to the state,[22] and modern New Confucianism proposes that conscientious self-restriction will open the way to science and democracy. These again are not necessarily so. And interestingly enough, the more highly regarded intuitionist thought in Western philosophy also has aspects similar to this. G. E. Moore held that goodness is like the color yellow. It is an intuitive self-evident principle that cannot be defined or explained. Therefore what is important is examining the connotations, uses, and functions of morality's many terms, concepts, and judgments. This initiated metaethics' decades of academic hegemony, which continues to this day.

But is moral psychology actually just intuitive judgment? During discussions of aesthetics in the 1950s, especially in "Meigan liangchongxing" 美感两重性 (The dualistic nature of aesthetic sensibility),[23] I worked on the issue of aesthetic intuition. Aesthetic intuition is much clearer and more pronounced than moral intuition. However, the result of these discussions seems to have been that many scholars praising practical aesthetics have asserted that both beauty and the sense of beauty come from human practice, and that the sense of beauty is neither indefinable nor an animalistic biological instinct. There is not, moreover, a self-evident algorithm for beauty. Rather, it remains a product of *a posteriori* cultivation that takes place on an antecedently given biological foundation. This is also the case with moral intuition.

Many modern thinkers, including Michael Sandel, see intuition as a foundation for considering moral and ethical issues by way of critical, rational reflection, and believe that these are informed by historically

34 | The Humanist Ethics of Li Zehou

particular, communally shared views and customs that in some ways include bias and falsity. Nevertheless, these shared, historically accumulated views are largely what culture—along with ethical and moral tradition—consists in. Whether right or wrong, intuition is formed from the accumulation of history, custom, and tradition. This is to say that the internalization of external ethical norms of "common opinion" into individual psychology, over time, produces our intuitions. In terms of internal psychology itself, however, John Doris and his research team published *The Moral Psychology Handbook* in 2010 (which was reprinted several times over the following years),[24] showing the experimental research of contemporary moral psychology to strongly affirm the interaction of the "affect-intuition system" and the "conscious-cognitive system." Doris's team concludes that there is no single psychological process of moral judgment. On the contrary, moral judgment relies on interaction among various psychological systems. The book repeatedly puts forward questions such as whether what we call intuition is in fact intuition, whether intuitions are reliable, and whether moral judgments can be understood as direct responses of pure sensibility. The book does not tell us the precise manner in which the conscious-cognitive system and affect-intuition system interact simply because today's empirical scientists do not know.

What we see, then, is a processual cultivation of the emotio-rational structure through history and edification, from the "self-regulating" of early ancient humans to today's moral behavior and psychology, and certainly not acts based on inherent, antecedently fixed intuitions. Only in this way is it possible to fundamentally explain how such tremendous and rapid shifts are possible in the demands of contemporary external ethical norms and the internal moral psychology of individuals, whereas other species of animals exhibit no such change. This is because morality never was a matter of either natural evolution or *a priori* innate nature.

So then, is there good and evil in human nature? How should we understand the famous debate between Mencius and Xunzi, typically described as a debate over whether human nature is inherently good or inherently evil? In my *Ethics* (*Lunlixue gangyao* 倫理學綱要),[25] I express clearly the position that human nature inherently possesses neither good nor evil. Good and evil are a set of concepts that have been produced within the formation of human history. Animals themselves express loving attachment, coordination, meekness, cooperation, and other aspects of so-called "goodness" as well as coercion, conflict, aggression, murder, and other aspects of so-called "evil." ("Good" and "evil" here are also conceptual labels added by humans.) Xunzi emphasizes the reduction of evil traits by repressing and extinguishing the latter natural human tendencies, while Mencius stresses the expansion of goodness through cultivating and developing the former. They differ in emphasizing the expansion of goodness or repression of evil, but they share the more important emphasis on edification. Like modern scientific theory, Xunzi is clearly more precise and powerful in his logical argumentation and theoretical speculation, while Mencius more easily persuades and convinces through his more emotional analogical and associative theory. Viewed in terms of later history, the achievements of School of Principle Neo-Confucianism expressed in the emphasis of Zhu Xi 朱熹 on "preserving heavenly principle and eliminating human desire" actually carry forward the thought of Xunzi under the banner of Mencius (in terms of the objective structure and practical function of the theory, not as regards Zhu Xi's self-conscious intention). It stresses repressing human emotions and desires via relational ethics. In this light, it is not surprising that many scholars see Zhu Xi's teachings as in line with those of Xunzi. Mou Zongsan 牟宗三, the great proponent of Mencius, harshly criticizes Zhu Xi for teaching "heteronomous morality," and from the perspective of the movement from external to internal, this criticism is not unfounded. Tan Sitong 譚嗣同 characterized the two millennia of Confucian tradition as following Xunzi, and Mao Zedong 毛澤東 stated, "A hundred generations have all carried out the government institutions of Qin."[26] Both are quite right. The use of education that "eliminates human desires" to manage and control the populace and to consolidate the great unification of this autocratic empire was a matter of historical necessity. Thus the actual main thread of Chinese ethical tradition ran from Confucius through Xunzi, Dong Zhongshu 董仲舒, and Zhu Xi. Wang Yangming 王陽明 and School of the Heart-Mind Neo-Confucianism also developed this logically and historically in a manner that moved toward early modern individualist theory, as seen in their notion that heavenly principle lies within human desire. Equating the moral heart-mind (*xin* 心) with principle (*li* 理) and equating moral conscience (*liangxin* 良心) with substance (*benti* 本體), they moved toward a naturalistic human nature and psychology.[27]

Understanding Zhu Xi as Xunzi clothed in Mencius brings us back to the second and perhaps most important reason why the theory of innately good human nature came to predominate Chinese tradition. This is also the reason that presenting one's ideas as following Mencius, even if in substance they were closer to Xunzi, served an important function.

36 | The Humanist Ethics of Li Zehou

For millennia, Mencius has been considered Confucianism's second sage, second only to Confucius himself. His position and influence have been far greater than Xunzi's, and they remain so today. Why is that?

I believe this is principally related to Chinese tradition's emotional cosmology. In my essay "On the Shamanistic-Historical Tradition" (*Shuo wushi chuantong* 說巫史傳統),[28] I argue that the Chinese notion of "heaven" (*tian* 天) has been dualistic since ancient times. It connotes heaven both in the sense of a non-personal god or divinity and in the sense of the natural sky. These dual connotations serve to affirm human life in both its spiritual and material aspects, and thereby inform a worldview in which people should approach life and this world, as well as their own nature and emotional relations, with an affirmative and optimistic, proactive emotional attitude. This is true of both the ethical norms of political philosophy as well as the individual cultivation of moral psychology. The *Book of Documents* (*Shang shu* 尚書) states, "Heaven sees as my people see; Heaven hears as my people hear."[29] The *Book of Changes* states, "generation (*sheng* 生) is the great virtue of heaven and earth"[30] and "the continuous generation of life is called change" (*shengsheng zhi wei yi* 生生之謂易).[31] With Dong Zhongshu this came to present the emotional cosmology of resonance between heaven and human, which identified the Way of heaven with the Way of humans and "heavenly heart-mind" (*tianxin* 天心) with "humaneness" (*ren* 仁). Much like the gratefulness a Christian feels toward God, Chinese people have always had a feeling of gratefulness toward heaven and earth, along with a cognizance of the virtue of heaven and earth. It is just that rather than a supernatural personal god, this heaven and earth represent the natural cosmos itself. Here humans are not meant to manage and control nature, as in the Bible, but rather to live in accordance or in coordination with it. This goes far beyond merely material existence, to include moral emotions and beliefs as well as emotions and beliefs that go beyond morality. Humans are meant to "assist in the transforming and nourishing processes of heaven and earth" and "form a trinity with Heaven and Earth,"[32] that is, participate in the work of heaven and earth and cultivate themselves.

The *Zhongyong* further explains natural human nature, which was originally seen as neither good nor evil, to be the morally good character bestowed by heaven. Mencius greatly developed this, and therefore the idea of the goodness of natural cosmic "heavenly" processes (as in "heaven's action is robust," *tian xing jian* 天行健[33]) and Mencius's notion of the innate goodness of human nature are closely connected in spirit.

On Ethics | 37

Both bestow strong affirmation on the emotions and have faith in human life. Therefore, although Xunzi is superior as a rational theory, Mencius provides the better teachings in terms of emotion. Mencius argues in a language that, although not logically satisfying, succeeds in strongly arousing one's emotions. Compared with Xunzi's more concrete and practical theory, Mencius's teachings are much more easily identified with and accepted on the level of emotion and belief, which is what allowed them to become a major component of Chinese tradition's religious morals and culture of optimism.

"Innate goodness" and "original sin" can be seen as representing a general and rather drastic contrast between Chinese and Christian traditions, reflected also in the contrast of the Chinese celebration of life with the Christian devaluation of this world. Today, my perspective of anthropological historical ontology in one aspect emphasizes that the natural products of human psychology were originally without good and evil, and that good and evil are conceptual definitions of *a posteriori* society and come from *a posteriori* cultivation and edification. In another aspect, since "supreme goodness" is identifiable with the continuous existence of the totality of humankind, the notion of the innate goodness of human nature can be understood as the individual's inherent contribution to the practical extension of the existence of humankind. Therein, the individual's innate goodness is established via the "supreme goodness" of the integrated totality.[34] The former idea affirms the basis of modern social morals, and the latter carries forward the religious morals of Chinese tradition.[35] This is what I have referred to as inheriting both Mencius and Xunzi and returning to their common origin in Confucius.

I should discuss also another issue related to innate goodness and intuition. This is the notion of going beyond morality within morality. In the West, moving beyond morality occurred mainly through religion. In China, however, there was the "mystical experience" I discuss in "Dialogue on Aesthetic Edification Replacing Religion" (*Guanyu "meiyu dai zongjiao" dawen* 關於「美育代宗教」答問).[36] This served as a common baseline for "the happiness of Confucius and Yan Hui" (*Kong-Yan lechu* 孔顏樂處) and spiritual realm of heaven and earth, and it is seen even in the notions of "intellectual intuition" (*zhi de zhijue* 智的直覺) and "transforming consciousness to become wisdom" (*zhuan shi cheng zhi* 轉識成智) that Mou Zongsan loved to discuss. This mystical experience is not present, or is rarely present, in daily life. Rather, it is achieved through the struggle of individual cultivation, as William James describes in *The Varieties of*

38 | The Humanist Ethics of Li Zehou

Religious Experience and as seen in Chan (Zen) Buddhist and Neo-Confucian teachings such as those that ask us to reflect on the original aspect of one's self that preceded birth (Chan Buddhism) and on that which is prior to the activation of emotions[37] (Neo-Confucianism). Anthropological historical ontology admits the existence of this type of mystical experience, and refers to it as "the mysticality of sensibility" (*ganxing de shenmi* 感性的神秘). However, it believes that with the further progress of brain science, this mystical experience will be fully reproducible within the lab. Even if that day lies in the distant future, today's research, however incomplete and inconclusive, already evidences this possibility, as seen in the following report:

> This effect underlies the profound altered state of consciousness that people often describe during an LSD experience. . . . It is also related to what people sometimes call "ego-dissolution," which means the normal sense of self is broken down and replaced by a sense of reconnection with themselves, others and the natural world. This experience is sometimes framed in a religious or spiritual way—and seems to be associated with improvements in well-being after the drug's effects have subsided.[38]

So then, what is still mystical about intuitions and experiences of this sort, which are both moral and beyond morality? There is, it thus seems, ultimately nothing more than what I call "the mysticality of reason" (*lixing de shenmi* 理性的神秘).[39]

Kant, Ethical Relativism, and Virtue Ethics

There is no getting around Kant in Western ethics. Yet disagreement over his ideas is widespread, and clear discussion of the issues at stake has eluded us for two centuries. I believe one of the reasons for this is the lack of distinction between ethics and morality. If we take the second formulation of Kant's categorical imperative, "humans as ends," as content for external ethical norms, and the other two formulations ("universal legislation" and "free will") to regard the individual's internal moral psychology, the distinction seems to help us get a handle on things. The former proclaims a humanistic aim, and the latter describe the shape of human nature, or human moral psychology. These psychological forms are absolute and have been necessary to humankind from ancient times to today. The call to value and treat "humans as ends," in contrast, is a substantive demand specific to certain societies and times, and it is restricted by historical particularity. It is certainly not a universally valid categorical imperative.

Practical reason has priority to[40] speculative reason, since the former is produced through the transformation of reason within practice, as mentioned above. It accords with regularity in the continuous extension of human existence, and it refers first of all to the particular importance of reason that manifests in the ethical demands of practical activity. Only thereafter does it exhibit epistemological regularity. Epistemological regularity at its root is also inextricable from what serves the continuous extension of human existence. Classifying Kant as an ethical absolutist illuminates this point. Kant asserts that each person ought to hold to a certain conviction in carrying out moral action: The way I conduct myself can be universalized to serve as an imperative for all people, all people ought to model themselves on me, and my behavior can be universally legislated. Viewed anthropologically, in terms of historical origins, this is basically the experience, semantics, and reasoning that first arose and has been preserved in the practical activities of the manufacture and use of tools. It forms and shapes people's internal heart-minds through absolute commands, moving from coercion and submission to conscious choice, gradually becoming rational governance of the self and subordinating pleasure and pain, fortune, life, experience, and sensible existence to a free will that is able to disregard them. This is what Kant referred to as a "Good Will." We see then that the "Good Will" principally refers to a type of individual moral psychology capable of "universal legislation." It is also what Kant calls practical reason, which is higher than, superior to, and prior to the understanding's speculative reason. This is more or less the original semantics of human language. The *Book of Changes* states, "To drum people into action all over the world is dependent on the phrases."[41] Beginning from early ancient shaman masters' incantations claiming connection to "the will of heaven" (*tianming* 天命), this preserves the series of demands, rules, and regulations that first arose in the practice of the manufacture and use of tools as inviolable sacred commands issued for the guidance, organization, and management of communal and individual activity. Shamanistic ritual ceremony thoroughly moved humankind beyond the realm of animals, producing society. Therein, language and

40 | The Humanist Ethics of Li Zehou

reason (order and regulation) were central. Its basis remained the various experiences of the manufacture and use of tools for hunting food (which involved acquiring mastery and knowledge of things of the external world) as well as sharing that food (the relationships and order between community and individual that facilitated survival). This meant language was not limited to communication. Rather, the vehicle of the human voice (and later the written word) carried forward rich and important historical experience that supported human survival. The notion that "Language is the house of Being"[42] has deep significance only when understood from this point of view, recognizing the millions of years of historical experience of continuous progress and innovation in the use and manufacture of tools. Thus, it is history and not language that I draw into metaphysics. It is history that possesses the ontological significance necessary and sufficient for the continuous survival of humankind. Herein lies the point of explaining Kant's practical reason through Chinese tradition and Marx.

Likewise, from a historical perspective, and as mentioned above, treating "humans as ends" is merely a norm for individual behavior demanded by modern society. A great deal of cultural anthropological research verifies that treating humans as ends is not a universal ethical notion. Nowhere did the ancient world have this "categorical imperative." It is a product of modern society. The foundation of modern morals, it has already been realized in the institutions and law of some regions and countries, which take people's equal individuality as fundamental and the source of value. In these places, it functions as the guiding principle of liberal political philosophy. However, globally speaking, this is far from the case.

Cultural anthropology makes clear that in different times, different societies, different cultures, and different traditions there have existed highly divergent ethical norms as well as highly divergent religious doctrines, customary ways of life, social institutions, and ritual ceremonies. These are full of discrepancies and conflicts. Conflicts among a single culture's ethical norms are also common, especially in modern times—from proscriptions against divorce to allowing homosexual marriage, from prescriptions to cover up head to toe, revealing only the eyes, to the nearly nude models of fashion runways, from asceticism to sexual hedonism, and all the various theories and practices that fall between these extremes. These have sometimes been held side by side without clashing and other times broken into passionate conflict, and such remains the case today. Treating humans as ends is far from having become a global ethic or moral. Still, the cultural pluralism and ethical relativism that

On Ethics | 41

liberalism has derived from this is now mainstream. Let me repeat: To treat humans as ends is not a universally necessary categorical imperative, but rather a modern social moral that possesses a kind of universality and idealism. Universal legislation and free will, on the other hand, are indeed universally necessary formal structures of moral psychology; they have shaped human nature from ancient times to the present. Perhaps using the term "framework" can make things clearer. I take the so-called "categorical imperative" to refer to establishing this type of "framework" within people's internal psychology, which thereby makes humans human. Any substantive morals, regardless of whether they are some form of religious morals or social morals, must have this framework in order to be morals. This framework also brings together emotions, concepts, and the will. The framework and the will are unchanging. Concepts and emotions, however, diverge, differ, and shift over time and across societies and cultures. Therefore, within certain limits anthropological historical ontology affirms ethical relativism, since as mentioned above, ethics are all rational products of historical particularity. The particular social and communal norms that individuals abide by in their various times (represented as the solid line from ritual regulations [*li* 禮] to rational principle [*li* 理] on the general table of my ethical theory)[43] along with their divergence from and opposition to these norms (the table's dotted line running back from rational principle to ritual regulations) are what regulate the course of history. One cannot judge the past me by reference to the present me. This seems to be an issue that is unnecessary to discuss again. The problem is that within the broader recognition of such moral relativity is a type of "unrestricted moral relativism" that sees various incommensurable ethical norms as entirely equal in essence and value. This precludes evaluative distinction as to what is superior and inferior, better and worse, advanced and backward, and makes drawing such distinctions politically incorrect. It thereby also rejects the accumulative nature of history and its affirmation of historical progress, including that of morality and ethics. Such progress is especially clear when it comes to women. Whether or not women have a right to education or can work outside the home or freely marry or choose abortion are all examples. Therefore, the modern social moral of "humans as ends" is, in regard to the entirety of humankind, still far from fully realized. As the *Communist Manifesto* states, "The free development of each is the condition for the free development of all."

Worth special attention is that under liberal governance in which the individual is the source of all value there have arisen various waves of

42 | The Humanist Ethics of Li Zehou

anti-historicist, anti-progressivist, and anti-Enlightenment thought. Perhaps here I ought to mention communitarianism and virtue ethics, which are to a greater or lesser extent related with these waves of thought. At present, China also has many scholars advocating virtue ethics. They share opposition to the fundamentality of the individual in liberalism (*geren benwei* 個人本位) and uphold the fundamentality of the community (*qunti benwei* 群體本位) found in various traditions. But the virtue ethics of communitarians roots itself in ancient Greece and follows ancient Greek thought in making free citizenship most fundamental, therefore making relationships of equality and amity characteristic of communitarianism. Even though it emphasizes that the community is prior to, originates from, and is higher than the individual, at its root communitarianism does not diverge greatly from the fundamental position liberalism grants the individual. This is not the case with China's virtue ethics, which presents a morality of hierarchically ordered human relationships centered in traditional parental love and filial piety. Liang Shuming 梁漱溟 discussed this quite thoroughly, as the fundamentality of ethical relations (*lunli benwei* 倫理本位). Herein, the individual fulfills diverse obligations and responsibilities within various ethical relations. This type of virtue is relational virtue.

However, at present China faces unprecedented social change. The rural population is urbanizing on a tremendous scale, and the free exchange of labor and contractual principles are "liberating" the individual both materially and spiritually from one's family, clan, and village. Daily life is being comprehensively modernized, the traditional family undermined, and familial clanship ceasing to exist entirely. The traditional institutions and spiritual guidance of the "three cardinal relations and six major virtues" (*sangang liuji* 三綱六紀) cannot be revitalized or reemerge. Individual equality, freedom, independence, and rights have replaced traditional relationism (*guanxi zhuyi* 關係主義) and role ethics. Where do we look, then, in search of a foundation for Chinese virtue ethics?

This has already become a major issue. It seems to me the only solutions lie in promoting the outlook of "emotion as substance" (*qing benti* 情本體)[44] and appreciating the emotions of human psychology, and in transformative creation of how we shape emotions and psychology based in the constitutive principles of ethical roles and relations. The three cardinal guides are no longer around, and hierarchical relationships are now established on a footing of individual independence. In terms of abstract theory this can be described as amity between ruler and subject, amity between father and son, amity between husband and wife, and amity among elder and junior siblings (to borrow a point from Tan Sitong). A superior can fire a subordinate, and that subordinate can express his contempt and quit in indignation. The times in which "no parent under heaven is wrong" (*tianxia wu bu shi de fumu* 天下無不是的父母) and "even if the ruler does not fulfill the duties of ruler, the subject should fulfill the duties of subject" (*jun bu jun, chen bu ke bu chen* 君不君臣不可不臣) are gone and will not return. Contractual principles and the fundamental role of individuality have already come to characterize modern social morals. However, the interpersonal social roles and relationships between superior and subordinate (ruler and subject), father and son, husband and wife, and elder and junior siblings, and especially their emotional relations, nevertheless remain very much unable to be equated with simple amity between individuals. Therefore, role-specific virtues and obligations such as "humaneness of the ruler and loyalty of subject," "loving care of the parent and filial piety of the child," and "kindness of the elder sibling and respect of the younger sibling" can still function within emotional roles and relations. For example, the way we think and feel about using material rewards to encourage children's learning can and should differ sharply from how we think and feel about distribution according to labor and economic stimulation in a factory. The two ought to be seen as fundamentally different. As long as civic education remains prioritized over the *Three Character Classic* (an easily memorized text from which children learn Confucian morality), we ought to still recognize the importance of filial piety and respecting our teachers, of seniority and order, of diligence and fondness for study, of reverence for elders and caring for children, and of reading history and valuing experience. These teachings can serve to transcend material interests and guide pure equality, coordinating relationships, conflicts, and disputes among absolutely free individuals and preventing the market economy from becoming a market society in which everything is viewed in terms of money. The market economy, commodity production, and the free sale of labor are all based on fair exchange and rational calculation. The human is a rational animal, but is certainly not the product of simply adding reason to an animal. Rather, reason permeates into originally animalistic emotions, desires, and even instincts to thereby bestow humans with their emotio-rational structure.

Liang Shuming wrote, "ethical relations are relations of emotional affection," "ethics follows emotions and thereby has righteousness," "when one's emotion is increasingly deep, one's righteousness is increas-

44 | The Humanist Ethics of Li Zehou

ingly strong,"[45] "morality is a matter of rationality, and its achievement is self-conscious human autonomy," and "Confucius deeply loved reason, and deeply believed in reason." Liang Shuming's use of the term "reason" or "rationality" (*lixing* 理性) is, as he emphasizes himself, an "integration of emotion and reason" (*qingli* 情理) and not pure intellect as in the rational calculation of physical laws. It is not reason in that narrow sense. He emphasizes the complete permeation of feelings into self-conscious and autonomous intellect, an achievement integrating reason and emotion. The rightness (obligations and responsibilities) generated by this sort of integration of emotion and reason obtains in any and all places, and also grants people what Liang calls "stronger vitality." We thus see that Chinese people's accordance with emotion and reason—their achievement of reason through emotion—and the connection between feeling morally at ease and attaining moral principle are far more than the simple sum of emotion and reason. Rather, they involve the unification of emotion with the rational will, originally determined by the intellect and conceptual ideas, through their inter-permeation and blending, so that therein the moral duties affirmed through the intellect seem to be generated from emotion. This is precisely the important unique aspect of Chinese tradition's unified cultivation of the rational understanding of right and wrong and the emotional senses of like and dislike, attraction and repugnance. This differs from Kant, and differs as well from Hume.

Next it seems we might as well look at the virtue ethics of traditional Confucianism, and how it sedimented and was practiced in people's daily lives.

The Deep Structures of Confucianism

I have the habit of quoting from my earlier writing. While I feel a bit sorry about this, no one has strongly criticized me for it yet. I do so for reasons I have stated before: Rather than repackaging old ideas in new phrasing, I prefer laying out the old ideas directly and trying to sell them again. This is what is called "having a broomstick but prizing it as a pile of gold."[46] My article "Preliminary Remarks on the Deep Structures of Confucianism"[47] seems worth referencing here. By "deep" I refer to the conscious and unconscious individual emotio-rational structure. Here is a long passage:[48]

What I am interested in is primarily exploring the Confucius who has melded into the thought, consciousness, customs, conventions, and behavior of the Chinese people over the last two plus millennia. I would like to look at what kind of impression he has left on the Chinese people as well as the strengths and shortcomings this has brought to the cultural-psychological formation of our culture. This Confucius is alive and well in the thought of you, me, and Chinese people generally. . . . Because of this, even though China's vast population of farmers do not read the *Analects* and may know very little about Confucius, nevertheless it is Confucius and Confucianism, not Daoism, Legalism, or Buddhism, that is infused and sedimented into the conscious and unconscious levels of their behavioral norms, conceptual models, mode of thinking, emotional disposition, and so forth. Of course, there are elements of these other schools of thought, but most of them have already been absorbed, integrated, and dissolved within Confucianism. . . .[49]

This also involves the deep structures of Confucianism I will discuss here. Thus, what I call the structures of the "surface level" of Confucianism refer to the teachings of Confucius to his disciples as well as the political systems, legal institutions, ethical principles, life order, ideology, and so forth of Confucianism since the Qin and Han dynasties. These are expressed as social and cultural phenomena and are basically the theoretical manifestation of value structures or a system of knowledge and power. *The "deep" structures of Confucianism are the outlook on life, habits of thought, and emotional orientation that see the Way as something that "functions for the common folk on a daily basis, yet they are unaware of it."[50] These cannot be purely rational, but rather are complex composites of emotion and desire nevertheless intertwined and integrated with reason.* Basically, they are individual psychological structures of sensible manifestation centered in the integration of emotion and reason. I call this composite the "emotio-rational structure." In it, desire, emotion, and reason (rational knowledge) reside in complex interrelation within a type of structure. These relationships do not merely involve reason and rational knowledge's control, governance, and guidance of emotions and desires, as ancient Greek philosophy advocates. More important is that "emotion" resides within "reason" and "reason" within "emotion." That is, emotion integrates, permeates, and is united with reason and rational knowledge, and vice versa. I believe this is one of the principal characteristics of China's cultural-psychological formation, which was established primarily through Confucianism. This is not simply a theoretical notion; it has long been a practical reality.

These "deep structures" are not my own innovation. They have existed, in fact, as a long-standing truism often discussed as the characteristics of the Chinese nationality, the spirit of the Chinese people, cultural tradition, and so on. They simply have not been identified with the term "cultural-psychological formation" or examined in terms of the complex relationship between the surface and deep levels and structures of Confucianism. Of course, the differentiation of what I call "deep" and "surface" levels is not easy. First, *the "deep" levels form through the long temporal process of sedimentation of the "surface" levels.* This includes conscious cultural education (such as ancient government policies of moral edification (*jiaohua* 教化)) as well as unconscious customs and conventions. The relations between these are various and complex, with the conscious and unconscious intertwined and interacting, which makes them very difficult to cleanly separate from one another. Secondly, *as the "deep" levels include unconscious elements and emotion, it is very difficult to describe them accurately through conceptual discourse.* Their distinction from the "surface" level can only be roughly or generally pointed out.

Then, what are the basic features of these "deep structures"? China's "culture of optimism" and "pragmatic reason," which I have described previously, remain two very important aspects. These both appear in the cultural characteristics of the surface level and constitute the psychological characteristics of the deep levels. The summarization of these two aspects of Chinese thought occurs in the notion of China's "one-world" (or one-life) outlook that I have focused on in recent work. This is the principal characteristic of the deep emotio-rational structures formed through sedimentation of Confucianism and Chinese culture (including Daoist, Legalist, Yinyang, and other thought). Whether or not it has been previously recognized and regardless of whether we are aware of it, this "one-world" outlook has and continues to serve as a foundational psychological structure. Through this, Confucianism (and Chinese culture) differentiates itself from other cultural psychologies, such as those of Judaic, Christian, Islamic, and Hindu traditions. Chinese culture has not denied the existence of deities (including God, ghosts, and spirits). This is seen as early as Confucius himself, who "did not speak of prodigies, force, disorder, and gods" and who stated, "You are not able even to serve man. How can you serve the spirits? . . . You do not understand even life. How can you understand death?"[51] Chinese culture simply believes these things cannot be definitively discussed and so submerges them in emotional states permeated by rationality. The *Analects* tells us, " 'Sacrifice as if present' is taken to mean 'sacrifice to the gods as if the gods were present.' The Master, however, said, 'Unless I enter into the spirit of a sacrifice, it is as if I did not sacrifice.' "[52] That Confucianism is neither the pure speculation of philosophical induction and deduction nor a purely emotional faith is due to this interpermeation and intermelding of emotion and reason in its cultural-psychological construct. This is also the reason that it possesses both the moral function of religion as well as a rational outlook that respects the empirical. Confucianism has continuously developed this fundamental "one-world" conception, remaining ultimately oriented toward human life within present actuality and neither seeking happiness in an afterlife nor aspiring toward salvation of the pure soul. Importantly, by "human life within present actuality" I do not refer to the life of the individual self but rather of the community, from the family to the state and even "all under heaven" (humankind). To ordinary people in this tradition who also believe in the Bodhisattva or ghosts and spirits, the realm of the divine, of God, or of spirits remains part of this world and human life. These realms exist for this world and human life. People burn incense and worship Buddha or pray to the divine and practice divination in hopes of acquiring peace, health, fertility, and prosperity.

48 | The Humanist Ethics of Li Zehou

Due to Confucianism's "one-world" outlook, people lay great importance on human relationships and emotion. In managing sorrow at the vagaries of life and death and the brief temporality of life, they see the meaningfulness of life as lying within the human realm, understanding the notions that "the infinite resides within the finite" and of "engaging with the world in striving to move beyond it." This "one-world" outlook leads people to focus on strengthening themselves ceaselessly and persisting in their struggles. Confucius famously celebrates the person "who keeps working towards a goal the realization of which he knows to be hopeless"[53] and stated, "Only when the cold season comes is the point brought home that the pine and the cypress never lose their leaves."[54] Through this "one-world" view Confucianism asserted tremendous emotional affirmation of nature and the cosmos. The *Book of Changes* states, "The great virtue of heaven and earth is called 'generation,'"[55] as well as "In its capacity to produce and reproduce we call it 'change,'"[56] "Heaven's action is robust," "generous virtue carries everything,"[57] and so on. Here we see the use of this "philosophy" full of positive emotion to sustain people's lives, which thereby allows people to "form a trinity with heaven and earth" and their commonality therein to constitute "ontological substance." This is what I call China's "culture of optimism." The mode of thinking of this "one-world" outlook lays greater emphasis on practical efficacy and less emphasis on fantasy and reverie. It promotes inclusivity (accepting the useful and reasonable) while discounting emotional passions and fanaticism (not clinging to certain emotions, beliefs, or ideas). This is what I call China's "pragmatic reason."

As for the origin of this "one-world" (or one-life) outlook, it has deep ancient sources that of course precede Confucius himself. It may be related to the excellent natural environment along the ancient Yellow River (which can be compared to Babylon, Egypt, and Greece) and people's development of basic feelings of intimacy, gratitude, and reverence toward "heaven and earth" rather than fear and thus separation. This has been pointed out by many others (such as Mou Zongsan). However, I believe China's ancient shamanistic tradition to be a much more significant factor. Shamanism involves the active coercion of spirits by humans rather than passive prayer to them. The precocious rationalization of China's shamanistic practices is seen in Strategist and Daoist thought, and went on to form the unique shamanistic-historical tradition. This is extremely important to ancient history and intellectual history, and is discussed in my essay "On the Shamanistic-Historical Tradition."

Due to its "one-world" outlook, the Chinese tradition also lacks the "fear" promoted by Judeo-Christian teachings, as well as the limitless striving of the Faustian spirit. The "one-world" view also led China to produce firm political institutions and a cultural tradition of the "tripartite unity of ethics, politics, and religion." "Unity of heaven and human" became unity of public and personal, which made it very difficult for true individuality and individual personality to arise. Thus, in one aspect Confucianism promotes the absolute rule of a system of power and knowledge under the banner of "heavenly principle," and in another aspect it also promotes a sort of self-interest and complacency arising from contentment with the transient present. In all, as the emotio-rational structure of this "one-world" view does not clearly separate reason from emotion, and conflates instrumental rationality with value rationality, it cannot give rise to modern science and democracy.

The task before us thus lies in clearly recognizing this issue. This clear recognition requires further understanding how Confucianism constructs this emotio-rational structure on the surface level. Confucianism has always taken human nature as foundational, seeing ethics, politics, and religion as fundamentally issues of human nature. Whether understood as "ritual regulations" or "humaneness," whether following Xunzi or Mencius, the issue of human nature has always been crucial to Confucianism. Human nature is directly related to individual sensibility and psychology. It is only through this that China was able to produce the construction of the emotio-rational structure.

Confucius states, "Men are close to one another by nature. They drift apart through behavior that is constantly repeated."[58] He states as well, "Would you feel at ease? . . . If you can feel at ease, do it."[59] Mencius and Xunzi both greatly stressed the differentiation of human from animal, which forms the crux of

50 | The Humanist Ethics of Li Zehou

human nature. Thus both theories of human nature as innately good (that people possess innate "sprouts" of goodness) and as innately bad (natural animalism) emphasize the necessity of education, through which people return to (as in Mencius) or acquire (for Xunzi) human nature. This education requires the infusion of rationality into emotion, transforming people's animalistic emotions and desires into "human" emotions. For example, in the animal realm motherly love is a biological instinct. While Confucianism presupposes this biological instinct, it emphasizes its "humanized" qualities; that is, it stresses that not only the mother but also the father ought to love their children (*fu ci* 父慈). More importantly, it emphasizes that this must be a reciprocal love, that is, that children also ought to love their parents (filial piety). The Confucian emphasis on this kind of love cannot involve only the external order of ritual etiquette or institutional norms, but includes also the fostering of internal emotional attitude. Confucius states, "Even hounds and horses are, in some way, provided with food. If one shows no respect, where is the difference [between providing one's parents with food and providing horses and dogs with food]."[60] Confucianism takes the emotional psychology of human nature as its starting point, and takes this reciprocal love between parent and child as well as between siblings (family members) as its axis and foundation. In this way it erects all of society, moving from the ethical to the political ("Inside the family there is the serving of one's father; outside, there is the serving of one's lord"[61]) and religious (the three-year mourning period and worship of ancestors). Thus, when Confucius states, "Being good as a son and respectful as a younger sibling is the root of one's enaction of humaneness,"[62] it is not at all some kind of philosophical speculation of pure reason, nor is it some kind of moral norm of practical reason. Rather it constructs an emotio-rational structure of sensible psychology. Various religions strive to erect their own emotio-rational structures. They often take transcendent mystical substance as their object of faith and emotional grounding. Or they take reason as independent and self-sufficient, absolute and true, and see rational knowledge as sufficient to discuss the existence of the divine (such as through ontological, cosmological, and teleological proofs). Or on the contrary they emphasize the need for faith due to absurdity or human shortcomings and thereby reject reason and appeal directly to emotion. In these views the relationship between and structures of emotion and reason differ greatly from Confucianism. Confucianism does not construct its grounding in the divine or in reason (truth), but rather does so in the integration of emotion and reason within human nature itself. Therefore, it does not stress opposition and conflict between reason and emotion, spirit and corporality, or the afterlife and this life. Rather, it demands that psychology itself, which occurs through the sensible corporeal body, become the object of metaphysical striving. That is, it seeks the completion and perfection of the sedimentation of sensible corporality itself. This is what Confucius means when he states, "Be inspired by the *Poetry*, take your stand through the help of the rites, and be perfected by music."[63]

This is also the Confucian tradition of emotion as substance. Because of this, both the aims of external human culture (including ethical norms) and the formation of internal human psychology (including individuals' moral psychological states and actions) are inseparable from this "one-world" view. This "one-world" thought sees the interpersonal human relations of daily life as the true substance (*benti* 本體) that human existence cannot do without. The above discusses interpersonal emotions of caring in relationships between parent and child, spouses, siblings, and friends within this "one-world" view. Do these differ in certain aspects from the interpersonal emotions of "two-world" outlooks, such as "loving God and God's grace"? This is a subject worth further study. The interpersonal emotions of the former can themselves constitute substance, which is not the case in the latter. In many two-world views, substance must be God, even if God is present within the human world. This is the difference I discussed previously between *Dream of the Red Chamber* (*Hong lou meng* 紅樓夢) and *The Brothers Karamazov*. The Christian aim of salvation of the soul differs from the Confucian scholar-officials' aim of saving the people from disaster and hardship.

Proponents of the New Confucianism prevalent in Hong Kong and Taiwan as well as advocates of the rise of religious Confucianism in Mainland China have not recognized the emotio-rational structure of this "one-world" outlook through which the Chinese people have viewed the

52 | The Humanist Ethics of Li Zehou

world (without being conscious that they do so) for the last millennium, and they have overlooked especially the importance of its actual existence and great power as substance. The system of this emotio-rational structure, emphasizing relationships and human emotion, can serve as the basis for traditional religious morals and virtue ethics and thereby offer a remedy and corrective to the market values that let human desire run amok. The lonely, the addicted, the directionless, the hedonistic, and the youth drowning in an artificial world, following occasional indulgence in individual romanticism, can snap back and pursue true happiness of the soul within human reality. To this day, Chinese society remains richly infused with emotion, its personal interactions frequent and its relations many and close. Customs of visiting friends and relatives as well as reciprocal gift giving continue to structure central parts of life. Although this is related with the large population of Chinese people and close proximity in which they live, their tradition of a "one-world" outlook and "emotion as substance" remains the basic character of society's soul. Regarding political philosophy, my 1999 essay "On the Integration of Confucianism and Legalism" also pointed out the emphasis on emotional relations in "bending the law to extend emotion" (*qu fa shen qing* 屈法伸情), "taking the heart-mind into account in determining guilt" (*yuan xin lun zui* 原心論罪), "acknowledging the importance of carrying out discernment" (*zhongshi xing quan* 重視行權), and "avoiding legal suit" (*bi ye wu song* 必也無訟). To this we can add "atoning for wrongs through good deeds and meritorious achievements" (*dai zui li gong* 戴罪立功 and *jiang gong shu zui* 將功贖罪), which goes beyond judgment according to merely isolated, formal, external facts and punishment according to merely formal laws.

Related to this is the point that, like many scholars, I also once discussed Christian "ultimate concern" alongside Chinese tradition's ideal of "placing oneself morally at ease and establishing a sense of spiritual belonging" (*an shen li ming* 安身立命),[64] conflating the two in a manner that is, in fact, wrong. Of course, there are many various denominations and theories within Christianity, and Paul Tillich's "ultimate concern" is not necessarily acceptable to Karl Barth's idea of "the wholly other." Some Christian doctrines and schools emphasize that God exists precisely within this world, struggling along with humans, so as to erase the separation between the two worlds of corporeal and spiritual, body and mind, and heaven and human. Yet even so, the faith and emotions of worship directed toward a transcendent, non-material force—an ultimate reality that created and governs this world—remain predominant among the various Christian schools of thought. The Christian God remains different from the Chinese notion of "heaven" (*tian* 天), and therefore "ultimate concern" remains different from China's notion of "placing oneself morally at ease and establishing a sense of spiritual belonging." In terms of emotion, the latter takes horizontal relations and emotional care among humans as the ultimate grounding of belief, while the former continues to take the vertical love between humans and God as ultimate substance. Christianity sees salvation of the soul as its mission, whereas Chinese scholar-officials have taken concern for the wellbeing of the common people and universal peace as their responsibility. Achieving these aspirations, one shares in the happiness of the people; failing to achieve these aspirations, one becomes a hermit, or passes on teachings to disciples, or expresses oneself in writing and art, freeing oneself of excessive obstinacy as well as placing oneself morally at ease and establishing a sense of spiritual belonging. Often this results in regret or nostalgia for one's days of positive social and political engagement, referred to in the Chinese tradition as "being physically in the countryside, but in one's heart keeping to the palace." As Li Rui 李銳 poetically put it, "There is no greater concern than the affairs of court; One cannot observe idly with folded arms."[65]

In addition to this, according to the Christian theory of original sin, suffering and hardship are not the direct result of individual immoral acts and thoughts. The limitations of human existence and survival themselves are an expression of sin, and are completely unconnected to whether one lives morally or not. Thus, the suffering of the innocent has a type of ontological significance. The innocent suffer and pursue salvation, but are unable to achieve it, and therefore Christianity uses the notion of grace to transcend accordance with morals and the lack of correlation between virtue and fortune seen in the suffering of the innocent. This eliminates the secular desire that goodness be rewarded and evil punished, and transcends morality and ethics to root itself in divinity. This indeed leaves people in awe and feeling lofty reverence, but certainly does not accord with Chinese tradition. Historical ontology holds the position of Albert Einstein, who said, "I do not believe in immortality of the individual, and I consider ethics to be an exclusively human concern with no superhuman authority behind it."[66] Chinese tradition holds to the notion of historical judgment in which goodness is rewarded and evil punished within a "one-world" outlook. This unifies virtue and fortune—and unifies "the antinomy of history and ethics"—in future human generations rather than in the embrace of the divine. Anthropological historical ontology emphasizes

54 | The Humanist Ethics of Li Zehou

as well that only love and caring can dispel nihility. However, this caring does not break away from secular life and the natural world. Drawing history into metaphysics[67] gives a home to the insufficiencies, temporality, and limitations of individual life in the lofty aesthetic psychological realm of the progress of history, which is both moral and transcends morality. It is true: People live their lives often not by choice, yet seemingly mutual recognition and love grounds them. Buddhism may tell us the world is ultimately empty, but what of it? We must go on living. Confucius celebrates perseverance even when knowing its futility. What else is there? The only answer is to love this life and love this world—sorrow, awakening, cherishing, and emotional attachment—moving beyond yet also holding fast to this life. This explanation may be intensely attacked, but that does not bother me.

The Self

Since everything, including ethics and morality, is ultimately grounded in the individual, this individual self is the final concern of these additional comments. From the free individual to the atomic individual, Western philosophical discussions are myriad. They have included even postmodernism's notion that the human is dead, that the self is fragmented, and so on. Chinese scholars have followed suit, discussing ideas of no-self and similar issues a great deal. I would like to make a few simple remarks to clarify what is at stake in those discussions.

Firstly, is there a self? And is the self important? The answer: Yes, there is, and it is indeed important. However, anthropological historical ontology from its very beginnings (in *Critique of Critical Philosophy*) has used the notions of "greater self" (*da wo* 大我) and "lesser self" (*xiao wo* 小我) to argue that the individual self is a "greater self" in the sense of being a historical product of modern humankind. This is the extraordinarily important self-awakening of the "lesser self" in its economic, political, and ideological consciousness and emotions. The limitations of individual life along with the grasping of the importance of these limitations has led liberalism, which sees the individual as the source of value, to become mainstream modern thought. Kant saying that humans are ends is the most prominent and celebrated call for recognition of the self. The free sale of labor among all individuals in society is the actual foundation of this. This powerful historical torrent, even if it is often repressed, will eventually flow forth. The various appeals to traditional culture and fashionable theories attempting to obstruct and oppose this are necessarily extremely wrongheaded and stand against history.

Secondly, does Chinese tradition have this form of selfhood? The answer: No. As Yan Fu 嚴復 wrote, "In regards to liberty, it is true that the ancient sages and virtuous figures historically held a deep fearful awe of this, and did not attempt to establish it in their teachings."[68] Chinese Confucianism conceives of individual free will as described in the statement "the will of even a common man cannot be taken from him,"[69] but this is not the individual freedom of actual material life. On the contrary, Confucianism emphasizes that the meaning and value of individual life lies in fulfilling one's roles (*jin lun* 盡倫), which involves carrying out the duties and responsibilities of the "three cardinal relations and six major virtues." Chinese Daoism has the spiritual freedom of the soaring imagination of "roaming" (*xiaoyaoyou* 逍遙遊). But this again is not freedom of actual material life. The individual self of liberty, equality, independence, and human rights is a product of modernity.

Third, liberalism sees the individual as the source of value, but then is there an "atomic individual" in the sense of a self that is entirely independent of the community? The answer: No. Whether material or spiritual, belonging to the body or the soul, the self always has its origins. It is always situated within relations, existing with others and within its environment. An "atomic individual" or "unencumbered self" abstracted entirely from all relations is merely a supposition, and not something that actually exists. Therefore, to see the individual as the source of value—as is usually done in putting forth many guiding principles of liberal theory, including notions of divinely bestowed human rights and the equality of human life—is unsubstantiated. However, these theories and principles are extremely valuable and meaningful in the struggle against pre-modern autocracy and postmodern support for the absolute authority of things like ethnicity, nationality, and democracy.

Fourth, this being the case, does the fundamental position of ethical relations in Chinese tradition have significance today? The answer: Yes. Ethics originally has the two aspects of "what sort of person should I be" and "what should I do." Although these two questions are difficult to separate, they are, after all, certainly not equivalent. This is especially true with the sharp clashes and conflicts among today's various religions, peoples, cultures, ideologies, and religions, which make it nearly impossible to arrive at a shared understanding of the common good or good life.

56 | The Humanist Ethics of Li Zehou

Anthropological historical ontology puts forth the theory of two morals[70] precisely to deal with this situation. Modern social morals primarily (but certainly not entirely) deals with the right and wrong of "what should I do," whereas traditional religious morals concern "what sort of person should I be." The former establishes the role of morals and norms of right and wrong for various professional ethics, clarifying rights and duties, professional responsibilities, and honor and disgrace. Traditional religious morals pursue the moral character, conscience, and identity ("placing oneself morally at ease and establishing a sense of spiritual belonging") of "what sort of person should I be" through emotion and faith. Although the two morals have places where they accord, they are not the same; for example, they provide different approaches to how to people can communicate, be compatible, and connect so as to blend and avoid severe conflict. This is a major contemporary issue, as evidenced especially with Islamic regions. As described above, Chinese tradition pursues the establishment of the emotio-rational structure, melding emotion and reason within a one-world outlook, and this outlook has tremendous global value today as regards this issue.

Fifth, what will the self be like in the future? The answer: It cannot be known. In 1992 I wrote,

> No longer is it a dream of engineering utopian society, but rather a dream seeking the substance (*benti* 本體) of human nature, edification, and psychology. It therefore is also a dream of inquiry and study of "the humanization of nature" and "the naturalization of humans." . . . [And we ask] can carrying forward and reinterpreting tradition make a contribution to this dream?[71]

In 1999 my essay "On the new meaning of heaven and humans" (*Shuo tian ren xin yi* 說天人新義) put forth the issue of the "hardware" of the humanization of internal nature.

> What I here call the hardware of humanization refers to how to remake the nature (*ziran* 自然) of humankind itself, including human bodily organs, genetic inheritance, and so forth. The cloning and genetic technology of the twenty-first century is poised to turn a new page, developing aspects of the humanized hardware of internal nature (*ziran*) to new heights. This will

promote historically unprecedented human health, treatment for various diseases, extended life, increased physical strength, and heightened intelligence, reaching the greatest peaks of human development.[72]

In "Response to Paul Gauguin's Three Questions,"[73] I state my belief that the future will see a psychological turn more important than the linguistic turn in twentieth-century philosophy—for instance, the implantation of microchips in human brains, connected with neurons, or modification of an individual's genetic makeup. What direction will these developments lead humankind and each individual self? Will they hugely increase people's physical and intellectual capacity, extend length of life, and completely eliminate disease? Or will humankind and the individual selves that compose it vanish by transforming into homogenous machines, or through gradual destruction? Is this a euphoric dream, or a twisted nightmare? We cannot know. China's traditional culture of optimism maintains a positive and affirmative outlook on this. I have written, "Human psychology, emotion, and contingency are the fated qualities of the philosophy I hopefully anticipate, which will poetically unfold in the twenty-first century" (see "Di si tigang" 第四提綱, 1989).[74] The individual is thrown extremely randomly into the myriad tragedies of this world. As I wrote in *Historical Ontology*, "Its aim, prospects, and obstacles are certainly not fixed, and therefore unable to be predicted." The contingency of fate, the particularity of individuals, the limitations and fallibility of humans, and the transcendence of these fully unfold herein. This is life. This is the path. This is truth (*zhenli* 真理). This is "circumstance" and also one's self. It is my own and others' living existence and awareness of our own living existence. There is no atomic individual, nor is there *a priori* psychology, nor is there Heaven or Hell. The individual self can merely live an existence within the contingency of historical survival, and it is an existence that does not belong exclusively to itself. Ethics will see exceptionally heated and unending debate within this future contingency, and only those who live to see it will be able to truly discuss what it holds.[75]

Further Comments on Ethics

These further comments aim to better clarify two issues: first, the idea that morality does not consist in merely cognitive knowledge and, second, the way in which Xunzi's teachings were adopted and carried forward under the banner of Mencius's thought.

Comment 1. On Knowing, Acting, and the Will

Not long ago, Professor Yu Zhenhua 郁振華 of East China Normal University introduced me to Gilbert Ryle's distinction between "knowing that" and "knowing how." This distinction, along with the divergences between intellectualism and anti-intellectualism, between Humeanism and anti-Humeanism, and within the debate in China over Wang Yangming's 王陽明 conception of "enacting moral conscience" (*zhi liangzhi* 致良知),[1] all have important ethical implications. Here I would like to use them to clarify several points of my discussion in *Ethics*.[2]

In *Ethics* I argue that morality is not a matter of "knowing" (*zhi* 知) but rather of "acting" (*xing* 行). Morality involves knowledge (that is, ideas and concepts), but is not equivalent to knowledge.[3] Morality is a matter of acting itself, and therefore morality is neither "knowing that" nor "knowing how"—neither knowing whether to act nor knowing what way to act—and it is even less an issue of volition. It is not an issue of knowledge, capacity, or willingness, but rather of doing. While I identify three elements of morality—(i) ideas and concepts (or cognitive knowledge, which comes from experience), (ii) emotion, and (iii) the will[4]—I emphasize the primary importance and governing role of the will (*yi* 意)

60 | The Humanist Ethics of Li Zehou

therein. The crucial element in morality is the conscious choice of the free will: that is, the choice to act or not to act.

Only free will in this sense leads to moral action. One might know but not act, be capable but not act, or be willing but not act. There are many cases in which one knows one "ought to" act, and knows "how to" act, and is "willing to" act, but still does not act—cases in which one has good intentions but does not perform the corresponding good actions. As Ryle points out, there is merely a logical relationship between good intention and good action, not a causal one. Cognitive knowledge, whether "knowing that" or "knowing how," can be taught; emotion cannot be communicated in the same way, but can be affectively transmitted; the will can be neither intellectually communicated nor affectively transmitted. It is expressed through "establishing one's will" (*li yi* 立意) to act and actually acting. This requires self-conscious resolution through reflective choice and self-determination, which is distinct from the drives of animalistic instincts and desires, and often conflicts with them. It often requires hardship or struggle to achieve. Thus, knowledge and emotion are merely ancillary within the moral realm. Only the will is capable of making people actually act or not act as they ought or ought not. It is the will in which moral motivation consists. It is called free will because it possesses the capacity for conscious choice to act or not act. That one "ought to love one's parents" is merely observation; loving one's parents is emotion; only the realization of loving one's parents within action—that is, various concrete acts, attitudes, speech, countenance, and other forms of expression of care, protection, respect, and so on—constitutes morality. This realization primarily relies on the will, and not concepts (knowledge) or emotion.

Of course, the will does not act exclusively or entirely in the moral realm. In daily life and action generally, the will and the exercise or strengthening of the will are also necessary, as in the hardship and hard work that occur in physical labor, intellectual pursuits, physical training, military exercises, and so forth. However, whenever these acts directly bear on other people or communities (this is especially important: when they do not merely concern oneself) they thereby possess moral factors of a greater number of levels and degrees.

Within the moral realm, the role of the will is particularly prominent. Especially in times of hardship, and most acutely in facing death, people retain the capacity for persistence and undeterred perseverance to the point of sacrificing body and life for moral virtue, so as to thereby

Further Comments on Ethics | 61

become a moral exemplar. Clearly, placing morality within the sphere of epistemology, and thus removing emotion and especially the will from it, is a mistake. It strips morality of its substantive character (*benti pin'ge* 本體品格). In contrast, it is precisely the free will's role as driver of individual action that my practical philosophy of subjectality (*zhutixing* 主體性)[5] and anthropological historical ontology intend to emphasize. Of course, there are a variety of connections and points of alignment between knowing and acting—among knowing that, knowing how, willingness, and action—just as there are many places of conflict and contradiction. These require further research by moral psychology.

Comment 2. On Moral Knowledge

Because of this, I explicitly oppose the Mencian conception of innate moral knowledge and capacity (*liangzhi liangneng* 良知良能) captured in ideas like "knowing without contemplation" (*bu lü er zhi* 不慮而知) and "being capable without learning" (*bu xue er neng* 不學而能).[6] Likewise, I do not endorse Wang Yangming's teaching of the unification of moral knowing (or conscience) with acting, which states that acting is knowing and knowing is acting. Such a position not only ignores the differences, distance, and issues that lie between cognitive "knowing" and moral "acting," but also presents morality as the natural, heavenly bestowed capacity possessed by all humans, by which one "sees one's parents and knows (enacts) filial piety and sees one's seniors and knows (enacts) respect." This takes moral acts of being filial to parents and loyal to rulers and equates them with the natural biological sensory responses of "loving a lovely sight and hating a hateful odor" (*hao hao se, wu e xiu* 好好色, 惡惡臭).[7] Today, if we do not identify this with mystical or Christian divine grace, with what is bestowed by heaven, or with revelation, it can be taken as entirely confluent with the sociobiology popular in contemporary Western thought. This sits a great distance from Confucius, who taught that humaneness lies in "mastering oneself and returning to ritual" and that people are similar in nature and diverge through learned practice.[8]

In fact, only through "mastering oneself" can one "return to ritual," and only through learning and practice (that is, through conscious human effort) can one possess goodness. Thus Xunzi taught, "One's goodness is a product of human artifice."[9] Here, "artifice" (*wei* 偽) refers to being produced by conscious human effort (*ren wei* 人為). In addition to

62 | The Humanist Ethics of Li Zehou

knowledge (what I refer to as "conceptual elements"), this type of learning—or "mastering oneself"—and conscious effort depend primarily on cultivation of the self-conscious will. Wang Yangming emphasized "effortful action" (*lixing* 力行), believing that true knowing (*zhenzhi* 真知) and moral conscience (*liangzhi* 良知) occur only within "effortful action." In fact, what this emphasizes is precisely the steadfast persistence of will power within the "unity of knowing and acting" (*zhi xing heyi* 知行合一). However, due to his philosophy's theory of the innate goodness of human nature, Wang Yangming had a great deal of difficulty accounting for how one could possibly fail to enact or align with one's moral conscience as well as for how "enacting moral conscience" gives us a set of ethical social norms. Therefore, it became logically and factually necessary to produce teachings that lack objective norms, such as that "the people filling the street are all sages" and a working boy and a sage are equivalent in moral capacity.[10] Later followers of Wang Yangming ultimately moved toward naturalistic theories of human nature, telling us heavenly principle is implicit in human desires and even directly identifying human desires with heavenly principle.

Additionally, this led to the development of ascetic positions (such as that of Liu Zongzhou 劉宗周) understanding human moral essence in terms of "emotion" (*qing* 情) rather than innate "nature" (*xing* 性) and then strictly and absolutely separating "emotion" from "desire" (*yu* 欲). Thereby, followers of Wang Yangming sometimes successfully produced ideas that were liberating and opposed tradition, and thus of tremendous significance and value. But that was all they succeeded in producing.

In this way Wang Yangming's thought falls short of Zhu Xi's 朱熹. Zhu Xi emphasized recognizing and according with heavenly principle as well as the elimination of human desires, requiring the daily practice of "investigating things" (*gewu* 格物) so as to extend moral knowledge (*zhizhi* 致知).[11] This takes external, *a priori* heavenly principle (which was in actuality the "ritual regulations" of relationships between ruler and minister, father and son, husband and wife, elder and younger siblings, and friends—that is, external social norms) to control, manage, restrain, and normativize all natural human emotions and desires; and through continuous, accumulative daily exercise, one's will, conceptual understanding, and emotions are strengthened and cultivated in accordance with the moral ideal. Such movement from external to internal, from ethical norms to moral action—isn't this precisely the teaching of Xunzi? In Zhu Xi's thought, humaneness (*ren* 仁) is principle (*li* 理), and principle is innate nature (*xing*). The sprout of humaneness is the heart-mind, and compassion (*ceyin* 惻隱) is emotion. The heart-mind connects with and acts on both innate nature and emotion. In sum, Zhu Xi takes external, *a priori* principle to govern, internalizes it as the morality of the heart-mind and innate nature, and sees it as culminated in moral action. He promotes the notion of "a single principle with diverse manifestations" (*li yi fen shu* 理一分殊), which recognizes the differences among people's particular "material nature" (*qizhi zhi xing* 氣質之性; which has its foundation in natural biology) and their various degrees of clarity and turbidity (*qingzhuo* 清濁),[12] and thereby demands that each person ought to "transform" this material nature by way of controlling and restricting it. This brings people's various actual acts, in all their great diversity, under comprehensive normative criteria, setting up hierarchically leveled and sequentially ordered systematic regulations. More than this, it creates practically implementable and extraordinarily vast and intricate moral concepts and ethical standards that effectively govern people in both mind and body. As Tan Sitong once wrote, predominant Confucian tradition has followed Xunzi for two millennia. That very Confucian thought, as it developed from Xunzi to Dong Zhongshu 董仲舒[13] and then to Zhu Xi, reigned within Chinese ethics for two thousand years. Yet Zhu Xi preserved and reinforced the established role of Xunzian thought under the banner not of Xunzi but of Mencius, celebrating the Mencian ideas of the "four sprouts"[14] and innate goodness of human nature.

These issues arose, as well, several centuries ago among Confucian scholars in Korea, who in fervent debate split into camps over the notions of the "four sprouts" and "seven emotions" (*qi qing* 七情),[15] and delved more deeply and with greater subtlety into these teachings than Chinese scholars had. One position held that the "four sprouts" were rational abstractions while the "seven emotions" were natural emotions and desires, and advocated an interpretation of Mencius that called for the "four sprouts" controlling the "seven emotions." This is precisely what Zhu Xi taught. The Cheng-Zhu[16] tradition of thought understood the "four sprouts" as relating to the metaphysical heavenly principles of the "supreme ultimate" (*taiji* 太極). It also inverted the *Analects*' description of filial piety being the root of humaneness, reading it instead to claim that humaneness is the root of filial piety.[17] Both of these identify morality as aligning human emotion and action with external principle. Therefore, even though Zhu Xi celebrates the "four sprouts" and the innate goodness of human nature, his version of these teachings transformed them to align

64 | The Humanist Ethics of Li Zehou

with Xunzi. Originally, three of the "four sprouts"—those corresponding to distain, deference, and approval and disapproval, excluding only that corresponding to compassion[18]—were difficult to explain as forms of "innate moral knowledge and capacity" bestowed by heaven and possessed by all. These issues have further implications for many major aspects of the history of Chinese philosophy—too many to discuss in detail here.

Comment 3. On Emotion and Human Nature

What is crucial is, since I align myself with Xunzi and Zhu Xi, why do I advocate recognizing and carrying forward both Xunzi and Mencius? Since I hold that Zhu Xi followed Xunzi, why do I also consider the "banner of Mencius" to be important? What value, significance, and function does the "banner of Mencius" have? I have previously touched on these questions, but not yet discussed them in detail. Considering their importance, I ought to add a few further remarks. Let me point out as well that this same issue is what prompts me to emphasize emotional factors within the three elements of morality and is why I have stressed from the very beginning that we ought to supplement Kant with Hume.

Central here is that I see China as having a shamanistic-historical tradition, which is without religion. It is a "culture of optimism" with a "one-world" outlook. This worldview sees optimistic, proactive, and deeply emotional qualities throughout the entirety of the cosmos and human life. I call this "emotional cosmology."[19] The *Book of Changes* states, "heaven's action is robust, and the gentleman strengthens himself ceaselessly" (*tian xing jian, junzi ziqiang buxi* 天行健, 君子自強不息).[20] This "strengthening oneself ceaselessly" does not pursue elevation of the soul to heavenly paradise, but rather consists in courageous effort within this physical world. Therefore, the idea that human nature is innately good, which complements the notion that "heaven's action is robust," is extremely valuable: It provides emotional force supporting moral human action. As I presuppose the "highest good" (*zhishan* 至善) to lie in the extension of the existence of humankind and its actual practices (see *Ethics*), then on the individual level we may also adopt emotions and beliefs that presuppose the "goodness of human nature" understood as our inherent participation in the extension and practices of human existence. The presence of certain animal instincts, when developed and deployed positively, supports realization of this philosophical presupposition in

Further Comments on Ethics | 65

practice, through *a posteriori* moral edification. The emotional cosmology of Chinese philosophy believes that all things, including the growth and development of humans themselves, requires reason (pragmatic reason) while still being "established through ritual" (*li yu li* 立於禮).[21] However, what supports, drives, and assists in the completion and perfection of this growth and development are the optimistic (*leguan zhuyi* 樂觀主義) emotions of this world, both secular and non-secular. The religious morals of Chinese Confucianism take the emotional force of affirming innately good human nature to establish a steadfast notion of human perfectibility. This permeates pragmatic reason into emotional elements of human psychology. At the same time, it also remains a matter of emotional faith, not of rational, logical deduction.

Precisely because of this, the ancillary force of emotion possesses importance. That is why my writings on ethics repeatedly emphasize that Chinese tradition should be understood as taking the "emotio-rational structure" as the root of humanity and emphasizing the integrated cultivation of "likes and dislikes" (*hao wu* 好惡) (as emotions) and "right and wrong" (*shi fei* 是非) (as concepts). Or as Wang Yangming put it, right and wrong are nothing other than forms of likes and dislikes of the heart-mind, especially in their practical application through the cultivated and resolute power of the will. This is the character of Chinese ethics. It can also be said to be the "integration of Confucianism and Legalism" within Confucianism itself, using emotion to facilitate reason in regulating behavior, and unifying personal cultivation with political governance, religious morals with social morals. This is also why theories of the goodness of human nature have been predominant throughout Chinese tradition while the emphases in imported teachings on "original sin," the transcendent, and pursuit of "emptiness" have had such a hard time shaking this pillar of tradition.

In the future, Confucian tradition might possess greater universality, bearing on humanity worldwide. It is neither intellectualist nor anti-intellectualist, neither Humean nor anti-Humean. Thus, as I have written, today we need analysis, deconstruction, and reconstruction of this tradition, which will take the cosmology and religious morals of emotion as substance to regulate and properly constitute the modern social morals of public reason. The same point could also be put another way: The social morals of public reason present a modern version of Xunzi's teachings, and the religious morals of emotion as substance present a modern version of the Mencian banner. Both await human creation. The principal

66 | The Humanist Ethics of Li Zehou

questions lie in how to properly distinguish and then reconcile the modern and ancient. Modern society is founded on individuality and the free sale of labor (which constitute Western substance, *xi ti* 西體), while the ancient teachings were founded on clan-based agricultural production and community (which constitute Chinese function, *zhong yong* 中用). How ought we relate modern social morals and the teachings of Xunzi and especially their Mencian veneer?[22] This is the issue I address in advocating the "theory of two morals" and the "new Way of inner sageliness and outer kingliness."

So then, is human nature ultimately good or bad? As I have answered before, from a scientific perspective, it is neither (see *Ethics*[23]). We thus have to be careful about how these concepts are used across various domains of inquiry. Humans naturally possess animalistic instincts that include tendencies toward communal assistance, cooperation, affection, and caring as well as correlative tendencies toward combat, harm, enmity, and murder. Discussions of the goodness or badness of human nature refer in actuality to the cultivation and development of the former tendencies and the repression and eradication of the latter, so as to become "human" (on the individual level) and protect the continuous existence of the totality (on the level of humankind). Innate goodness, innate badness, original sin, and so on are all forms of traditional religious or quasi-religious emotional faith. Today, you and I can both accept and reject this type of belief, holding only that our unknowable universe has "knowable" principles with which we can accord. We can thereby maintain—through optimistic emotion and faith—that humankind can control and create its own fate. This places extreme importance on the various choices and decisions we make through our own free will. This is discussed a good deal in *Outline of a Philosophy*, so I won't get into it here.

Comment 4. On the Self and History

I have mentioned several times above that good action goes beyond good intention. Generally speaking, having good intentions is prerequisite to good acts, but certainly bad acts are sometimes performed with good intentions and bad intentions sometimes have good results. I have often discussed "the antinomy of history and ethics" and that "history proceeds in the midst of tragedy." This brings us beyond discussion of morality as

Further Comments on Ethics | 67

individual behavior and psychology and comes to bear on the realm of external ethical norms and political philosophy. I distinguish morality and ethics, and moral psychology from political philosophy, partly to facilitate clear discussion of this. Individual behavior, especially the social effects and historical function of individual behavior within various social roles, is one of the central points in need of discussion in political philosophy and philosophy of history. Therein, the contingent nature of history is crucial. Thus, even if the economy is the foundation of social life, political figures have always played major roles in determining history.

Additionally, in the modern West, the core topic of discussion in utilitarianism, liberalism, communitarianism, and virtue ethics has been the idea of the "self." My previous work has expressed and defended my own position that this idea of the "self," in terms of both external behavioral norms and internal psychological pursuits, is an extraordinarily important achievement of individual awakening. It cannot be denied or rejected. Rather, it ought to be strongly protected and developed, and the diverse potential of individuals brought out and promoted. These are important aspects of the future prospects of humankind. However, the so-called "unencumbered" "atomic individual" has in actuality never existed. The theory of self in my own ethics is a form of historicism that sees movement from the "greater self" (*da wo* 大我) to the "smaller self" (*xiao wo* 小我). It therefore both opposes the concept of the individual as understood in liberalism as well as opposes the devaluation or denial of the individual in communitarianism.

One thing I would like to point out here regards the opposition to the individualized self—harbored within opposition to modernity, rationality, the Enlightenment, and progress—that has become fashionable within the contemporary academic world. As I see it, the matter is actually quite simple: Without the notions of self and progress—including progress in medicine, health, and lifespan—implicit in the rise of modern technology and the Enlightenment, those fashionable figures opposing modernity would be unlikely to have the time and health to rally against such ideas. Of course, what is important is that when the further advances of genetic research and artificial intelligence have the potential to threaten the ultimate good of the continuous extension of humankind, how to deal with such products of alienation indeed presents crucial philosophical questions, especially in ethics. The future is vast and unclear, and the concerns it presents are multitudinous and wide-ranging. China's traditional culture

68 | The Humanist Ethics of Li Zehou

of optimism believes in the continuous ability of humankind to resolve its problems. The path of that resolution will be long, and certainly will not follow the seemingly lofty but ultimately vacuous calls of anti-modernists.

Comment 5. On Moral Psychology

Here I discuss a few related issues.

1. Desire: Much of my writing on ethics differentiates emotion from desire. "Desires" refer primarily to the needs, pleasures, and satisfactions of material demands and pursuits. They are based in the natural biological sensations of pain and pleasure, and are found in basics of human survival: food, clothing, shelter, activity, sex, health, longevity, and delight. I see no direct relation between them and morality. Desire is capable of driving people's behavior, but that behavior is not necessarily moral behavior. Desires are not and cannot be the source of moral action. They have never been the principal motivation or ancillary force in morality. So then, how should we understand Mencius's teaching, "the desirable is called 'good'" (*ke yu zhi wei shan* 可欲之謂善),[24] or Wang Yangming's teaching that enacting goodness is the greatest happiness (*wei shan zui le* 為善最樂)? As I see it, the sorts of "desire" and "happiness" in these passages are not those that I have just described. They do not refer here to naturalistic emotions, biological needs, or material enjoyments and pursuits. Rather, they refer to a kind of higher-level spiritual, emotional, and psychological state cultivated by humankind. These are the kinds of higher pleasures that I discussed in connection with John Stuart Mill in *A Response to Michael Sandel and Other Matters*, such as the desire to read, to pray, and to appreciate art.[25] Within the moral realm, this includes the desire to perform good acts, the desire to contribute to one's community and country, the desire to participate in virtuous activities, and so forth. Mencius's "the desirable" and Wang Yangming's "ultimate happiness" (*zui le* 最樂) refer to spiritual pursuits and satisfactions, the highest realm of which—for

example, the exultation some Christians feel upon bearing the cross and the elation some heroic martyrs feel upon facing their suffering or death—differs entirely from, and sometimes stands opposite, the naturalistic emotions and desires described above (such as in the contrast between the self-starvation of a hunger strike and being driven to beg by starvation). Often this is precisely the withstanding, repression, and even elimination of naturalistic emotions and desires, which may involve suffering of the physical body. It is not and cannot be what we generally refer to as pleasure, satisfaction, and desire. In their positive aspect, and as Wang Yangming discussed, truly good acts or enacting goodness are like the naturalistic responses of "loving a lovely sight and hating a hateful odor." Yet it is only for sages that morality or virtue is as natural as the responses of biological senses. Such a state is extremely difficult to achieve. Even "worthy persons" (*xianren* 賢人) are barely able to do so. This state of cultivation of course also includes, but is far from limited to, the aforementioned highest moral realm associated with Mencius's "the desirable" and Wang Yangming's "ultimate happiness." From this we see that morality is certainly not a matter of the general desires and emotions "possessed by all humans" (*ren jie you zhi* 人皆有之).[26]

2. Emotion: First, what is emotion? I distinguish emotion (*qinggan* 情感), as external expression of what is internal, from feeling (*ganqing* 感情, in recent writing also *qingxu* 情緒), as internal response to what is external. This helps to differentiate distinctly human emotion from animalistic feelings (which are also predominant in infants). Moral emotions are, of course, the former. But what, still, is moral emotion? This term is not at all clear. Does it refer to the emotions that precede moral action, such as Mencius's "feeling of compassion"[27] and Hume's sympathy? Or does it refer to emotions generated through moral action (either within or following moral action), such as being pleased with oneself, proud of oneself, or respected and admired by others? Or does it refer to loving and hating

70 | The Humanist Ethics of Li Zehou

people and events that are associated with right and wrong? Kant tells us the proper moral feeling is respect, which ought to be understood as the main emotion of oneself and others in moral action. As for the more vivid emotions of love and hate, Confucius teaches, "Only the person of humaneness is capable of truly loving others and hating others."[28] He also tells us one ought conduct oneself with a sense of shame (*xing ji you chi* 行己有恥),[29] and the *Zhongyong* likewise states, "To know shame is akin to courage."[30] These emotions come close entering into the will and action, as seen in Mencius's notion of the "heart-mind of shame and dislike" (*xiuwu zhi xin* 羞惡之心),[31] which he associates with righteousness (*yi* 義). These considerations are precisely why I have emphasized "storing goodness in beauty" (*yi mei chu shan* 以美儲善).[32] They are also major issues of moral psychology, although they can merely be mentioned here, and not dealt with in detail. As for the idea that certain emotions such as compassion and sympathy are the source of morality, I have explained previously that as naturalistic feelings, these are no more than valuable ancillary forces, and provide neither the true motivation nor origins of morality. I have also stated previously that I maintain the traditional Confucian distinction between human and animal, and reject the notion that animals also have moral emotions. There is no need to explain this again here.

3. Ideas: My ethical theory emphasizes the formal force of the will. The content of this will is made up of ideas, or knowledge (including "knowing that" and "knowing how," which include knowing to do or not do something and knowing how one ought to do or not do it). These ideas include standards and norms. They also can be right or wrong, good or bad; and precisely because of this people's free will can do good as well as do bad. Ideas of good and bad differ across times, cultures, and religions, and these changes possess historical particularity and cultural relativity. However, through the long processes of history, the various cultures, religions, and societies of humankind

Further Comments on Ethics | 71

also gradually accumulate universal and absolute ethical ideas from within these relative and particular concepts of good and bad. For example, we have progressed away from murder and exile of the elderly in primeval tribes and away from murder of captives, women, and children in war. Female infants are no longer drowned and female feet no longer bound. This shows that not only does internal will possess absoluteness, but external ethics also accumulate absoluteness. They become necessary pillars of the extension of the living existence of states, peoples, and the human community. I have expressed this position for well over a decade: Ethics and morality possess absolute value.

We also see from this that good and bad in moral action are not entirely determined by the free will's decision to act or not act, but rather determined by the inter-permeation and unity of the free will with ideas that are good and bad. (Good and bad are originally a matter of human concepts and ethical norms; acts believed to be beneficial—to oneself, but primarily to the continuous extension of the community—are good, and those opposite this bad.) Above I have emphasized that the formal (and active) force of the free will is the primary component of ethical action, and is identifiable with the categorical imperative, that is, with believing that one's actions can be "universally legislative" in the sense that others all ought to take them as a model. It is precisely in this sense that I have previously stated that the terrorists of the September 11th attacks can also be said to have morality. They sacrificed their lives in jihad (which is understood as "good" by their conceptual and value scheme), and therefore people in many Muslim regions hailed them as heroes at the time. Yet conceptions of good and bad also, as described above, shift among cultures and religions, and especially with the times. Today, such a choice by the free will to self-sacrifice can be generally rejected from being "good" (right) and seen as "bad" (wrong). Therefore, the September 11th terrorists are not heroes. They are villains. Despite having the heroic spirit of will to self-sacrifice, they committed the heinous wrong of killing innocent civilians. This happened because their conceptions of good and bad were completely mistaken. And this illuminates an important aspect of morality: that the formal force of the free will is limited by the

72 | The Humanist Ethics of Li Zehou

concrete content of ethical ideas. This is also the crux of Hegel's criticism and emendation of Kant.

However, bad acts are not limited to this single type. They go beyond committing evils when one thinks one has chosen goodness. There are also cases in which one fully recognizes the act is bad and chooses to carry it out anyway. This second type makes up the majority of bad acts. Moreover, some bad acts succeed in valuable ways, and may even benefit the masses, a state, or an entire people. Herein unfolds a complex aspect of historical progress. In theory there arises "the cunning of reason" and the notion of evil as the lever of historical development.[33] In actuality, however, we have cases like those I discuss in my previous writing, for instance with Tang emperors Taizong and Suzong. Moreover, because of this, many theologists have taken self-choice of free will to be the source of evil. Kant stated that "radical evil" is not naturally inborn, but rather lies in the human capacity for freedom: "the source of evil . . . can lie only in a rule made by the will for the use of its freedom."[34] My advocacy of "lauding achievements but not extolling virtue" (*ge qi gong er bu song qi de* 歌其功而不頌其德),[35] the "antinomy of history and ethics," and that "history proceeds in the midst of tragedy" all intend to highlight this. I emphasize that although ethics and morality are produced within human historical progress, they nevertheless possess independence and absoluteness—aspects in which they are not dependent on particular time or place in history. Zhu Xi referred to this as "heavenly principle," and Wang Yangming discussed it as "moral conscience" (*liangzhi* 良知). In reality these absolutes consist in historical accumulation sedimented within the human heart-mind. The nature of this accumulation needs further study to be precisely understood.

This view illuminates the various complex and multifarious aspects and conditions of human life. It shows history's contingency, and also highlights the important role of ideas in moral behavior. Of course, this even more clearly expresses that reason (including its intellectual content and its formal component of the will) serves as moral motivation only where it operates independently of instinct, desire, and emotion. At the same time it also captures the importance of pragmatic reason's prowess in "the art of proper measure" (*du de yishu* 度的藝術) within the tragic unfolding of the antinomy of history and ethics, which cannot be delimited by abstract principles established *a priori* by reason, as put forth in various forms of liberalism.

Comment 6. On the Emotio-Rational Structure

To conclude I will add a few words regarding the "emotio-rational structure." As I see it, the formation of the emotio-rational structure is precisely what establishes human nature. I continue to happily follow the classical way of putting this, primarily in terms of the three elements of *zhi* 知, *qing* 情, and *yi* 意, associated with ideas, emotions, and the will, respectively. Each of these three, moreover, itself has conceptual, emotional, and willful aspects, and the three are also mutually interpenetrating. Knowledge consists primarily in ideas, aesthetics primarily in emotions, and morality primarily in the will. These consist in diverse connections, structures, modes, and schemata that are formed by diverse neural pathways, networks, and signals, all of which operate in a variety of ways on a variety of levels. The richness of variation, magnitude of distinctions, intricacy of modes, and complexity of schema—the exquisite subtlety of it all—will only be understood in its profundity by subsequent generations. Yet this quite possibly is crucial precondition for the future challenges of genetic enhancement. In sum, philosophy today is capable merely of providing perspectives and inventing concepts through which to clarify certain issues and problems we face. It introduces ways of approaching things, and no more.

To clarify my points, I have written these short notes, although brief and unrefined, and perhaps unnecessary.

History, Ethics, and Metaphysics

History Has Three Qualities

Liu Yuedi:[1] This conversation aims to help organize and clarify ideas you and I have discussed in recent years. It can be seen as an extension of our earlier conversation in 2018.[2] How about we begin from your statement, "The quintessence of Chinese philosophy is history entering metaphysics"?[3]

Li Zehou: Great. Yes, humans are historical beings.

Liu: How exactly is this idea of "history entering metaphysics" related to your similar notion of "experience becoming *a priori*"?[4]

Li: I have discussed history a great deal. In contrast with the Abrahamic notion that "in the beginning there was the Word," I have often emphasized that "in the beginning there was the Deed."[5] Here "Deed" (*wei* 為) refers to the deeds of humankind, that is, history. China's shamanistic-historical tradition[6] drew history into metaphysics. Metaphysics most often refers to *a priori* or transcendent existence, truth, or reality, which are insensible and beyond space and time. Saying "history enters metaphysics" fully tears down the separation between the *a priori* and empirical. My ontology takes "humans living" as its first premise,[7] and my epistemology takes "proper measure" as its primary category. These are of course nothing other than manifestations of human "deeds" and "history."

Liu: This is what is crucial.

Li: Indeed.

Liu: In our previous discussion you mentioned that if we were to write a book together, we might as well call it *On Fate* (*Lun mingyun* 論命運).

Li: In 1978 I discussed philosophical study of fate, and of prognostication of fortune and misfortune. I elaborated on the Chinese dialectics

76 | The Humanist Ethics of Li Zehou

of the *Laozi* and the *Changes* being more empirical and concrete than Hegelian dialectics, as a form of "pragmatic reason."[8] This is relevant here. Fate possesses contingency. This is because history possesses contingency.

Liu: You emphasize contingency, and not necessity?

Li: Correct.

Liu: Then history does not possess necessity?

Li: Necessity is contained within what I call accumulation.

Liu: How's that?

Li: Are you familiar with my discussion of "the three qualities of history"?

Liu: Not really. If history has three qualities, let me guess them.

Li: Guess away.

Liu: First, it is practical. Second, it is developmental. Third, it is contingent.

Li: The three qualities I assign to history are particularity, accumulation, and contingency.

Liu: Oh? So there is no necessity?

Li: The first of these is particularity—of certain times, places, and conditions. Hegel and Marx laid special emphasis on this, and it is indeed extremely important. That is why I place it first. All things, beings, and fate must be examined and discussed within their particular contexts.

Liu: Their certain time and place—history always occurs within certain time and place, with no exception.

Li: I discuss "ideas" as one of the three elements of morality (*daode san yaosu* 道德三要素).[9] These ideas include ethical norms, and they are historical products of the conditions of certain times and places. They possess changeability, difference, and relativity. What I absorb from Hegel and Marx is just this. Historical particularity is extremely important. Hegel's critique of Kant's "formalism" principally points to Kant's moral law lacking regulativity and normativity for actual actions, which is also its lacking historical particularity. Many scholars pay far too little attention to this, instead discussing Confucian virtues such as humaneness and filial piety always in an abstract, general manner.

Liu: This is what you refer to in advocating "a tremendous sense of history"?

Li: The second quality of history is accumulation. People often view ethical concepts such as humaneness, rightness, and justice as foundational, identifying them with "substance" (*benti* 本體) or the "Way of heaven" (*tiandao* 天道). In fact, these are accumulations of history. They do not exist outside history, but rather remain always interconnected with the empirical accumulation of particular communities over long periods. While indeed they may transcend particular concrete experiences and situations, they cannot transcend the collective concrete experiences and situations of the totality of humankind.

Liu: Accumulation and what is accumulated are very important. Is this related with your theory of historical sedimentation?

Li: What I just discussed is precisely sedimentation, which is the accumulation internal to history. History also has "external accumulation."

Liu: Accumulation can be distinguished into internal and external? What do you mean?

Li: External accumulation refers to the developmental nature of history. This is also what is called necessity. Necessity in this sense is established on the need to eat to sustain human life. It is the existence and improvements of food, clothing, shelter, behavior, reproduction, health, longevity, and pleasure. Through the manufacture and use of tools—that is, technology—humanity maintains and develops this existence, and hugely improves it. This is seen in widespread increases in life expectancy and decreases in military conflict, among other measures. Steven Pinker discusses this at length, and I strongly endorse his views.[10]

Liu: Sure. Without historical development, we could not identify progress or regress.

Li: We have previously discussed the notion that the world has recently fallen into a period of regression.

Liu: As I see it, on both global and local scales we are seeing historical regression.

Li: Yet this present period of regression still has aspects in which we find progress.

Liu: And what are those?

Li: Well, technology is still advancing rapidly. Thus, the present regression is better than comparable periods in the ancient world, and will probably be short lived. Premodern periods of regression could last for centuries. Even these, however, were mere instants from the perspective of human history. It is a shame and pity that any one person lives only so many decades.

Liu: That's true. But how do you know we really are more civilized than people in primeval times? Isn't there widespread agreement that modern technology has brought with it all kinds of harm?

Li: There certainly is this side to things. However, the benefits mostly outweigh the harms. Advanced technology remains a force impelling historical progress.

78 | The Humanist Ethics of Li Zehou

Liu: You still haven't answered my previous questions. How do you know we are more civilized than people of primeval times?

Li: Didn't I just mention food, clothing, shelter, behavior, and so on? Would you be willing to live in primeval society? You almost certainly would not have managed to live this long, and would not be here to have this discussion with me. This is why I endorse Pinker's attack on the postmodern tendency to deny progress and reject Enlightenment principles.

Liu: Pinker is quite concerned with historical progress, and has all kinds of data and analysis supporting him.

Li: The postmodern denials of history and progress emphasize cultural relativism. They have been very fashionable, and even now many continue with that hubbub. I have opposed this since the 1980s.

Liu: Historical relativism indeed has many problems, as does absolutism.

Li: We cannot treat them as equivalent evils—although I know you love to do that. History distinguishes these as forms of social advancement and backwardness.

Liu: But postmodern relativism itself rejects a linear view of historical improvement, instead upholding a vision of pluralist coexistence.

Li: Opposition to linearity is also fashionable in postmodern theory. You are always so fashionable. Do you think the cyclical theory of five elements in Han Confucianism is superior to contemporary linear theories? I admit that progression and regression are not simplistically "linear" matters. In addition to emphasizing the free will (as an expression of the internal accumulation, or sedimentation, of history), my ethics also highlights the role of ideas (which are also accumulative, and even more historically particular). I thus add Hegel to Kant. Hegel's is a theory of historical progress. In fact, Kant's is as well.

The Way of Heaven and Way of Humans as Historical

Liu: And what about the third quality of history, contingency?

Li: I cannot discuss contingency this time around. I have emphasized the antinomy of history and ethics as the tragic fate of humankind. We remain merely able to strive to adapt through accordance with proper measure. This is a profound aspect of history, and is closely connected with contingency. The antinomy of history and ethics is also related with historical particularity, and the cohesion of ethics and history has to do with their accumulative quality. The contingent quality of history greatly complicates pursuit of the "Way of heaven," in which history enters metaphysics. Especially in modern circumstances, living under pressures of the technological capability to wipe out the totality of humankind, the importance of maintaining control over our own fate is even more pronounced.

Liu: If we say that history possesses contingency, then what about human life? In the past you have emphasized the contingency of human life and fate in this same manner. So which is it? Are you referring to the course of history or the course of particular people's lives?

Li: The two are fundamentally interrelated. If they were not, history would not be human history. History is most basically the existence, life, and fate of various relations among individuals, groups, societies, nations, and humankind. All of human life arises contingently.

Liu: In what sense is it contingent?

Li: History is contingent in the sense that control over our fate is within our grasp!

Liu: This is your "historical ontology"?[11]

Li: Thus, historical ontology is a matter of history entering metaphysics. That is, the physical and metaphysical are inseparable and indivisible from one another. The Way (*dao* 道) cannot be independent of its vessel, just as principle (*li* 理, and here principle is equivalent to ritual regulations) cannot be independent of its manifest constitution (*qi* 氣). The natural cannot be independent of the human, the *a priori* arises from the empirical, and rationality is established through history. History is the rich and vibrant constituted vitality, dynamic existence, and experiential process of billions of people and their billions of interactions, both joyous and tragic. It is not fixed and rigid in the way people often conceive of human psychology, human nature, moral principle, material constitution, or the Way. We can thus say that my theory of "emotion as substance" is comparable to a theory of no substance.[12] It takes the rich and vibrant, changeable and profound emotions of the individual as what is fundamental. This is the basis for attachment to, affection for, recognition of, and cherishing of the self—this weak and infinitesimal contingent life—and thereby also the basis for striving to bestow grounding for its life and fate. Once history has entered metaphysics, we still distinguish the Way from its vessel. But what the "Way" of history is becomes an especially profound question demanding deep exploration.

Liu: How impressive of history, to become metaphysical—to create metaphysics.

Li: This history is not just a collection of events. . . . Events are merely "vessels." The historical "Way" first and foremost demands ideas of historical truth, objectivity, and the value of history. These are major

80 | The Humanist Ethics of Li Zehou

issues that are tough to affirm and confirm. Is there a "true" history? Can history be "objective"? The complex axiological relations of coherence and conflict between history and ethics or history and morality all constitute major issues of the ontology of historical philosophy.

Liu: How is this historical metaphysics related to what you have advocated as "aesthetic metaphysics"?

Li: History should be understood as including the various emotions of human life. Only then is it concrete history. This is what I refer to as emotion being substance, isn't it? And ultimately, doesn't this take aesthetic emotional experience as constituting the "realm of heaven and earth"?[13] I will return to this point later. In terms of history's particularity, as emphasized above, it is the interactions, both joyous and tragic, of all people in their concrete lives that constitute history.

Liu: Of all people?

Li: All individuals. That is, billions of people, and countless generations.

Liu: I see. History becomes substance, and this is a dynamic living substance. It is not the substance of Western ontology, but rather what is foundational—what Chinese describes as the "embodiment" (*ti* 體) of the "root" (*ben* 本).[14]

Li: Chinese tradition describes the Way of humans in terms of the Way of heaven, and the Way of humans is historically constituted, or even is history itself.[15] This is why I describe this outlook as "historical ontology."

Liu: But according to "new historicism," history is also a kind of fiction. The historical narratives of traditional Chinese histories, as represented in the *Records of the Grand Scribe* in particular, have a certain fictional quality.

Li: In *Historical Ontology*[16] I discussed this, pointing out that while there is a fictional aspect to these narratives, archeological studies show that they are not entirely fictions. Histories are not purely works of literature. If they were, there would be no "Way" to pursue. So I reject the idea that all history is fictive. "New historicism," in my view, is another postmodern fashion.

Liu: So then, it is precisely within history that we should seek the Way (*dao*) and pursue metaphysics. We cannot find it through empty ahistorical discussion.

Li: Being the Way of heaven or nature, it cannot be generated by the human subject's imagination. Yet this Way of heaven or nature is, nevertheless, generated by the labor and exertion of humans themselves.

Liu: And this is why you are so concerned with the matter of fate?

Li: Fate is controlled by humankind itself. This is an affirmation of the great wisdom and importance of the Confucian notion of "establishing one's fate" (*li ming* 立命).[17]

Liu: Right. This view describes pursuit of the Way of humans from within history, correct?

Li: We should pursue the Way of heaven within history, but it will remain extremely difficult to find. The "flourishing of the three Chinese dynasties" that Confucians pursue is like the historical necessity discussed in communism in that both search for the Way of heaven within history.

Liu: The Way and its vessel are ultimately unified. Many people believe the two are inextricable from one another, and that the separation of the physical and metaphysical is mistaken. This is a sort of dialectic.

Li: Western postmodernism has a trend of opposing dichotomies. It is fashionable.

Liu: So you oppose that opposition to dichotomies?

Li: What I mean is, some things objectively can be split into dichotomies, and yet many of these ultimately turn out to be difficult to sharply divide. Can you say at exactly which minute of which hour day turns to night? The same goes for old age and youth, life and death, and so forth. So then, many dichotomies are established out of necessity by humans for the sake of convenience in their actions and lives. I have long used the issue of traffic lights to discuss this. How would we avoid car crashes without distinguishing red from green lights? This distinction is a requirement and normative standard in human activity. It is not merely a matter of static conceptual understanding. Moreover, these dichotomies are all concrete historical products. They cannot be simply denied or annulled.

Liu: Practical, although artificial, dichotomies remain necessary.

Li: This "artifice" first of all aims to regulate action. Isn't this the point of all of ethics, to regulate what is right and what is wrong, what should be done and what should not, and so forth?

Liu: Ha, an interesting "rejection of the rejection of dualism." And indeed, postmodernism already seems to be in decline, not only in China but throughout the world.

Li: Postmodernism—beginning from Nietzsche's "revaluation of all values," which was actually a form of skepticism and the rejection of all historically created reality—reached an outer limit with the deconstructionism of Foucault, Derrida, and others' opposition to reason, and has been difficult to continue forward with.

Liu: Postmodern thought has come to an end.

82 | The Humanist Ethics of Li Zehou

Li: Central characteristics of postmodernism include the rejection, destruction, and suspicion of history and reality. Of course there are also some good things about postmodernism. For example, postmodern architecture is great.

Liu: You remain a modernist.

Li: The outlooks of Steven Pinker, John Searle (leaving aside recently uncovered problems of Searle's personal character and conduct), and others seem relatively healthy and positive.

Liu: Searle wants us to abandon skepticism.

Li: Well, skepticism in the sense of the postmodern deconstruction of everything, at least. Pinker and others have two "healthy" attitudes. One is their clear opposition to the various fashionable trends of postmodernism, as seen in Pinker's bald criticisms of many famous thinkers, including his severe denunciation of Nietzsche.[18] The second is concern with reaffirming the fundamental status of the individual promoted in Enlightenment rationality. Pinker makes his point through statistical analysis of large amounts of data, while Searle concerns himself with the distinction between "we" and "I," and so forth.

Liu: Postmodernism is a contemporary form of skepticism. The basic principle of postmodernism is "Everything goes!"

Li: Up to Paul Feyerabend's *Farewell to Reason* (1987), "everything goes."[19] The postmodern style of argument is labyrinthine and convoluted, in which a simple principle is tediously contorted.

Liu: What is most important in today's discussion: Humankind must control its own destiny!

From the Pre-Conventional and Conventional to the Post-Conventional

Liu: You have already written no small number of essays on ethics. Yet mostly these do not deal with the diversity of other contemporary ethical theories and schools of thought. Why is that?

Li: I primarily discuss formal aspects of the philosophical structure of the entirety of ethical discourse. These essays seldom directly bear on the substantive content of ethical discussions, and do not discuss much in the way of particular ethical and moral norms or the like.

Liu: Why is that?

Li: I believe it is important to establish these larger formal structures first. These bear on issues of methodology. They are prerequisite to exploring the various concrete matters, problems, and theories of ethics, as well as various forms of normative ethics, political philosophy, and moral psychology.

Liu: But your theory of two morals[20] already begins to bear on the concrete normative content of ethics, as well as on issues such as the relation between religion and morality. Your theory of the three elements of morality and distinction between ethics and morality,[21] along with your explanation of the internalization of external norms,[22] of course further bear on commonly discussed questions of whether morality is learned or innate (either naturally so, as an evolved genetic aspect of humans, or as the command of a transcendent divinity, or as *a priori* human nature). These can be interconnected, for example, with Lawrence Kohlberg's three levels and six stages of moral development, which Kohlberg puts in terms of conventionality.

Li: Right. I am mainly targeting and rejecting theories of *a priori* human nature and of natural biology (which tell us animals also have morality) as the basis for morality. I believe Kohlberg confirms my explication of the internalization of external norms.

Liu: It seems discussion of your emphasis on the source of moral laws should actually begin from the relation between morality and religion. Therein, Kierkegaard's interpretation of Abraham's willingness to kill his own son in the Bible is apropos. Absolute obedience to God's command—based in the belief that God is omniscient, all powerful, and goodness itself—here becomes the origin of the absolute quality of the moral law as well as the ultimate grounding of human nature. This kind of divine command theory, along with the sanctity of certain religious morals, were attacked by Enlightenment thinkers. Thereafter, on the one hand it took on various new guises of expression, such as the aforementioned political religion of obedience to the leadership of a personal god, and on the other hand there arose a great number of ethical theories embracing cultural relativism and rejecting such sacredness and absoluteness. What is your view of this?

Li: I agree with your basic portrayal of things. But I also have already answered that these are all "conceptual" categories that form part of the three elements of morality. That is, they are all formed and transformed through human ideas, such as in no longer believing in an omniscient, omnipotent, omnibenevolent God, not believing outdated laws are absolute or sacred, not believing in the authority of conventions, or maintaining one's faith but shifting its object. In the 1950s I witnessed devout

Christians transform into devout Marxists, ready to struggle and sacrifice themselves for the communist cause. In the '80s I again saw many of those same Marxists transform into followers of Christ—and in all of this they were entirely true and sincere. The objects, content, and ideas of "faith" could change, but the psychological disposition for "faith" did not change. The former is relative, and the latter absolute. Yet, there are also many with no such "faith" in anything who are nevertheless kind-hearted, upstanding persons as well as good citizens. This shows that there lies much value in exploring whether morality needs to be founded in religion or some kind of religious or other belief, and what the true nature of the relation between morality and religion is.

Liu: Herein, of course, lie questions of ideological change. But ideas consist in rational concepts, while religion is a matter of emotional belief.

Li: And this is exactly where things get complex. The "Way of heaven" understood within history by political religion seems to be a matter of political ideas supporting emotional faith. In fact, however, it is a matter of staunch "religious" faith, which is deeply affective and motivating, and involve absolute submission to a religious figurehead such as God. These support ideology and cause catastrophe, as seen with Nazism, Marxism, the Islamic State, and so forth. Of course, this kind of impassioned faith remains guided and grounded in certain ideas. Marx and his radical followers manufactured a political religion of intensely passionate faith and then forced those beliefs on others, creating tremendous global catastrophe. That tragedy continues to this day. In the past I have often argued that the notion of "abstract labor" discussed in the first chapter of *Das Kapital* is unsound, and conclude from this that communism is a transcendental illusion of sorts.[23] There is no necessity to it, and it is not the Way of heaven found within the Way of humans. In fact, then, emotional faith generally still requires a cognitive foundation, that is, a foundation of rational concepts and ideas. Animals and infants also have emotion, but are they capable of religious belief and religious emotion?

Liu: You still argue that morality is neither a natural instinct nor a heavenly (divinely) bestowed moral conscience.

Li: Correct. As one of the three elements of morality, "ideas" should be understood—as they are within my general scheme of ethics[24]—to denote ethical norms, including all social morals and religious morals. The diverse forms of normative ethics and political philosophy, then, discuss various "ideas" that constitute this element of moral psychology (and thus moral action). Studying the historical course of moral ideas—in terms of

History, Ethics, and Metaphysics | 85

the concrete processes by which various moral ideas are produced, upheld, and developed or reversed, overturned, and decline—I therefore believe to be extremely important. The study of human culture and the recent rise of historical anthropology can provide robust resources for this.

Liu: This is because these are all conscious or unconscious historical products of humankind situated in conditions of particular time and place?

Li: Right. This is the view I advocate under the name "historicism," affirming the concrete and accumulative nature of history.

Liu: You have discussed both the relativity and changeability of ideas as well as the absolute and unchanging nature of the will and of some ideas where they are constitutive of human psychology. We can summarize this as proposing that psychological forms are absolute and ideological content is relative. However, the ideas that adhere to the forms of the absolute will are also accumulative, as in your own discussions of loyalty, honesty, not lying, and so forth. Some of these accumulate to become "*a priori*" or "transcendent" divine commands or heavenly principles.

Li: The particular ideological content of being loyal changes, but the psychological disposition[25] for loyalty does not change. Kant states that morality ultimately leads to religion for more or less this reason. Since morals serve as absolute laws regulating individual conduct, they seem to always require an absolute and stable foundation in order to set our conscience at ease and to feel secure in the rectitude of fulfilling moral duties and responsibilities. With this emotional assurance, we acquire spiritual comfort and grounding.

Liu: The notion of "setting our conscience at ease" seems to also have grounds in Confucian moral psychology.

Li: Morality and religion consist of a set of issues that are difficult to fully divide into one or the other. They both involve placing oneself morally at ease (*an shen* 安身) and finding the sense of spiritual belonging of "establishing a sense of spiritual belonging" (*li ming* 立命),[26] as well as take up the matter of "ultimate concern." However, it is also not the case that all moral acts and psychology necessarily require religious belief to provide a sense of spiritual grounding. As with the kind-hearted and upstanding "good citizens" I mentioned earlier, we don't necessarily need to ask what someone believes in. This is what my "theory of two morals" states. On the whole, Kohlberg's second level of moral development is sufficient. There is no need to demand that every person reach the mental states of the third level, especially those of the sixth and highest stage. Civic virtue can rest on the second level or the fifth stage.[27] Only personal virtue usually demands the third level and sixth stage. Religion then pursues a seventh stage. Of course, there are also other views of this. I have stated previously that I endorse the third level but am skeptical of the sixth stage. Kohlberg also did not discuss issues related to instinct, the unity of knowledge and action, and so forth. His third level merely affirms, through the approach of educational psychology, my own major discussions of the internalization of external norms and the movement from ethics to morality.

Liu: You have said that what you call religious morals are in fact the medium, or outer casing, of social morals, while social morals are shaped by the economic, political, cultural, and other conditions of society in a particular time and place. These social morals can be conscious matters of refined etiquette or unconscious practices of custom.

Li: Sacredness within history often sheds its halo and transforms into everyday customs. Moreover, the particular content of religious morals likewise shifts and evolves. For example, Christian priests are now often allowed to marry, which is a major change from the centuries of predominant Catholic regulations requiring clerical celibacy. The accumulative and concrete nature of history on the level of individual psychology has a certain complexity. For example, to view the five major Confucian virtues (humaneness, rightness, ritual regulation, wisdom, and trustworthiness) as independent of the five major Confucian relations (ruler-minister, parent-child, husband-wife, elder sibling-younger sibling, and friendship) can only be a conceptual disposition or structure accumulated through history and attached within the individual will. The five major Confucian virtues originally formed on the basis of the social norms and interpersonal relations of the role-ethics of ancient China's five major relations. Through their practice over time these became engrained so that they seemed to be independent *a priori* principles or aspects of moral conscience originating from heaven or "original nature" (*ben xing* 本性). Here we see the adherence of ethics to history. I see Feng Youlan as having made two major contributions to philosophy. One is his proposal of the four realms of human life. The other is his method of abstract inheritance. Yet Feng begins from a New Realist "world of principle" (*li shijie* 理世界),[28] whereas I begin from the sedimentation (dispositions) of psychological forms, which is even less "abstract." I give the "abstract" a material foundation (through the direct connection of psychological and

History, Ethics, and Metaphysics | 87

neural activity). This exhibits the internal accumulation in which ethics closely adheres with history.

Liu: In recent centuries, the moral norms or particular rules of the five major Confucian relations have already gradually broken down and even disappeared. Take, for example, the "ritual" of three years of mourning for a parent, or the "propriety" of widows burying themselves with their husbands, or the priority of having children among matters of filial piety, or the taboo against widows remarrying. The particular social content of other "virtues" has also changed. However, in another respect, "ritual," "propriety" and other psychological dispositions also possess their historically accumulative quality. The tension and conflict between the changeability of these shifts and the regularity of accumulation make for an extraordinarily complicated picture that has fostered a great variety of ethical and moral theories.

Li: That is precisely right. The ideas of "loyalty" and "trustworthiness" I mentioned earlier as being quite distant from animalistic instincts are changeable in their content as well as accumulative in their form (as psychological dispositions). Emphasizing the former draws us toward various sorts of ethical relativity; the latter pursues "ultimate concern"—placing oneself morally at ease and finding a sense of spiritual belonging—within ethics and morality, which draws us toward religion and ethical absolutism.

Liu: Kant opposed theological morality but presents a moral theology. Kierkegaard places religion above morality, Levinas places ethics as first philosophy, Kohlberg suggests a religious seventh stage of moral development, and Mou Zongsan 牟宗三 identifies moral principles as cosmic laws.

Li: In these views, religion comes to orient and ground morality. Both are seen as matters of transcendent or *a priori* principals, raising human psychology and human nature to become part of sacred heavenly decree or divine will. In Confucianism, such views take "humaneness" as the root of filial piety and respect for elder siblings. They ground the psychological structures the Mencius discusses as the "four sprouts" (compassion, shame, deference or respect, and rightness) (*Mencius* 2A6, 6A6) in an *a priori* aspect of the major virtues (humaneness, rightness, ritual propriety, and wisdom; *ren yi li zhi* 仁義禮知).

Liu: You oppose these theories and reject this Chinese version of transcendental theory.

88 | The Humanist Ethics of Li Zehou

Li: Not only this "Chinese version"—I likewise reject the transcendentalism of Kant and other non-Chinese philosophers. I am willing to see Mencius's "four sprouts" as a "good nature" that is in fact shared in common among humans and animals and which is elevated through the supposition of the "Way of heaven" in Confucianism's "emotional cosmology." However, I still emphasize "learning." Confucius tells us to "learn what is below to reach what is above" (*Analects* 14.35), Xunzi gives "an exhortation to learning" (title of the first chapter of the *Xunzi*), and Mencius declares we must seek our "lost heart-minds" (*Mencius* 6A11). All of these emphasize that moral achievement remains the fruit of *a posteriori* learning. The four major virtues and "four sprouts" are not inherently possessed. Would you say that infants and children simply "know without contemplation" and "without learning are capable" of deference, respect, and rightness?

Liu: This returns us to our discussion of Kohlberg's theory of three levels of moral learning—pre-conventional, conventional, and post-conventional. What is your view of these?

Li: As I stated already, I agree with Kohlberg's description of three levels (retaining reservations regarding the six stages) and see them as according precisely with my own description of external social ethics transforming into internal subjective morality.

Liu: And more specifically?

Li: The pre-conventional first level begins from punitive and coercive demands and regulations. These use specific ideas and emotions to order and restrict the animalistic aspects of the human mind. The advance of an individual's psychological level from low to high just so happens to be interconnected with changes in these ideas and emotions from ideas of the interests of individual existence (pre-conventional) to ideas of the customs of individual and group life and norms of conduct (conventional) to ideas of beliefs that transcend the self and even the life of the group (post-conventional). This is also precisely the path from morality to religion.

Liu: The Chinese Confucian tradition has no religion of a personal god or metaphysical philosophy.

Li: Humans are not gods, and cannot become gods. Beginning in the 1970s, in discussing issues of human nature, I emphasized the animalistic aspects of the human. My ethics continues to recognize the importance of this side of things. For example, in my theory of two morals I point out that the Enlightenment ideology of modern social morals in fact already highlights issues of "desires"; yet because it is established on rational principles, although there are emotional elements therein, nevertheless their conceptual content is predominantly rational. For this reason, we now have the rise of anti-masculine and anti-individualist feminist sentimentalist ethics. This is one of the good things postmodernism has brought, although it remains mostly marginal. Postmodernism is a complicated thing. It is often destructive and negatory while also possessing reasonable and important positive aspects. This is an issue of historical particularity. However, postmodernism's main characteristic is denial of the accumulative quality of history. I believe this is a mistaken direction to take.

Liu: The way you draw on Kant's idea of "regulative" function in your theory of two morals is, I think, extremely important.

Li: The reason I see great significance in the regulative and properly constitutive function of China's traditional Confucian religious morals in relation to modern social morals is that it happens to include China's major ideas of mutual complementarity and interpenetration of *yin* and *yang*. And this of course involves the sort of emphasis on emotions that is characteristic of feminist ethics, including sympathy, concern, and recognition of humanity in response to the helpless and forlorn. I thus emphasize that ultimately "harmony is higher than justice." "Justice" is a matter of rational judgement, and while harmony includes rational elements, it goes far beyond being merely rational.

Liu: China's global contribution to ethics mostly lies in this.

Li: This is the nature of virtue for China. It differs from the four Greek virtues, which lack humane love. Of course, we still need to get rid of the gender inequalities of traditional Chinese interpretations of *yin-yang* complementarity.

Liu: You proposed your theory of two morals in the 1990s through explication of Chinese tradition. What about the West?

Li: In Europe and America, all major philosophical views—including forms of utilitarianism and liberalism as well as virtue ethics based in Aristotle's notion of equality in friendship and advocated by postmodern trends such as communitarianism—are forms of androcentric individualism and rationalism. As Alasdair MacIntyre tells us, these outlooks fail to pay attention to the dependent and weak animalistic aspects of humans, and therefore also require traditional religious morals such as the Christian morality of God's love. Although the theory of two morals is a product of Chinese modernity, it has a universal character applicable to the world.

90 | The Humanist Ethics of Li Zehou

Liu: I also strongly endorse the views MacIntyre puts forth in *Dependent Rational Animals*. However, it is unclear to me what contribution Chinese thought is able to make from this. Looking at Chinese ethics from the perspective of Michael Slote, it offers a *yin*-like ethics distinct from the *yang*-like ethics of the West.

Li: I fundamentally do not endorse this way of putting things, and do not agree with Michael Slote's theory of "empathy" more generally. I have repeatedly stated why elsewhere. However, we must also take into account that China's hierarchical ethics and morals, which are centered in the degrees of intimacy in familial relations, indeed do differ from Christian ethics and morals which see all persons as "equal" (somehow traditionally excepting females) and which center on the relation between God and man.

MORAL CONSCIENCE IS NOT MERELY COGNITION

Li: What level of opposition have you received in response to arguing that "moral conscience is not cognition" (*liangzhi fei zhi* 良知非知)?

Liu: There has been criticism, especially at the conference on "Conscience and Cognition" (*Liangzhi yu renzhi* 良知與認知) at Renmin University.[29]

Li: Was "moral conscience is not cognition" your title?

Liu: Yeah.

Li: How about "moral conscience is not *merely* cognition"? Just add a word and you won't be attacked.

Liu: Why's that?

Li: Well, I discuss there being three elements to morality, not just knowledge. . . .

Liu: What do you mean?

Li: Of the three elements, only ideas are knowledge.

Liu: Knowledge in what sense?

Li: To be filial and respectful to your father, you must first know who your father is. When a mother teaches her child she should love her father, listen to her father, and so on—isn't this knowledge? This is the most basic knowledge.

Liu: Sure. But knowing to be filial and respectful and knowing who your father is are not the same kind of knowledge.

Li: In determining your regard for, demands on, and conduct toward another you must always first know what kind of person this person is.

History, Ethics, and Metaphysics | 91

Your conduct differs from person to person. Toward your parents, siblings, and friends you do not act the same, and toward different friends your conduct also differs. Any ethical norm or moral action has its particular regulations and demands, and these are forms of cognitive knowledge. Any moral idea has cognitive elements.

Liu: Then moral conscience is cognition, after all? If I remember correctly, you have already rejected that idea!

Li: It is like this: moral conscience expresses knowledge through intuitive forms. It is not merely cognitive. Moral conscience also needs the support of intentional consciousness and emotions.

Liu: Then it is latent?

Li: It has latent dimensions, but is not entirely latent. There are those aspects that we are clearly aware of, and those we are unaware of. It seems as though it does not pass through conscious thought, but in fact it has transformed into habitual consciousness through the subject's long-term development within a particular environment. This includes the fortification of intentional consciousness (as in the notion of "overcoming oneself" in *Analects* 12.1) as well as emotions. It is "education" in the broad sense, and education of course cannot be separated from "knowledge."[30]

Liu: Moral conscience is indeed cultivated, which mostly occurs *a posteriori.*

Li: This is commonsense. As I mentioned earlier, something like "filial piety" is not an abstruse and empty abstract notion. Filial conduct always has particular content, which includes a large component of cognitive knowledge (that is, ideas) while also including intentional consciousness and emotions.

Liu: And that is the important point.

Li: The important point is often quite simple. My discussion of the three elements of morality is quite simple, and quite important.

Liu: All three are important? Which is most important?

Li: Haven't I already said so repeatedly? Most important is the will.

Liu: In wanting to do good, or in actually doing good?

Li: If one wants to do something, one does something. I emphasize that morality is a matter of action, and not of some sort of cognitive knowledge or thought, or how one knows or thinks.

Liu: Ah, the unity of knowing and doing—ultimately it must transform into action.

Li: To put it simply, if you do not act but only think of acting, that does not count as morality. To think of doing something and then be

92 | The Humanist Ethics of Li Zehou

capable of doing it relies on willful resolve. Kant believed that if one truly knows what to do then one can do it. But that is not, in fact, the case. The way Kant conceives of reason is simply far too "pure."

Liu: This is the crucial point. Conscience is expressed in one aspect through intuition, and in another aspect through the drive of one's will.

Li: Ideas and emotions are expressed through willful resolve as intuitions, which we call conscience. You all love to discuss Mencius, and especially his notion of the four heart-minds of compassion, love, and so on. I emphasize Mencius's statement that moral demands "test one's resolution, exhaust one's sinews and bones, and expose one to hunger and hardship" (*Mencius* 6B15). That is, only through continuous cultivation and exercise of the free will does a person resolve to "go forward against thousands and tens of thousands" (*Mencius* 2A2). I emphasize Mencius's spirit of "three proscriptions": one ought "not fall into excesses when wealthy and honored, not swerve from one's purpose when poor and obscure, and not bow before superior force" (*Mencius* 3B2).[31] It is precisely this spirit that has fostered the many exemplary and virtuous members of China's intelligentsia. It is what Lu Xun 魯迅 (1881–1936) called the backbone of China. For more than two millennia, this spirit has been carried forward. That kind of longevity and strength stand out among cultures.

Liu: Qing dynasty scholar Ling Tingkan 凌廷堪 (1757–1809) stated, "In times of its prospering, one or two extraordinary persons rise up to give [morality] new life, while thousands of common folk indignantly struggle against it; in times of its decline, thousands of common folk sit by and let it waste away, while one or two extraordinary persons maintain and prepare for it."[32] This is what it means to walk one's own path and to "go forward against thousands and tens of thousands."

Li: That's precisely right. I emphasize exercise of the will. The unity of knowing and doing advocated by Wang Yangming 王陽明, it seems to me, is just this. The intuition and capacity for moral goodness are products of sedimentation. The fruit of sustained effort over long periods becomes seemingly natural or innate.

Liu: Indeed. This is your theory of historical sedimentation. Moral conscience is formed through sedimentation.

Li: I have discussed "sedimentation" for several decades now, and people have often criticized me by saying this imposes reason on emotion and restricts individuality. I have pointed out that the situation is quite the contrary. Since what is *a priori* as well as *a posteriori* for each individual

History, Ethics, and Metaphysics | 93

differs, therefore what sediments is also distinct for each person. This is a tremendous promotion, expansion, and development of the unique nature of the individual, and its expression in morality is quite manifest.

THE MATTER OF THE "FREE WILL"

Liu: This touches on the recently hotly discussed issue of whether artificial intelligence has free will.

Li: In our previous discussions, we have already mentioned my view that free will is not an issue of the natural sciences or brain science.

Liu: Then it is only an ethical matter?

Li: Any technology operates within causality, and has never possessed the "freedom" of independence from causality. Freedom in Kant's thought is placed alongside the spirit and God as a valuable "transcendental illusion."

Liu: Right.

Li: But then, what does it mean to say that, ethically, people possess free will? Even though you have free will, you also have causality. And yet in regard to the relations among individuals and between individuals and groups, things are different. We face the issues of "freedom" as free choice.

Liu: In what sense is it freedom?

Li: Because it is not a matter of the individual or the individual's brain. It involves relations among individuals and between individuals and groups. This is not a scientific question; it is a social question.

Liu: Free will is of course carried out in social choices. But contemporary Western psychology and philosophy of mind are highly focused on explaining the nature of free will through scientific principles.

Li: In relations among individuals and groups, you decide whether to do something or not do something. The decision to act or not, this is causal. Thus, in lawsuits, lawyers seek to outline what acts a criminal has done as well as the various causes that lie beyond the control and choice of the criminal herself, such as the loss of normal mental faculties, duress or coercion, momentary impulse, and so forth. This shows that any act, including acts of free will, remain regulated by the laws of causality. They have causes. Thus, when we say "free" in the sense of casting off causality, we mean casting it off in the sense of not worrying about or being concerned with consequential considerations of one's own benefit or harm: knowing there are tigers on the mountain, but traversing the tiger mountain anyway. This is unconcerned with the categorical limitations and determinations of knowledge of the actual world of phenomena within space and time, causation, relations, and so forth.

Liu: This is social causality. Doesn't it naturally have no causal determination?

Li: A lot of people fail to parse this issue clearly. It is not a matter of the individual's neurology. Regardless of what causes beyond your control or awareness lead you to act one way and not another, that very "act" arises from the "freedom" of your three elements of morality impelling you—what we refer to as "free choice."[33] You must take responsibility for this "freedom." This is "free will." Does your decision benefit or harm society? That is determined by ethics! Thus, free will is not a matter of whether one's brain activity is determined or not: All of these decisions are determined by the brain, and the brain's decisions have their own causes. Whatever those causes, you choose this or that action and are thereby responsible to society and the community for the choice, making it an ethical issue.

Liu: Responsibility of course is an ethical issue, and "ethics of responsibility" are flourishing these days.

Li: From the view of society, this is an ethics of responsibility. From the perspective of the individual, it is moral obligation. Responsibility and obligation are both determined by ideas, and ideas change and differ with time, place, and history. Therefore, this is a matter of ethics rather than epistemology. It is not an issue of epistemological causation through neurology, consciousness, or otherwise. Identification of supposed "free will" in artificial intelligence is in fact encompassed within the complex causal chains of human software design, and is thus unrelated to "free will" in the sense I discuss it.

Liu: So you oppose the contemporary approach of using scientific method, as in brain science, to affirm the existence of free will, and also oppose the approach of philosophy of mind in providing a theoretical foundation for free will.

Li: Brain science has it right. It shows that there is no free will!

Liu: Right. That is an alternative scientific theory.

Li: I say that free will is meaningful only in terms of ethics, and not in science.

Liu: This is your view. But I have recently been reading up on speculative realism, which presents a position entirely unlike your own.

Li: I am not very concerned with what others say, even quite popular and influential voices.

Liu: But don't you say that "beauty is the form of freedom" and so forth?

Li: Here I am discussing only the issue of "free will," which does not bear on the other meanings and uses of the term "freedom." "Freedom," it is said, has over 200 meanings.[34]

The Three Basic Approaches to Ethics and Morality

Li: Returning again to ethics, where do you think ethics and morality come from?

Liu: You're asking about their historical origin? This is a distinctive aspect of your thought.

Li: As I see it, it all comes from history. Ethics are the external accumulation of history, and morality is the internal accumulation of psychology. There is correspondingly sedimentation of the cultural-psychological formation and of the individual emotio-rational structure. Social ethics must manifest in individual moral action, and the virtue ethics theories prevalent today in particular elaborate on the importance not of what people ought to do but of what kind of persons they ought to become. They thus aim at individual cultivation and effortful, embodied achievement of virtue. How are we able to be moral and to become sages and worthies? Perhaps through what is called "learning of the heart-mind" (*xin xue* 心學).[35] However, I believe that looking to their grounds and origins, there are only three approaches to understanding ethics and morality.

Liu: What three?

Li: Actually, this reiterates much the above discussion of conscience and intuition. The first is through animality.

Liu: Instinct!

Li: Animalistic instincts.

Liu: This is a foundational way of approaching things.

Li: Chinese scholars are generally not very receptive to discussions of animalistic instinct. Scholars from other cultures tend to be more receptive, some even believing that animals possess morality and that human morality is merely developed from it.

Liu: China has long upheld a distinction between man and beast. What is the second?

96 | The Humanist Ethics of Li Zehou

Li: Second is heavenly origination. Thus, there is much discussion of the *a priori* and transcendental, which has long been academically predominant. However, where does the "*a priori*" come from, and how? No one has ever been quite able to explain this. Is it bestowed by heaven? When exactly did that happen? Does "heaven" immediately "bestow" it when a person is born? If so, how does it then differ from animalistic instinct?

Liu: This view formulates a type of transcendental illusion, in both China and other cultures.

Li: Transcendental illusions are a different matter. We should not confuse the issue. In two recent conferences[36] heavenly origination has proven the predominant position.

Liu: Another question has bothered me for quite a while: Was Song Confucianism ultimately a version of one-world thought or two-world thought? This topic falls under your discussions of Chinese wisdom and its cultural-psychological formation being one-world. I have debated this issue with friends from Tsinghua University. They say Song Confucian conceptions of the Way of heaven are part of the human realm, making them also one-world outlooks. Immanent transcendence is a form of one-world thought. I responded by pointing out that the two-world character of Christian thought is unquestioned, and that immanent transcendence presents merely a distinct form of two-world thought. Otherwise, to where would we transcend?

Li: I have been asking that very question for quite some time, in arguing that Song Confucianism's pursuit of the transcendent and attempt at a two-world outlook fails.[37] You don't seem to quite grasp my basic point, or perhaps still waver between the two positions, trying to reconcile them. Also, the recently published Tsinghua bamboo slips further highlight that the essence of Confucian teachings lie in theories of the heart-mind and human nature (*xinxing lun* 心性論), and show the mistake of those famous four authors of the Manifesto[38] and of the New Confucianism of Hong Kong and Taiwan generally. When teaching in the US, I discussed Chinese intellectual history directly in terms of the "cultural-psychological structure," pointing out that this living tradition has its strengths and its shortcomings. I did not merely discuss ancient theories, or those of dead people. I also contrasted the way criminals in the West will repent to a residing priest for the sake of the ascendance of their soul, whereas in China one must be sent off on one's final journey

History, Ethics, and Metaphysics | 97

full of a hearty meal of fine drink and food. The students chuckled, and understood the difference between one-world and two-world outlooks.

Liu: When I was debating one-world and two-world outlooks with my friends, I found myself unexpectedly a bit irate. They said that Song Confucianism has a one-world outlook, as does Mou Zongsan. All of Chinese thought does. On the whole, it is all one-world thought, and although Song Confucians diverge a bit from this, that is not representative of the traditionally main aspects of Chinese wisdom. Rather, it resulted from changes following the arrival of Buddhism. Many people in Chinese intellectual and philosophical circles hold deep and unwavering faith in the movements of a transcendent Way of heaven. When this belief is questioned, they often respond with radical refutation; and in debating aspects of this belief, many issues become simply unapproachable. Dogmatism has arrived.

Li: Theirs is simply an emotional faith in the Way of heaven. But what is the substantive content of Way of heaven? Let's hear what they have to say about that! Didn't the Song Confucians tell us that the Way of heaven is the Way of humans? Yet that "Way of heaven" is also the hierarchical relational norms of the "three cardinal relationships and five constant virtues" (*sangang wuchang* 三綱五常), which include extremely specific feudal ethical norms. I also believe in the Way of heaven, and that the Way of heaven is the Way of humans. But this "Way of heaven" is not itself the Song Confucian set of relational and virtue norms, and thus even if we say that Song Confucianism has a one-world outlook, it differs greatly from how I understand the early Confucian one-world outlook, in which the thing-in-itself just is the material world, and not a soul, heaven, or God separate from body and matter. The Song Confucians pursued a world of principle (*li* 理) that is "prior to" material constitution (*qi* 氣). Zhu Xi told us "principle is substance" and that "prior to there being heaven and earth, first there was principle." That is, he tells us that there is an *a priori* "world of principle." However, Zhu Xi also consistently emphasized that principle cannot be separated from material constitution. Kant's realm of "rational" substance transcended humankind and was fully independent of the phenomenal world of causality and material constitution. Song Confucians desired to elevate the relational set of norms and virtues (i.e., the conduct and dispositions proper to rulers and ministers, fathers and sons) to the "pure and empty realm" of "principle." This is eternal and unchanging, and congruent with all things. You could even describe this view as seeking that history enter the Way of heaven, only they conceived of this "Way of heaven" as unchangeable concrete feudal roles, which would thereby make "history" static, in fundamental contrast with my own views. Also, we are unable to ourselves "transcend" to that realm of principle, since that realm transcends experience as well as material constitution and concrete form. Such a view follows precisely from people's (including the Song Confucians') rejection and repression of China's longstanding and powerful shamanistic-historical tradition. The difficulties faced by the theories of Zhu Xi and others are quite apparent. Today people are forced to explain these views as asserting only the "logical priority" of principle; but that then gives these theories little actual meaningfulness. This is why I say that they "failed."

Liu: Exactly. This is where the fundamental difference lies. Everyone "believes" in this transcendent Way of heaven, but how can heaven and earth, as we naturally find them, be moral? They conflate the "starry heavens" above with the "moral law" within—but how exactly is that possible? To also draw the Way of heaven back into the human realm after projecting the morality within us out into the natural world—how is that possible?

Li: It is possible in Kant having faith in a form of reason that transcends humankind, and it is possible in my having faith in an unknowable material thing-in-itself that transcends humankind.

Liu: This is the difference between you and Kant—Einstein's cosmic divinity!

Li: So in contrast to Stephen Hawking's human-dependent schema of the cosmos, I state in *Pragmatic Reason* that Einstein believed in this divinity, Chinese tradition believes in this divinity, and I believe in this divinity![39]

Liu: Of course, this is also a sort of "faith," haha. So that is what Hawking believes? Does it not align with Kant?

Li: Nope.

Liu: How so?

Li: That the existence of the cosmos depends on humans? The manner in which something exists is not the same as the cause of its existence. The former is legislated by humans, not the latter. Thus, Heidegger and Wittgenstein both marveled at why there is something and not nothing. This is not a question of how but of why, and it cannot possibly be solved.

Liu: An inquiry like why there is something and not nothing sits at the foundation of metaphysics. On this point, you move toward a "rational mysticism." You mentioned there are three approaches to ethics and morality. What's the third approach?

History, Ethics, and Metaphysics | 99

Li: I have already discussed it: sedimentation becoming intuition. This is why ethics is prior to morality, and not the inverse.[40]

Liu: I endorse that view. We should follow this approach to things. You have put things quite clearly this time.

Li: So you can push your friends to answer, what exactly are the Way of heaven, heavenly intention, heavenly decree, and other such notions they talk about? What kind of things are they? Which are *a priori*, and which are not *a priori*?

Liu: Right. I will ask them.

Li: For example, filial piety. We already discussed that this involves a great many specific norms, such as the "three forms of obedience and four virtues" (*sancong side* 三從四德), "no parent anywhere is wrong," "do not travel far when your parents are around," and so forth. Which of these are *a priori*? Which are not *a priori*? What standard do we have for distinguishing the one group from the other? Many ancient norms of filial piety have changed today. Are they still *a priori*? We could list all the different specific views of filiality. Over the last century, these ideas have transformed dramatically. In fact, what ought to be written is a history of the development of ethical ideas and norms as an examination of the issues of what is *a priori* and *a posteriori*.

Liu: They really should be viewed historically.

Li: Which views do we understand as *a priori* and right? In the past, free love was considered immoral and abhorrent.

Liu: Western views of love migrated to China.

Li: Which view is *a priori*? Which is the *a priori* "good"?

Liu: Moral conscience is not fixed and unchanging—you're arguing for historical materialism here?

Li: The various peoples and cultures of humankind's existence share certain common ends in the most basic aspects of life—food and clothing, shelter and conduct. They thereby also tend to have similar and even equivalent regulations in terms of interpersonal relations, social restrictions, and ethical norms. Some of the ideas therein have changed only very little throughout history. I have already mentioned this adherence of ethics to history a few times. It involves history's elevation of ethics. Thus, within the processes of antinomy between history and ethics—within the particularity, relativity, and contingency of history—we paradoxically find the constitution of the absoluteness, supremeness, and universality of ethics and morality. This is also the path—profound and complex—by which the "Way of humans" is elevated as the "Way of heaven" and history constitutes metaphysics. My views aim precisely at progressively reducing

100 | The Humanist Ethics of Li Zehou

the antinomy between history and ethics, that is, of making the Way of humans into the Way of heaven, removing evils and pursuing goodness, and thereby drawing history into metaphysics. Of course, for the community and society this is a long and gradual process. Therefore, the individual's emotional grasp of temporality and pursuit of the emotio-rational structure is increasingly important. This is far from being a matter of language. It is a matter of moving from language toward examination of how historical sedimentation enters human psychology.

Liu: Between the absolute and the relative—perhaps there is no absolute, but moral relativism has its own problems.

Li: I am pretty sure I already discussed this earlier. This is an issue of the "cultural-psychological formation."

Liu: In terms of human psychology, Mencius emphasized the heart-mind of compassion as one of the "four sprouts" of virtue, whereas Wang Yangming took the heart-mind of approval and disapproval, or right and wrong, as the foundation of moral conscience. This is the difference between Mencius and Wang Yangming.

Li: These kinds of specifics are not of great interest to me now. Mencius's heart-mind of compassion has been given an extraordinary number of interpretations. The discussions among Korean scholars of the nature and relations of the four heart-minds and seven emotions present especially robust scholarship on this.

Liu: These became known as the "Four-Seven debates."

Li: But more important is that we firmly grasp the crucial issues, such as whether these are *a priori* and the relation of history with ethics and morality. You all love to discuss the heart-mind of compassion as humaneness, and Zhu Xi stated "humaneness" to be "the principle of love"; but Zhu placed even greater emphasis on "humaneness" being the "comprehensive virtue," meaning that "humaneness" refers to the totality of the various diverse aspects of virtue. This is actually similar to my own discussion of the "structural formation" (*jiegou* 結構) of humaneness. So is humaneness the principle of love, or comprehensive virtue? Zhu Xi stated both. How are they related? Which is more important? This is what is crucial.

China's Emotional Cosmology

Li: Since we are returning to ethics, my *New Sketch of Ethics* (*Lunlixue xinshuo shuyao* 倫理學新說述要), including the appended dialogue with yourself, although quite concise, is important.

History, Ethics, and Metaphysics | 101

Liu: In that work you elaborate on the empirical becoming *a priori*.

Li: I focus on the origins of history (ethics) and education (morality), and so emphasize Confucius and Xunzi's "exhortation to learn."

Liu: Our dialogue is short but sweet.

Li: In it I discussed moral conscience as intuition. I said that in Chinese tradition, the heart-mind of right and wrong (or approval and disapproval, *shi-fei*) and the heart-mind of liking and disliking (*hao-wu*) are melded together.

Liu: The melding of the heart-minds of right and wrong and liking and disliking—that's the "unity of emotion and reason"! In right and wrong there are judgments of liking and disliking, and in liking and disliking there are judgments of right and wrong.

Li: Because Western tradition emphasizes rational ideas, those advocating the importance of emotion, like Hume, end up denouncing reason, calling reason a slave of the passions. They do not pay attention to the structural interrelation between the two. That is why I put forth the idea of the "emotio-rational structure." This term does not seem to appear in Anglophone discourse.

Liu: From Plato to Kant, there is a general overemphasis on reason.

Li: Because the West has a "two-world" outlook.

Liu: Does China really lack a tradition of transcendence?

Li: Not at all. More or less any culture, including China, will have ideas and sentiments with tendencies toward, and aspects of, transcendence and another world. China does as well, but comparatively speaking, these aspects are vague and insubstantial.

Liu: But nevertheless, there is this tendency.

Li: As I have already repeatedly emphasized, Chinese people believe in the Way of heaven, heavenly will, heavenly decree, and so forth. They believe there is something that transcends humankind. But what kind of thing, exactly, is it? What particular content and form does it take? In contrast to many religions, these are not at all clear and definite. We do not have the explicit, recorded words of God or of Jesus Christ. Of course, there are things like the Jade Emperor in Chinese Daoist religion, as well as belief in mythologized historical figures like Guan Yu 關羽, in folk deities like Ma Zu 媽祖, and in various other deities and spirits. However, these present no doctrinal teachings to follow; there are just traditional folk customs. The "heaven" of Chinese Confucian thought is both spirit and matter, as I have often quoted Wang Guowei 王國維 telling us.

Liu: In the Bible, God speaks a great deal, whereas in China, Confucius asks, "Does Heaven say anything?" (*Analects* 17.19) Yet, haven't you

102 | The Humanist Ethics of Li Zehou

also argued for a materialist explication of Kant's reverence at "the starry heavens above me" (Ak 5:161)?

Li: This is my own interpretation of Kant. The thought of Kant himself seems to still mainly emphasize a form of reason that transcends humankind and governs all. I view this as an unknowable thing-in-it-self—cosmic noumenon, if you will.

Liu: This still uses Kant's categories.

Li: An unknowable "thing-in-itself"—this is precisely how we should understand the "Way of heaven." Its content is supplied by the "Way of humans," including its explanation of the cosmos.

Liu: This is the synergistic co-existence of humans and the cosmos?

Li: Right.

Liu: This seems an even more elevated notion.

Li: It provides a prerequisite, a necessary supposition, for theories of the goodness of human nature.

Liu: How so?

Li: The predominant Chinese outlook is "one-world," and has faith that this world is good. Of course, in the West Leibniz also asked why there is something and not nothing, discussed pre-established harmony, and saw this world as the greatest of all possible worlds. The Bible also tells us that humans are created in accordance with the image of God, and therefore should be viewed as fundamentally good. However, these views still differ from China's emotional cosmology. The influence of the notion of original sin remains strong. In contrast, this Chinese cosmology is far more thoroughgoing and constitutes a core and original aspect of the development of Chinese tradition. It is a longstanding strength of this tradition that has been carried forward over the centuries.

Liu: China's "culture of optimism"![41]

Li: We can see Mencius's four heart-minds as an important contribution to this "emotional worldview."

Liu: This is not something you have said before. I thought you rejected the theory of four heart-minds?

Li: I haven't elaborated on this at length, because you all place far too much emphasis on "learning of the heart-mind" already.

Liu: You do not reject the notion of a fundamental heart-mind of compassion?

Li: When have I ever rejected the heart-mind of compassion? What I oppose is the idea of simply "being capable without learning and knowing without contemplation." All I said is that this compassion is no more than

History, Ethics, and Metaphysics | 103

animalistic instinct, not a form of *a priori* morality bestowed by heaven. Mencius and especially the Song Confucians elevated this to *a priori* status as part of their conception of the traditional Chinese emotional worldview. Mencius and Wang Yangming discuss innate moral conscience as an intuition of the free will that avoids choosing to do evil and instead does good. I believe this is better understood as a cognitive and behavioral capacity for goodness formed through edification of the will—a "good will." The free will is the capacity to self-legislate universally applicable morals. For Kant, this is a form of reason that transcends humankind. In the context of Chinese tradition, it is part of an emotional cosmology.[42]

Liu: This indeed seems like a positive direction to pursue.

Li: As I have mentioned, there have been many changes in ideas of good and evil, which often differ due to variances between the past and present and between cultures. Because of its emotional worldview, Chinese tradition saw heaven as good and "heaven's action is robust" (*tian xing jian* 天行健).[43] Thereby human nature was also seen as good, in the sense that the generation and existence of humans is a good thing. Humans have no original sin; we are fortunate to have life, and are not burdened or punished in it.

Liu: In contrast with the West's "culture of guilt."[44]

Li: This can be viewed alongside the theory of original sin and Kant's "radical evil," since they are on the same level. That is, they transcend the level on which we discuss good and bad aspects of animalistic instincts, and refer to the good or bad nature of humans on a higher level.

Liu: What do you mean? A higher level?

Li: Good and bad are originally two different aspects of people's descriptions of animalistic nature. I have elaborated on this many times already. When discussed in terms of original sin and emotional cosmology, they are unrelated to animalistic nature.

Liu: What about people's personalities? And original human nature?

Li: The difference between Mencius and Xunzi fundamentally arises from these two aspects of animalistic nature, with Mencius and especially Song Confucians elevating the goodness of human nature to a metaphysical level far removed from animalistic nature. That view has remained predominant to this day.

Liu: That is true. Mencius and Xunzi differ, and Xunzi's views are far inferior to those of Mencius.

Li: Mostly it is just that Song Confucians elevated Mencius to such heights. Of course, Tang-dynasty scholar Han Yu and others initiated that

104 | The Humanist Ethics of Li Zehou

movement. But really it is not of great import whether human nature is good or bad. Confucius himself put it best, telling us, "By nature, people are nearly alike; by practice, they come to be far apart" (*Analects* 17.2). It all relies on learning and practice.

Liu: You hold that humans are neither good nor bad by nature?

Li: Humans are like animals, as mentioned earlier. Animals have good "instincts" (such as those for cooperation and caring for others) as well as bad ones (to harm and even kill others). Of course, here good and bad are still defined by humans.

Liu: Even animal ethics are proposed in regard to humans. These two types of instinct both serve the survival and flourishing of the species. Where there is good, there is bad; where there is shade, there is light.

Li: Humans made these designations of good and evil, and on that basis we label human nature good or bad. Mencius elevated one set of animalistic instincts to the *a priori* status of an originally good human nature. I summarize this as the emotional worldview of China's shamanistic-historical tradition. Let me add a few comments on Mencius. He proposes the "four heart-minds" alongside one another. Of course, these include rational aspects therein, most obviously in the heart-mind of right and wrong and the heart-mind of respect and reverence. You all mainly emphasize the heart-mind of compassion, as humane love (*ren'ai*) or "humaneness" (*ren*). I, on the other hand, understand Mencius's elevation of the feeling of compassion to become the foundation or starting point of "humaneness" as the "comprehensive virtue," which directs people to pursue, establish, and realize the meaningfulness of the "Way of heaven" in human life, and to do so in a deeply emotional manner and within the historical processes of tragedy and happiness of human life lived within its concrete limits. Precisely for this reason, history enters metaphysics to form an aesthetic metaphysics. This is Mencius's tremendous contribution to the emotional worldview of China's shamanistic-historical tradition, in which no personal god arises. We can top off my construction of an anthropological historical ontology with this. This is an extraordinarily high appraisal of Mencius.

Liu: True. Mencius's historical origin lies in the shamanistic-historical tradition.

Li: This is sufficient. Here we have a one-world outlook which can be compared on the same level with Western views of original sin.

Liu: As religious suppositions, right?

Li: Original sin is a religious supposition. Chinese people do not believe in such a thing as original sin. However, China's emotional cosmology involves emotional faith in a kind of non-religious religious supposition.

Liu: Sure. Its notions of repentance are lacking.

Li: Right. Chinese culture lacks sufficient awareness of repentance. This is a shortcoming. In Western cultures, many people believe in original sin. The sentiments of original sin are part of the particular content of the cultural-psychological formations that developed within the context of Western traditions. China did not have them.

Liu: Chinese culture's optimism made it so.

Li: China emphasized precisely that humans—

Liu: Humans are fundamental?

Li: In Christian teachings, humans were driven out of the Garden of Eden into hardship, suffering, and death. Only through the Last Judgment will they be allowed to enter Heaven.

Liu: That's correct.

Li: This is quite unlike the views found in Chinese culture. Chinese people have believed we are fortunate to be born into this world. As long as we strive to do our best, we can also rise to heaven, although this is a quite vague notion of heaven. In the original version of Judeo-Christian teachings, not matter how great people's efforts, there could be no assurance they would enter Heaven. It was for only God himself to determine who the "chosen people" were. Chinese people, in contrast, have aspired to live a life of happiness, and believed that as long as people do good in their lives, they can ascend to heaven. Ascending to heaven, moreover, they bring with them all those aspects of their worldly lives. This may seem quite banal, but it may in fact be anything but.

Liu: The influence of Wang Yangming's thought over the last five centuries really ought to abate.

Li: The way you have been attacked for saying so, it's pretty impressive that you have not yet capitulated.

Liu: What reason would I have to capitulate?

Li: Are you sure you can withstand their attacks?

Liu: I don't really worry about it. I am willing to face that school of thought head on.

Li: Their position is mainstream, and their emphasis on the heart-mind of compassion, interpreted as no more than emotion, seems quite suited to your tastes.

Liu: I am not a sentimentalist. Your theory of "emotion as substance" is a good example of understanding reason as central and emotion as auxiliary.

106 | The Humanist Ethics of Li Zehou

Li: Reason permeates morality and emotions in my theory. It is not a matter of what is central and what is auxiliary. That is why I refer to moral psychology as the "emotio-rational structure." For various reasons, both inborn and developmental, each person has a distinct emotio-rational structure. Also, sometimes emotion is central and reason auxiliary. That is why I call it a "structure." Structures can take many diverse formations. A garden flourishes with flowers of all types.

Liu: Reason enters into emotions.

Li: Humans are rational animals. This ancient definition is correct.

Liu: It is quite ancient a definition. Aren't humans symbolic animals?

Li: Ernst Cassirer defines humans that way. But symbols are products of reason. The issue turns on how we understand reason. How are humans able to generate reason? My writings on epistemology address this. To say that humans are emotional animals is not accurate. Other animals also have emotions.

Liu: Yet the relation between emotions and desires remains a problematic issue to this day.

Li: The relation between emotions and desires is a matter of how we differentiate them, as well as an issue of how various particular emotions are related with various particular desires. Some emotions are closely related to animalistic desires, while others are not, and yet others are even fundamentally unrelated to desires. The same is true of ideas. Erotic love and marriage are not the same thing. The latter is predominantly social. The fourth stage of Confucianism I propose[45] differs from the transcendent conceptions of the heart-mind and human nature that characterize the third stage. I probably should elaborate on this, but I cannot bring myself to do that again here.

Liu: So what is the secret formula for their mutual complementarity?

Li: This is particularly complicated. To completely understand how people's many animalistic instincts are structurally integrated with reason is likely to take centuries of further research in the natural sciences.

"PHILOSOPHY WITH HUMANS" AND "PHILOSOPHY WITHOUT HUMANS"

Liu: At present, Chinese philosophy is quite popular, while there seems to be declining interest in Western philosophy.

Li: There is nothing strange about that. In recent decades China has risen in wealth and power, and scholars have shifted their attention accordingly.

Liu: The situation was quite opposite in the 1980s.

Li: Many of the scholars who intensely opposed tradition in the '80s have now reversed to intensely embrace tradition.

Liu: In a sort of ethno-nationalism.

Li: Which is actually the wrong direction to take. They think there is no need to learn from other traditions.

Liu: Of course, we should practice the approach of taking what is useful from other traditions.[46]

Li: They think that Confucius is supreme, and stands above all else. This is entirely mistaken.

Liu: Esteeming Confucius, we still cannot return to the past.

Li: Haven't you been particularly interested in my more recent distinction between "aesthetics with humans" and "aesthetics without humans"?

Liu: I just wrote an essay on "Taking the Way of 'Aesthetics with Humans' to Construct a School of Chinese Aesthetics."

Li: We should actually move from there onto a discussion of "philosophy with humans" and "philosophy without humans."

Liu: Shouldn't we be critically reflecting on anthropocentrism?

Li: I myself am an anthropocentrist! What of it? Hahaha.

Liu: You have been consistent in this, at least, from your "subjectality-based practical philosophy"[47] to your "anthropological historical ontology."

Li: It is a fundamental part of those views.

Liu: There seems to be something wrong with this emphasis on anthropocentrism.

Li: Perhaps, but then, how wrong could it really be? Discussing the world, nature, and the cosmos separate from humans has no philosophical significance. Specific questions of how the world actually is, such as how to explain black holes and so forth, are matters of science. I have in the past consistently discussed how anthropocentrism is characteristic of Western thought.

Liu: Why is that?

Li: In the very first chapter of the Bible, God grants humans custodial responsibility for nature. This of course presents us with an anthropocentric view.

Liu: Sure, but this is a religious outlook.

Li: Of course, Enlightenment rationality is culpable on the same count. It likewise demands humans conquer nature. However, my own anthropocentrism merely states that we are to view things from the

108 | The Humanist Ethics of Li Zehou

position of humankind, rather than, say, from the position of mammals or primates more generally. And even more so, we are not to view things from the position of all animal species. What is wrong with that? I place the continuous extension of the living existence of humankind as the most important substantive reality and highest good. What is wrong with that? Although this substantive reality and good also require the natural world, nevertheless, our study, exploration, and understanding of the natural world is ultimately human oriented. Separate from humans, this natural world is without meaningfulness and value.

Liu: A bold, unflinching statement of things, indeed. I see your point.

Li: This is my version of anthropocentrism. In this, moreover, we can respond to Hume's famous philosophical problem: that "ought" (a normative, ethical matter) cannot be derived from "is" (a descriptive, epistemological matter). Indeed, that "this is a good book" (a value judgment: we "ought" to read a good book) cannot be derived "this is a book" (a neutral statement, without judgment of value). However, traced to the source, books are published for people, and the reading of a good book may help cultivate good humans and good affairs. At their ultimate source, ethics and morality can be united with epistemology. They do not necessarily need to be thoroughly separated. I know that both reading and not reading this book may influence me, and because of this I recognize that "this is a book" can be connected in its ultimate source to "this is a good book," even though this derivation may not be direct.

Liu: This is not animal centric.

Li: What matters here is the relation between knowledge and action (ethics, morality). Put simply, this "centrism" is not that of the Bible, which gives humans command over nature and places them in antagonistic relation to it.

Liu: Yet that humans should conform to the natural world is also not quite the right view of things, and not entirely possible.

Li: For the sake of the continuous extension of its own living existence, humankind should indeed seek harmonious forms of interrelation with the myriad things. Even if we are to control and utilize those things, we should still relate harmoniously with the natural world for the sake of the continuous extension of our living existence.

Liu: To recognize our relations to other people and things, and thereby care about them, is of course possible.

Li: Only in that way can humankind, as a species and communal group of living organisms, live well and continue to extend and protect its own life as a species.

Liu: This sees people as fundamental. Centering on humans in this way makes it an ideology of human existence.

Li: But I am not talking about existentialism, or the value of existence. Without the living existence of humankind, nothing has meaning. Knowledge serves survival. Yet this can be said only on the level of the totality. It should not be interpreted as the pragmatist notion equating use or function with truth. This is the crucial element of anthropological ontology's reverence for the "Way of heaven" and for pursuit of this metaphysical "Way of heaven" within the phenomenal realm of history and the Way of humans.

Liu: Stephen Hawking tells us that extraterrestrial civilizations will become a threat to humanity.

Li: I am not so convinced. There doesn't seem to be sufficient evidence of this threat. But in terms of discussing the cosmos, the Way of heaven, God, and so on—what do these matter independent of humanity? Of course, you can still examine things from the perspective of natural science. But things that may harm the living existence of humankind must also be identified and studied. Science may be unconcerned with that, but ethics needs to be. That is why we have medical ethics and other forms of normative ethics and political philosophy.

Liu: Meaningfulness and value are human products.

Li: Global warming might be detrimental to chimpanzees and other plants and animals, yet it might also prove beneficial to certain flora and fauna, microorganisms, bacteria, and so on. So you have to consider which species' standpoint you are speaking from. I view things from the position of humankind. If you want to call that anthropocentrism, I cannot say that you are wrong. The continuous extension of the living existence of humankind ought to be seen as the central issue for humans. It is a matter of our own fate.

Liu: And of course such a view would provoke criticism. Destruction of the natural environment needs to be halted. The loss of ecological balance is already irreversible.

Li: Of course I oppose the environmental destruction of modern big industry, including global warming, the rise of sea-levels, deforestation in the Amazon, and so on. These are tremendous mistakes made by

110 | The Humanist Ethics of Li Zehou

humankind, and are also great harms to the living existence of humankind itself. Aren't we starting to realize that now, and attempting to change course?

Liu: We are talking mainly of harmony between humans and nature.

Li: Humans will get many things wrong. When we make these mistakes, we gain experience and strive to correct things. This is precisely the pursuit of the "Way of heaven" within history.

Liu: There is always a cost for each step of human progress.

Li: Maybe not "each step." But the antinomy between history and ethics is something I proposed long ago. Engels told us that unrestrained deforestation and other practices by primitive societies sometimes left them with no means of survival. Later peoples had to learn from such experiences. Mencius likewise told us, "If the axes and hatchets enter the hills and forests only at the proper time, the wood will be more than can be used" (*Mencius* 1A3). Trees must still be cut down, but we should do so in the proper measure. It is just that we should "enter the hills and forests only at the proper time" so as to protect the regrowth of the forests. On the whole this remains oriented by human concerns.

Liu: Slash-and-burn practices, which destroy large sections of forest to make way for arable land, were the first major instances of human air pollution.

Li: At first these practices served human survival. Later, the situation changed. This is a case of learning from historical experience. Proper measure is fundamentally important because only it can establish the proper "Way of humans" as the "Way of heaven," regarding the natural world and human relations (such as those of the antinomy of history and ethics) within history. The reason that certain qualities of "shamanism" are important is that the history of humans, as participants alongside heaven and earth in co-creation, possesses a sacred quality. In this way, it is only the "Way of humans" that can possibly be the "Way of heaven." And it is in this that we see history enter metaphysics. Seeking the "Way of heaven" from within history is a matter of significant difficulty. Yet historical ontology, which takes "humans living" as its first premise, still aims to reiterate this fundamental point of view. It does not agree with the three major approaches—divine creation, genetic mutation, and the possession of language—to explaining how humanity has been made possible. I see this as explained only through the use and manufacture of tools. Although primitive axes and hatchets destroyed forests, and although some people continuously respond to this view by pointing out that chimpanzees and other animals (such as birds) also manufacture tools, I still maintain that only humans are capable of the universal necessity of the use and manufacture of tools. This is true today, but also has been true from our very beginnings, when tools were both a necessary condition (without tools we could not survive) and a sufficient condition (through the diversity of the use and manufacture of tools) as well as a precondition (in the biological evolution of the body and neural structures of primates) of human life. Reason arose from this, history was established from this, and thereby the quality of human life came to far surpass that of other animals. The distinctively human use of language, which passed down semantic content primarily encapsulating the interactive (with objects and other humans) experience of the practical activity of the use and manufacture of tools, thereby became humans' most important symbolic tool and power. In this sense, we see the astuteness of saying "That which stimulates[48] the movement of all under heaven resides in the words" and Heidegger's statement "Language is the house of being."[49] I have long held that it is the practical activity of using and manufacturing tools that established the distinctive semantics of human language. The technologies, bodily movements, processes, and so forth of our use and manufacture of tools are constitutive of the language we use to communicate, and this differs from the communications of animals. I see the use of hand gestures in primeval human languages as extremely important.[50] Many primeval languages of hand gestures were based primarily in the technologies, bodily movements, methods, processes, and so forth of the use and manufacture of tools. Later, speech subsequently became the typically human form of language. Today philosophy ought to move beyond analysis of language toward a focus on historical sedimentation in individual psychology.

Liu: But then how do we prevent there being a "cost" to nature in all of this?

Li: What does it mean for there to be a "cost to nature"? I don't understand. In any case, we make mistakes, and then we correct those mistakes. The earth is warming, and now we should follow the Paris Agreement. This is the Way of humans, and also the Way of heaven.

I think the present Coronavirus pandemic, in fact, evidences the importance of my "philosophy with humans." My historical ontology takes human life, in its existence and continuing extension, as its primary concern. It also takes proper measure (*du* 度) as the primary category of its epistemology, since humans rely on proper measure to live—as they have at least beginning with primeval production and human relations. Today

112 | The Humanist Ethics of Li Zehou

everyone has thrown themselves into discussing what the economy will be like after the pandemic, and these are precisely questions of "how to live" and how to live better.

Let me take this opportunity to openly rescind the label of "Marxist" I once adopted for myself. Although I continue to agree with and absorb the core of Marx's historical perspective on social and economic tools, technologies, and forces of production as well as his view of the economy as fundamental to human existence, these points of agreement no longer seem enough to call myself a Marxist.[51] I have already indicated this indirectly in the preface to *A New Approach to Kant*. There I discussed the ways in which I am and am not Marxist, pointing out three ways I am not and only one way I am. That ratio of three to one points clearly in this direction, but still I have yet to say as much outright. At this point, I should address the issue directly. To this day I maintain the belief that Marx is extraordinarily important and was a tremendous historical philosopher. However, the catastrophes of human life he brought about seem to have exceeded his academic contribution. I am sure that Marx and Engels themselves would certainly not have endorsed—and even would have opposed—the kind of political religion that developed from them. Still, ultimately they provided the theories on which intense belief in the political religion of "communism" was founded, which their followers espoused with unwavering faith. Of course, that connection is very oblique. We see this in Eduard Bernstein and the latter developments of the Second International, as Europe's Social Democratic Party, who abandoned faith in this political religion, instead understanding "communism" to be potentially fallible and possibly unrealizable in practice. Thus, any responsibility born by Marx himself for the political religion of communism and its disasters is extremely indirect. Marx's academic theories retain very high standing, and since the core of his philosophy remains valid, I remain convinced by it to this day.

Toward "Aesthetics as First Philosophy"

Liu: Let's talk a bit more about the structure of your ethics.

Li: As I stated already, my ethical philosophy, including its distinction between ethics and morality, its identification of the three elements of moral psychology, and the theory of two morals are all merely suppositions regarding the formal structures and conceptual categories of ethics.

Liu: This is a particularly minimal, or bare, framework.

Li: I understand utilitarian and liberal social norms as part of normative ethics and political philosophy, and the emphasis on cultivating personal moral character in virtue ethics, both Chinese and Western, leads us to begin from moral psychology.

Liu: This seems to relate to the distinction of public and private, or perhaps your distinction of social from religious morals.

Li: Let me reiterate, in neither direction do I discuss the specific content of things, such as how the various views in normative ethics and political philosophy differ in certain ways in accordance with different eras, cultures, and traditions.

Liu: You just lay out a broad outline. This is a bit of a pity. We still haven't discussed contingency as the third quality of history here.

Li: We also haven't at all touched on the three elements of human psychology and how the cultivation of their particular structures makes the formation of individual virtue possible, among other things. All of this still requires further explication, without which discussing historical contingency is not possible. People can look at the expanded edition of my *From the Duality of Aesthetic Sensibility to Emotion as Substance*,[52] where I explain this a bit. Actually, contingency can only be spoken of by later thinkers. This is because history is not merely the abstract knowledge of events, people, and statistics separate from oneself, but also involves the embodied emotional experience and grasp of the particular fluctuations of happiness and tragedy and various feelings of countless persons in the past. Especially in modern times, we see people gradually ceasing to regard human beings and human life instrumentally. We are seeing a gradual shift from subjectality of the "greater self" (as humankind, the nation, and so forth) toward subjectality of the individual, despite the individual's necessary connection with the greater self. After all, the individual is only a teeny tiny component of the great ego.[53] What needs emphasis at present is that each person is creating history, and its contingent aspect is constantly expanding. Uncertainty is likewise increasing. A philosophical explication of this is not something that can be done today. Philosophy ought only point out the relevant issues in a timely manner.

Liu: Leave that to later scholars, then. It seems this involves the relation between morality and religion.

Li: Since the title of this discussion includes ethics, let me say a bit more on it. Kant told us that morality ultimately leads to religion. I have similarly discussed morality and its connection to something that transcends morality. The latter refers precisely to religion (Christianity, Islam,

114 | The Humanist Ethics of Li Zehou

and so forth) and the aesthetic realm of heaven and earth (in traditional Chinese thought).

Liu: In saying that these things transcend morality, what sense of "transcendence" is this?

Li: In the sense that the ultimate answers to the questions of "why should I be moral"—such as "what should I sacrifice myself for"—ultimately involve questions of why life is meaningful.

Liu: Why life is meaningful? Does this question have an answer?

Li: The meaningfulness of life fundamentally has no definite answer. It arises from individual choices and decisions. This is also "free will."

Liu: You have always been a determinist regarding free will, right?

Li: Since the vacuity of human life is clear and pronounced in this, why live at all? For that matter, why die? Therefore, to act and to follow and carry out or to reject and violate particular ethical norms, and to exhibit certain moral or immoral acts (as well as what the standards of morality are)—these are determined through each person's thoughts (ideas), emotions, and especially beliefs. In the 1970s I stated that philosophy is a combination of science and poetry. Philosophy is not merely epistemology and the pursuit of truth. It is related to the realm of human life.

Liu: Oh, by this you are referring to the dimension of things that "transcends morality"?

Li: Because of this, the highest aim of ethics and morality for Kant, whose thought is grounded in Christian tradition, is the alignment of prosperity with virtue. But in actuality this is not possible. It is potentially able to be realized only in an unknowable other world. That is why he had to maintain transcendental illusions of God and the soul.

Liu: And in China? How is prosperity aligned with virtue?

Li: In China's shamanistic-historical tradition, which equates the Way of heaven with the Way of humans and has no personal god, Song Confucians pursued morality and that which transcends morality as the "happiness of Confucius and Yan Hui," which could be realized only within aesthetics of a lofty "spirit of happiness" within the "unity of heaven and human" and "unity of oneself with the myriad things," and not separated from the actual world. The notions of pure spirit and a supreme metaphysical realm entirely independent of the human world with its vagaries of tragedy and happiness and the various human emotions—as I emphasized in my essay "On Aesthetic Education Replacing Religion"

(*Meiyu dai zongjiao* 美育代宗教)[54]—are in fact extraordinarily uniform, homogeneous, impoverished, and empty.

Liu: This is one of the ideas of yours I most strongly endorse. We should move toward an "aesthetic metaphysics"!

Li: Historical ontology inherits this tradition, taking Confucianism's melding of nihilistic elements with affirmation of existence—the outlook that even if the world is empty, as the Buddhists claim, we must still live—as a precondition of moral action and placing it within a presupposed *a priori* belief in the harmonious coexistence of humans and the cosmos. Since philosophy studies fate and here history enters metaphysics, pursuit of the Way of heaven within history leaves us with a virtue ethics that instructs us in what kind of persons to be to shoulder the historical responsibility, or calling, to "establish one's destiny in the life of the people."[55]

In sum, humans are historical beings, and history enters metaphysics, which fill Confucian tradition's melding of nihilistic elements and affirmation of existence with the rich emotions of the various vicissitudes of happiness and tragedy in the world of human relations. These also elevate the many feelings of actual human life to the height of substantive reality, where they serve as embodied aesthetic apprehensions and experiences, and do so without leading us toward hermeticism and asceticism, cessation and oblivion, or self-righteousness. It is within the aesthetic realm, which transcends the limits and variability of the individual, such as with the coexistence of feelings of substantive reality and feelings of nihilistic vacuity toward ruins and rubble, which are the existential experience of human limitations and contingency. Apprehension of the Way of heaven within the richness of the common world, in contrast, creates an aesthetic metaphysics. So I have proposed Chinese aesthetics to be a "Great Aesthetics" (*da meixue* 大美學), which does not align with and is not equivalent to Western aesthetics.

Liu: This is not merely a view in which history enters metaphysics, then. It also moves metaphysics toward aesthetics.

Li: In this way we see aesthetics as first philosophy. Ultimately, everything returns to nothingness. However, humans still must live. So the question is, how to live? By "knowing the impossible nature of the task but carrying it out anyway"—that is, by nevertheless striving forward, living up to the fortune of possessing life and to the greatest reality and highest value of the continuous extension of the living existence of humankind.

116 | The Humanist Ethics of Li Zehou

Liu: Ah, alright. This is the question I have been wanting to pursue: How is it that aesthetics becomes first philosophy? How is it not, as Levinas told us, that ethics is first philosophy?

Li: In prefacing the new edition of *Reading the Analects Today*, I wrote, "The years move in on their horizon and already I have found frailty of age; the days to come are no longer many, so why not venture out brazen and bold?" The ancients tell us human value lies in clarity of self-knowledge, and I know I am just an aged old man, beyond his years, rambling on about his views—especially today, having discussed again so many things already explained often in the past. The copy of my short article "On 'The Way of Internal Sageliness and External Kingliness'" that you sent me was published in 1994—and if they would let me, I would publish it again without changing a word. This shows I am indeed as stubborn as ever. Since I am unwilling to change with the times, perhaps I shouldn't continue on like this. Please let me take this opportunity to bid my audience farewell, wishing everyone health and longevity. Happy Lunar New Year![56]

Postscript to the English Translation

Appended excerpt from "Belated In Memoriam for Feng Youlan" (1992):[57]

Philosophy always sets out from what is most fundamental, from the "primordial phenomenon"—that is, it starts from the beginning. I believe this beginning, what is most fundamental, and the primordial phenomenon are the fact of "humans living."

All else—including language, God, pure consciousness, the objective world, and so forth—is derivative of or subordinate to the fact of "humans living."

"Humans living" then generates or includes three major questions: How to live, Why live, and To live in what way.

On an individual level, to be living is to be thrown into "Being-with-others" within the world. Yet humans also always exist as single members of a particular biological species (humankind), and this is not something that the individual can choose or determine.

"Humans living" in this sense consists in daily life, forms of life, and social existence.

We see, then, that the first implication of "humans living" lies in "how to live." . . . "Living" is prior to the meaning of life, and inauthentic existence has priority to authentic existence. This is because it is only by living that we have the question of the meaning of life.

Thus, we must first investigate how people live. Living requires food, clothes, shelter, and activity, and these involve methods of production and ways of life. I emphasized this over a decade ago when I proposed the manufacture and use of tools to be foundational to communal practices. This is anthropological subjectality—or we might also call it historical ontology. As I see it, language and many other things are all generated from this, and therefore, it is the use and manufacture of tools rather than language that is fundamental to "how to live," and that is the true "house of Being." I maintain this view to this day. The approach through language—syntax and logic—is generated from the needs and regulations of "how to live" (which primarily also remain the use and manufacture of tools) as "Being-with-others" (in which being human lies in the activities of communal existence). Through this, syntax and logic become laws, but they are first of all patterns of human interrelation, and only thereafter become epistemological and cognitive. The deeper and more profound question lies in how this is possible, and what it means.

Nevertheless, matters of "how to live" are no substitute for "why live." As I have elsewhere stated, there is no scientific view of the ends of human life. Understanding the rules of society and demands of the community do not resolve the question "What do I live for." The subjectality of humankind at large is prerequisite to the specific subjectality of the individual, but it certainly does not replace the latter.

That people just happen to be born, thrown into this world, leaves life rather meaningless. But humans are also animals, and possess love of life and attachment to it. Even when we are world weary, cynical, and full of ennui, we must live on. But what do we live for?

All kinds of religious beliefs, ethical theories, and social moralities provide answers to this question. Some people live for God, and others live for their grandchildren. Some live for

118 | The Humanist Ethics of Li Zehou

their race, their nation, their party, or even for other people generally. Some live for their own reputation, status, fortune, and enjoyment, while others live just for the sake of living. Some people live without worrying about why they live. . . . For all of these outlooks there are certain literary and artistic expressions, and they all have certain theories and philosophies to support them. Yet, none of them is necessarily able to definitively answer the question. Why live? This remains up to you yourself to pursue, to choose, to determine. Especially in the days to come, when "how to live" (the ability to live on) is largely no longer a problem, once the meaningfulness and motivation of continuing the fight for survival has gradually disappeared as a reason "why to live," this issue will become even more pronounced.

Appendix

A Response to Michael Sandel and Other Matters

Section 1: Reason and Emotion

1.1 Starting from the Beginning

Question: Are you familiar with Michael Sandel's work?[1]

Li Zehou: Yes, I am. In the '90s I read several books on communitarianism, including Michael Sandel's *Democracy's Discontent*.[2]

Q: What do you think of communitarians?

Li: I discussed communitarianism in my books *Five Essays from 1999* (*Jimao wu shuo* 己卯五說) and especially *Historical Ontology* (*Lishi bentilun* 歷史本體論),[3] more than ten years ago. My views haven't changed since. Simply put, I see communitarianism as a product of the long-standing liberal traditions of developed countries. It has value in reference to those traditions, but can be quite dangerous if directly and indiscriminately adopted in non-liberal societies.

Q: In recent years Sandel has become very popular. Throughout Europe and Asia, he receives very warm welcomes and huge audiences turn out for his lectures. He is now widely known as an academic superstar. Would you be willing to respond to his philosophy along the lines of your own ethical theories, such as your "theory of two morals" (*liang de lun* 兩德論)?

Li: I'd be happy to. Not long ago I read two of Sandel's more recent works, *Justice: What's the Right Thing to Do?* and *What Money Can't Buy: The Moral Limits of Markets*.[4] In these books he points out that many countries, including America and China, are shifting away from market

120 | The Humanist Ethics of Li Zehou

economies (which he approves of) and toward "market societies" (which he opposes). In market societies everything can be bought and sold, leaving morality little if any role. This is something about which Sandel expresses deep concern, and he brings up many real-life examples to illustrate his concerns. While China has not reached the level of a market society, it is moving down this path, and so we should give his arguments careful consideration. Of course, the problem in China is more complex. Also, China's market is not yet fully developed, so there is still time to take steps to alleviate and prevent these issues, and this is precisely why I put forth the "theory of two morals."[5]

Q: Sandel's *Justice: What's the Right Thing to Do?* is an international best seller. What do you think of it?

Li: I admire the way he avoids overly academic terminology and the clarity with which he discusses quite profound and important points. However, the theoretical aspects of this work present very little original thought. What I want to point out most of all, though, is that Sandel relies on examples from historical and contemporary America, which is not even three hundred years old, to make his points. There are vast differences between America and China, both historically and at present. I cannot and do not want to discuss all of the various arguments and examples Sandel gives in detail. I simply want to respond to Sandel's basic ideas as we might see them from the perspective of China's history and current circumstances. At the same time, I should also clarify that I intend this less as an academic argument and more as a general dialogue, and one that may not comprehensively address all the issues involved.

Q: Just now you mentioned your theory of two morals. You have also put forth notions of "the antinomy between history and ethics," "history advancing in the midst of tragedy," and "harmony being higher than justice."[6] Do these bear on Sandel's thought?

Li: They do. These ideas form a basis for responding to Sandel's more specific analyses of how markets and morals interact. But to elaborate on this we must look at my own philosophical background and begin with its traditionally Chinese notions, such as taking "emotion as substance" (*qing benti* 情本體). This is because the ideal of justice, as primarily a rational principle (*li* 理), differs from the ideal of harmony, which involves the integration of emotion and reason (*qing-li* 情理). In the preface to *Reading the Analects Today* (*Lunyu jindu* 論語今讀)[7] I argue that the core of China's "cultural-psychological formation" (*wenhua-xinli jiegou* 文化心理結構) is "the emotio-rational structure" (*qing-li jiegou* 情理結構). In *How Can Chinese Philosophy Go on Stage?* (*Zhongguo zhexue ruhe dengchang* 中國哲學如何登場)[8] I emphasize that the fundamental difference between Chinese and Western philosophy and thought has to do with the latter's concentration on logic (*logos*)—language—reason—two worlds, in contrast with the former's concern with action[9]—life—integration of emotion and reason—one world. I believe that viewing things in terms of the integration of emotion and reason, rather than merely in terms of reason and rational principle, is the philosophical basis of the divergence between Chinese ethics and Western ethics—Western ethics here including Sandel. This is also a key point of our discussion here of Sandel's view of markets and morals.

Q: Don't you always emphasize reason, though? You often discuss how Aristotle defines humans as rational animals, but then you also stress this difference between mere reason and the integration of emotion and reason.

Li: To explain this, let me go back a step. Emotion is interconnected with desire, and desires are animal instincts. Aristotle distinguishes humans from animals in that humans possess reason. But humans are still animals. We are not gods, and cannot completely rid ourselves of desires, which is why we have the matter of the emotio-rational structure. Aristotle and many other Western philosophers such as David Hume give various detailed analyses and descriptions of emotions and desires and the experience of them, but they do not get at the root of the issue. In contrast, classical Confucian texts stress the emotio-rational structure from the outset, and indeed take it as their starting point.

Q: But you yourself have pointed out that Han dynasty thinkers considered human nature (*xing* 性) good but emotions (*qing* 情) bad, and that Song and Ming dynasty theorists, especially of the neo-Confucian School of Principle (*lixue* 理學), generally advocated "preserving heavenly principle and extinguishing human desires"—seeing these as opposed. In these ways it seems that Chinese tradition has often had a negative view of emotions.

Li: That is why I say I want to return to classical Confucianism, which preceded those ideas. I draw on the pre-Qin ideas that "the Way begins in emotionality" (*dao shi yu qing* 道始於情)[10] and "rituals are generated from emotionality" (*li sheng yu qing* 禮生於情)[11] when I advocate a "fourth stage of Confucianism"[12] and the outlook of "emotion as substance."

Q: It looks as though we have to talk about reason and its integration with emotion before we get into Sandel. So what is reason and where does it come from?

Li: This will start us pretty far from our main topic, from the basics of my philosophical approach, in fact, and I will be reiterating ideas previously discussed elsewhere. In the past I've often noted that there are many diverse explanations of "reason." The general definition I give is that reason is the repeatable ordering, normativization, and formalization by human communities of their own activities along with the intellectual grasping of the objects of those activities, which, stored in the consciousnesses of members of the community through language and passed on to successive generations, forms the ongoing construction of the distinctively human psychology that separates humans from other animals. The basic activity of human communities, moreover, involves the material practices of manufacturing and using tools, which are necessary to survive, and which I call techno-social substance (*gongju benti* 工具本體).

Q: But at the same time you also emphasize the construction of this uniquely human psychology as part of your theory of "the dual substances" (*shuang benti* 雙本體).[13]

Li: Human psychology is an extremely large and complex system. As I have said before, it includes three aspects: A) the solidification of reason (*lixing ningju* 理性凝聚) in which, as a result of social norms exhibited in linguistic commands, free will controls and dominates individual behavior and instinctual desires; B) the construction of reason (*lixing neigou* 理性內構) in which cognition, formed when actions become the deliberate manipulations of skill and art, also develops as logic and mathematics; and C) the melting of reason into emotion (*lixing ronghua* 理性融化), aesthetic appreciation in which order, rules, and forms permeate and interweave into individual sensation. In each of these three aspects, the structural relationships of reason and emotions differ greatly.

Q: You always trace human reason back to activities of the manufacture and use of tools. But don't some animals do this too?

Li: I have answered this question many times. The manufacture and use of tools are universally necessary for humankind. Their universality forms a necessary condition without which human existence would not be possible. Moreover, without diverse practices of manufacturing and using tools, human life would not unfold as part of a continual process of development. This diversity forms a sufficient condition the presence of which makes human existence possible. Together these make human manufacturing and use of tools distinct from that of chimpanzees and other animals. Only the universal necessity and diversity of the manufacture and use of tools, which are distinctive to humanity, produce reason as I have defined it above.

Q: This is why you emphasize the priority of learning (*xue* 學), in its occurrence as the very first character of the *Analects*. Manufacturing and using tools are not natural abilities. They can only be acquired and passed on to others through learning.

Li: The *Analects* emphasizes learning—not, of course, learning to make tools, but "learning to be human." This is an ethical teaching. The object of ethics is human action, and the normative regulation of behavior is prior to the normative regulation of thought, even in primeval conditions. I discussed this in the '80s. Ritual regulations (*li* 禮) are behavioral norms. Confucius talked continuously about ritual regulations, and his great advocacy of "learning" referred principally to learning ritual regulations. According to Confucius, people "establish themselves through rituals," and this requires "learning" (*Analects* 8.8). Confucius also tells us, "I was not born with knowledge. I love antiquity and diligently persevere in my studies" (*Analects* 1.20). He even states, "In a village with ten clans there will be others who are as loyal, faithful, and sincere as I, but there will be none who match my love for learning" (*Analects* 5.28). This type of learning consists not merely in the acquisition of rational understanding but also constructs and shapes the emotio-rational structure that makes humans distinct. This is why classical Confucian texts emphasize both music and ritual. For this reason I say that the ontological foundation of humanity does not lie in a mysterious "heaven" or in *a priori* "good"; rather, it lies in the diligent and continuous learning that forms our emotio-rational structure.

Q: You consistently emphasize that mere reason cannot replace the integration of emotion and reason, and that human psychology cannot be fully equated with logic and grammar. You say that the brain is greater than the mind, the mind is greater than consciousness, and consciousness is greater than reason.

Li: This is in line with traditional Chinese philosophy, which views humans as rational while also recognizing them as organisms with instinctual animal desires and natural needs. We cannot simply write off these important factors through looking only at rational moral concepts. The market economies we see today open this Pandora's box of instinctual desires. They effectively satisfy as well as produce various desires in people, even to the point of creating an overflow of materialistic desire. We

124 | The Humanist Ethics of Li Zehou

cannot adequately resolve this issue by engaging only rational principles and moral laws and failing to discuss the emotio-rational structure. Sigmund Freud discovered the suppression of the id by the superego, and the doctrines of many religions and ideologies repress emotions and desires with rational laws.

1.2 What Is Philosophy?

Q: You are a fan of philosophy of mind. Doesn't this sub-discipline research the relationship between reason and emotions?

Li: There are various schools of philosophy of mind, and I am most interested in that which relies on and works through linguistic analysis and unites these ideas with findings from brain science. Research in this area points us to the emotio-rational structure. For the specialized fields of philosophy this moves significantly toward displacing analytic philosophy, and accords with my idea that philosophy needs to "move beyond language," so I happily endorse it. Just as philosophy of language once greatly helped clarify issues associated with the semantics, use, and misuse of language, philosophy of mind is making similar advancements in human psychology, enlightening us about the relations among emotions, desires, thinking, and reason. However, philosophy of mind is also like philosophy of language in gradually becoming a kind of highly specialized, technical, and meticulous quasi-science understood only by very few. It no longer deals with larger philosophical issues. Questions like those Sandel puts forth regarding markets and morals are not generally brought up in philosophy of mind, whereas I think dealing with larger issues like this is the true task of philosophy.

Q: Great. Let us digress for a second. What is philosophy?

Li: G. W. F. Hegel laughed at his British contemporaries for what they called "philosophy." According to Hegel, philosophy consists only in abstract thought regarding truth or absolute concepts, which in fact refers to the strict logic of conceptual deduction and inference that began with ancient Greek thought. Thus Hegel completely dismisses Confucius's aphoristic teachings on human conduct as non-philosophical. But not everyone agrees with Hegel, and this issue has yet to be resolved. Books about "what is philosophy" continue to be published, and people have taken a great many positions on this question.

Q: What do you think?

Li: In line with Hegel we could say that philosophy is, in some sense, the philosophy of the history of philosophy. That is, philosophy often founds its new outlooks and ideas on the intellectual foundations laid by earlier philosophers. In terms of Western philosophy, there is an inherited gene of "reason" that follows the model established in Greek philosophy, especially by Plato and Aristotle. For example, their search for Truth and inquiries concerning Being are characteristic of the Western philosophical tradition. During the Middle Ages these investigations became slave to theology, and reason and logic were used to prove the existence of God. After the Renaissance broke free of religion, the height of modern Western philosophy as we know was born. On the other hand, this also began the division of philosophy into logic, ethics, political philosophy, legal philosophy, and aesthetics as well as today's philosophy of language and philosophy of mind. The field has become ever more scientific and specialized—separated into specific areas of expertise—and from this we have "the death of philosophy." After Martin Heidegger and Ludwig Wittgenstein, "philosophy" seems to have disappeared.

Q: Is there really no more philosophy?

Li: In actuality it still exists.

Q: In what sense?

Li: Like art, although philosophies are produced within various particular environments, they often transcend these to achieve lasting value, thereby drawing people to continuously return to them. Big questions regarding human existence, fate, the cosmos, how to live, why live, and to live in what way—these bother people, confuse them, and push them to seek answers and understanding, and probably always will. In different times and according with the changing ways people live, they come up with various outlooks and ideas that address these issues. For example, people are endlessly attempting to answer the questions "Why should one be moral?" and "What is morality?" That's why I say metaphysics always buries those who try to bury it. Famous works of science can be shelved when their times have passed, but today people still read classics like the *Laozi* and Plato's dialogues.

1.3 CHINESE PHILOSOPHY

Q: If we understand philosophy in this way, then traditional Chinese thought of course includes philosophy. In this view philosophy is not just the rational deduction and inference historically emphasized in Western philosophy.

Li: Bertrand Russell was quite ingenious, and unlike those before him titled his work to explicitly designate it only *A History of Western*

Philosophy rather than of all philosophy. And yet, the histories of Chinese philosophy produced by Chinese scholars in the twentieth century use Western models to interpret Chinese thought, and thereby lose sight of many essential elements of China's intellectual legacy, including, for example, the importance of the emotio-rational structure in Chinese thought. I can give an example from my own life to illustrate this. Some years ago, in discussing "emotion as substance," a very learned long-time colleague—one who specializes in Western philosophy—asked me, "Does this count as philosophy?"

Q: Does this motivate you to show that "emotion as substance" and "the emotio-rational structure" can contribute to world philosophy and thereby give Chinese thought a unique place in global philosophy, as well?

Li: My arguments are more aimed at the postmodern anti-Enlightenment and anti-rational trends popular in contemporary Western thought and often imitated in Chinese academia. As most people know, I have always opposed anti-Enlightenment and anti-rational thinking and strongly support reason and Enlightenment ideals. But at the same time, I emphasize that we cannot stop at reason and Enlightenment thought. In the '80s I pronounced my support of both upholding Enlightenment thought and moving beyond it. The relationship of reason with emotions and desires, as well as how this relationship produces human nature and human psychology, are questions of even greater importance. Postmodern anti-rationalism is destructive, whereas I put forth "emotion as substance" and "the emotio-rational structure" as a constructive way of discussing human psychology and human nature. These ideas draw on Chinese tradition and have universal significance. And I hope that these ideas and the practical development of modern China will intersect, cooperate, and influence one another. This has been my position since the early 1980s.

Q: Are your ideas about emotion as substance and the emotio-rational structure equivalent philosophical concepts?

Li: No. They emphasize different things. "Emotion as substance" declares the fundamental value and role of emotions in humans. *Benti* 本體 here is not noumenon, but rather the root, the substance. The "emotio-rational structure" refers to the concrete intersection of emotion with reason and emphasizes that emotion and reason exist in dynamic, constantly changing relationships of differing ratios and proportions with one another. This speaks to the complexity of human psychology or human nature.

Q: Today philosophy of mind produces detailed research on the mind. You address similar matters through your quite general ideas of emotion as substance and the emotio-rational structure, and you refuse to refine the specifics of these concepts. What possible significance can this project have compared with research in philosophy of mind?

Li: I put forth the broad ideas and questions of the emotio-rational structure and emotion as substance based on my investigation of the question "What is human nature?"—which in turn I look at through the problem "How is humankind possible?" This project can be put in communication with philosophy of mind but is not equivalent to it. I've already pointed out the differences between my approach and the narrow focus of philosophy of mind above. Broader perspectives like mine do not directly resolve questions, but rather attempt to illuminate and enlighten. I simply put forth the concepts of "emotion as substance" and "the emotio-rational structure," and I neither have investigated nor could investigate their concrete specifics. That falls under the scope of science.

1.4 EMOTIONS, DESIRES, AND MONEY

Q: So then, you are also saying you differ from Sandel in that you discuss issues like those of the market and morals in terms of the emotio-rational structure, which is an idea founded on traditional Chinese thought?

Li: You could say that. But my primary focus is on human nature in general, which I approach through asking in what ways a person is "human." This is also the main issue of ethics. I've said many times that I do not endorse the idea that God created humans or even that biological evolution is the basis for what makes us human rather than animal. I do not accept the idea that heaven endows humans with "innate moral conscience and capacity for good,"[14] regardless of whether "heaven" is understood as nature or God or "pure reason." So too with ethics and morals. Humans, including their ethics and morals, are established and created by humans themselves, not as atomic individuals but as societies and communities—the products of history, education, and socialization. I rather like early Heidegger and later Wittgenstein, who emphasize *Dasein* and the "forms of life" as the basis for language, respectively. I think that further investigation of "the forms of life" would reveal these to include the origin and development of ethics and morals, in which "action" (*dong*

動), "proper measure" (*du* 度), and "emotion as substance" are important links. Unlike many other scholars of Chinese philosophy who heavily emphasize tradition, I do not try to alienate, isolate, or maintain separation between Chinese thought and its Western counterpart. Rather, I advocate absorbing and incorporating useful elements of the latter as much as possible so as to further develop the tradition of Chinese philosophy. In this way we may also break beyond the global dominance of Greco-European philosophical discourse. For example, consider one way this might be possible with Michael Sandel's work. Sandel brings up many examples of what money cannot or should not buy, but he does not highlight that emotions cannot be purchased monetarily. For example, he elaborates at length on questions of surrogate pregnancy but does not discuss their close interrelation with emotions or the intense emotional complications and damage of the practice.

Q: Sandel highlights and opposes the market's pervasive infringement on morals, but certainly does not oppose the market economy itself. So where is the limit at which this "intrusion" occurs? Where should we draw the line between markets and morals, between what money can and cannot buy? He does not tell us.

Li: As I just mentioned, the line of demarcation, what we can and cannot buy, is a matter of emotions. Market principles such as "fair exchange" and "free trade," in contrast, are rational. This is why in responding to Sandel we had to start from the difference between mere reason and the integration of emotion and reason, and between Western and Chinese philosophy.

Q: Emotions are interconnected with desires, and money often can buy desires. The market can intrude on them.

Li: Emotions and desires are indeed linked, although this does not mean emotions are equivalent to desires. Desires can be bought, but for emotions this may not be the case: on the basis of rational principles, we can fairly or unfairly exchange and sell desires, but with emotions fair or unfair exchange is difficult or even impossible. Nevertheless, emotions and desires are generally intertwined and can be difficult to fully distinguish from one another, and below I will often discuss them together. On the whole, desires are directly connected with individual biological needs and pleasure and pain. These involve emotions and feelings, but also desires and needs much more so. Emotions, in contrast, have aspects that transcend individual biological desires. Liang Shuming 梁漱溟 (1893–1988) tells us, "In the midst of emotion, people have regard only for others and forget themselves; opposite this, in the midst of desires, people are only out for themselves and have no consideration for others."[15] The extremely complicated intertwinement of emotions and desires must be carefully investigated by philosophy of mind and analytic philosophy and can only be discussed generally here. In sum, what kind of relationships emotions, desires, and money have and should have are issues worth investigating. This is, moreover, exactly the type of problem that contemporary ethics should focus on.

Q: Some critics have said that your philosophy, especially in notions such as emotion as substance and the emotio-rational structure, concentrates too much on the internal mental aspects of a person at the expense of external social factors. Is this an accurate critique?

Li: Yes and no. I do indeed stress internal aspects, as I look closely at problems of human psychology. But I also emphasize that these "internal" aspects (of individual psychology) are constituted and constructed through "external" factors (of communal society). From externality we have internality, just as from "ritual" (*li* 禮) we have "humaneness" (*ren* 仁). As I state in "Additional Dialogues on Ethics" (Lunlixue dawen bu 倫理學答問補),[16] social norms ("ritual") are rooted in concrete and emotional situatedness (*qing* 情) and go on to produce reason (*li* 理). Yet it is this reason, and not emotion, that governs individual moral action. In terms of the community, ritual (ethics) come from emotionality (as situated and felt circumstance), whereas in terms of the individual, reason governs emotions. Now we are ready to discuss Sandel.

Section 2: Individualism and Relationism

2.1 Where Does Justice Come from?

Q: Can we start by talking about Sandel's book *Justice*?

Li: Before that we should begin by asking: What is justice? Where does "justice" come from? What is it composed of and what purposes does it serve? In the utilitarianism, egalitarian liberalism, and libertarianism Sandel discusses, as well as in Immanuel Kant and John Rawls, justice is always defined through abstract rational principles (for instance, as the greatest happiness for the greatest number of people, individual freedom of choice, the categorical imperative, or fairness). But why does the communal life of humankind need a rational principle of justice?

130 | The Humanist Ethics of Li Zehou

This is something they discuss very little. Of course, some have proposed its origins in cooperative agreement for the sake of personal safety and self-interest, but questions remain as to how such agreement is possible. It has no historical basis, and there is little more to say on it. It can be no more than a suppositional rational postulate.

Q: What is your view of this issue?

Li: I am a historicist. I see all of ethics and morals, including justice, as serving the continuous extension of human existence (*renlei de sheng-cun yanxu* 人類的生存延續) (as communities and societies) and understand justice as coming not from rational agreement among individuals but rather from the concrete historical circumstances of communal existence, including shared emotional experience. I explain the origin and formulation of principles of justice through classical Confucian ideas such as "rituals are generated from emotionality," "the Way begins in emotionality," "rituals are such due to human emotionality," and "the beginning is near emotionality, the end near rightness"—ideas found among the Guodian bamboo slips.[17]

Q: Can you further explain this?

Li: "Emotionality" (*qing* 情) here refers to the circumstances and conditions of life for humans (both individuals and communities). It is situation and context (*qingjing* 情境) as well as emotions and desires (*qinggan* 情感, *qingyu* 情欲). Emotions and desires are inseparable from actual life situations, and these situations are likewise inseparable from the human emotions and desires present in them (primary among these being the desire for life itself). These are all very concrete and historical. The concrete connections of circumstance with emotions and desires need to be specifically investigated. However, the Guodian bamboo slips and Xunzi have already given us very good philosophical direction here. My own "A Reevaluation of Confucius" (*Kongzi zai pingjia* 孔子再評價)[18] from 1980 cites Liu Shipei's 劉師培 (1884–1919) idea that ritual originates through customs and mores.[19] These customs and mores are the habits, conventions, rules, standards, institutions, and order generated in the situations, emotions, and desires of particular, actual life—that is, they are ritual. Ritual regulations are linked with law; they are unwritten laws. The abstract conceptualization of ritual regulations and their expression in language occur as rational principles or "reason." This shows that such rational principles or reason itself come from the living existence of humankind and are not *a priori*.

Q: That means that rational principles and reason itself are generated through the situated living existence of humankind (which includes emotions and desires). Thus, in terms of their basis or origin, emotions are higher than principles, correct?

Li: What exactly does "higher" mean? We have to look more closely at this, and cannot make such a general statement. We will come back to this issue later. Let us first address the question "What is justice?" In *The Origin of Abstract Ideas*, Paul Lafargue argues that the word "good" was first used in early tribal times in reference to courageousness, and "bad" to timidity.[20] "Justice" arose in matters of clan vengeance and fair distribution as extremely concrete and historical norms and standards of behavior. A great deal of research in cultural anthropology and early culture supports this conclusion. It was only later that the notions of "good" and "bad" were gradually abstracted and broadened into ethical categories and finally became concepts, ideal, principles, and values of universal standards, and even notions of "moral quality" or "character" that can be directly perceived but not specifically defined.

Q: You have often said that in everyday life "good" can have a variety of meanings, for instance "beneficial," "useful," "morally good," and so on.

Li: Some philosophers have tried to divide "good" into categories such as "intrinsic good" and "instrumental good," but these are difficult to fully distinguish. Particularly when they neglect concrete emotional circumstance (*qing*, as conditions, situations, and emotions), many holes and complications arise in this sort of analysis, ultimately obfuscating rather than clarifying things. For instance, Sandel uses the example of natural disasters and asks whether we should raise prices at such times[21] in order to get at issues of whether or not people should follow market rules or moral principles. I see this as an abstract "rational" discussion of justice that ignores emotional circumstance (the various situational conditions of time and place as well as concrete human emotions). This replaces concrete analysis of lived and felt human situations[22] with abstract rational arguments. As the concrete lived and felt circumstances of natural disasters all differ—the degree of catastrophe even varies within the same event and region—questions of whether or not to raise prices, the prices of which goods can be raised, exactly how much prices should be raised by, and whether or not free goods should be supplied to victims all require consideration of the specific lived and felt situations. This means both abstract principles and emotions related to moral principles need to be

132 | The Humanist Ethics of Li Zehou

consulted. How could one use only abstract moral rules to make such judgments? In his examples Sandel describes many concrete situations in detail, but his overall discussion is extremely abstract. This is particularly the case when he asks students completely unfamiliar with the details of a situation questions such as whether raising prices during such times is good or bad and whether we should follow moral principles or the laws of the market. Borrowing from Hegel, isn't this the same as asking whether rain is good or bad? Sandel ultimately concludes, "This dilemma points to one of the great questions of political philosophy: Does a just society seek to promote the virtue of its citizens? Or should law be neutral toward competing conceptions of virtue, so that citizens can be free to choose for themselves the best way to live?"[23] Sandel sees this as the divergence between classical (Aristotle) and modern (Kant, Rawls) thought. While I do not agree with the moral relativism of Hegel's position that what is real is rational, here I support the historicist methodology of Hegel and Marx, which states that values, justice, politics, and education all must be concretely analyzed and evaluated within specific historical conditions. Sandel argues that slavery is always wrong, and given America's history this may be correct, but in terms of history more broadly this is not how things have been. Compared with tribal warfare in primitive societies, where enemies were simply killed, the ancient use of slaves was less cruel. This was a major historical advancement, and in this way can be seen as just. Sandel himself brings up Aristotle's defense of slavery, which affirms the institution of slavery and sees each person as having an inborn nature of either master or slave quality. Mencius similarly tells us, "Those who labor with their minds rule others, and those who labor with their strength are ruled by others" (*Mencius* 3A4). Clearly, we cannot simply take the injustice of slavery and serfdom today and deploy that as an abstract conception of justice by which to judge the past. Likewise, we cannot indiscriminately judge all those who raise prices in times of natural disaster simply to be cruelly profiteering on the unfortunate and thus to be immoral or wrong. How does that clarify or solve anything? I believe it does not. Sandel's reminder that everyday life and behavior includes moral conflicts is valuable. However, taking abstract principles and applying them directly and homogenously across diverse situations is not the right method to adopt.

2.2 THE GENERAL DIAGRAM

Q: Does your advocacy of the "emotio-rational structure" include this particular methodology?

Li: Yes. This methodology can perhaps be cursorily summarized as emphasizing two things, historical particularity and grasping "proper measure" (*du* 度). These both are also of great importance to the fundamental notion of whether or not reason is supreme. This method rejects the idea of universally and directly imposing abstract rational principles on all particular objects, and it also rejects the idea that ethics and morals come from that kind of universal application of abstract reason. This is the methodological difference between "*a priori* reason" and the conception of "pragmatic reason" that I have put forward. I here have a diagram that gives a general overview of my understanding of ethics and morals, which principally involves rituals being generated from emotionality and reason governing emotion (figure A.1).[24]

I will refer often to the ideas in figure A.1. To first summarize, in terms of ethics there is important divergence between the traditional Chinese ideal of harmony, in which rituals are generated from emotionality, and the Western tradition's ideal of justice, in which reason is supreme.

Q: Why does this difference occur between Chinese and Western thinking?

Li: Once again my answer involves historical considerations. Of course life, institutions, and theories in the West all deal with the relationship between emotions and reason. However, in China this relationship has been far more pronounced and received much greater attention—consciously, theoretically, and philosophically. China's advanced level of development in the Neolithic period, based on small agricultural production and social ties of kinship, gave rise to a system of tribal clans and the rationalization of the shamanistic tradition that in turn transformed the ideology of "people as relations" into Chinese tradition's collective unconscious. In the West things have been different. Beginning with the free civil society of equal individuals in ancient Greece and strongly influenced by Judeo-Christian notions of equal final judgment before God as individual subjects, the Western notion of "people as individuals" has become that tradition's collective unconscious. This is the difference between relationism and individualism, representative of China and the West, respectively, which set them on two separate paths: one integrating emotion with reason and the other focused on reason alone. Of course, Western thinkers also argue that humans cannot survive apart from their communities, as when Aristotle famously claims that humans are political animals. But here "political" is built on the notion of each individual being free and equal, whereas Chinese thought is founded on the notion of the "five relations."[25] These are extremely different.

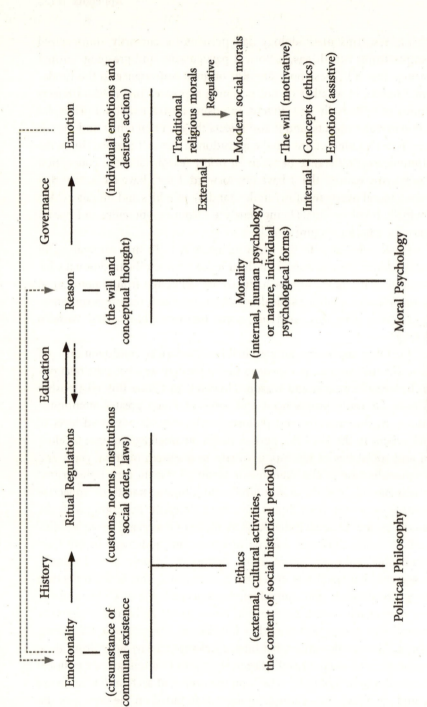

General Schema of Ethics

Figure A.1.

Q: What is "relationism"?[26]

Li: I didn't invent this term. Liang Shuming stated, "Human lives exist through a variety of interrelations (*guanxi*), and these various relations consist in various ethical roles (*lunli*)," and "Taking ethics as fundamental is the same thing as taking relations as fundamental."[27] My use of the term "relationism" is related to my notion of "emotion as substance" and should be contrasted with both individualism and communitarianism. People often describe China as communitarian and collectivist, but I don't think this is quite right. The term "community" can be just as well applied to a collection of equal individuals, whereas China heavily emphasizes kinship, and in these relations people are not equal. Rather, closer relations are more highly valued than distant relations, and thus each involves diverse relations of difference. Here "relations" are rationally ordered, but they are even more so matters of emotional identity, and are also born of lived and felt situations. Many communitarians, such as Alasdair MacIntyre and Michael Sandel, endorse and promote Aristotle's virtue ethics. Chinese tradition of course also presents a sort of virtue ethics, but it is quite a different sort. The essential distinction between the two has to do with their respective emphases on individuality and relations, which we can in turn connect to their respective emphases on desires and on emotions. Desires are directly linked to the individual's sensory and bodily feelings of pleasure and pain. As Liang Shuming tells us, affirmation of desires is affirmation of the individual. This means that theoretically one can elevate this to purely rational principles of absolute, transcendental selves or atomic individuals that are independent of other people. This is modern individualism. While emotions are often founded in desires, they are better understood as psychological reactions of interrelation with other people and things. As a rational theory this can be elevated to the relationism of the "emotio-rational structure." My proposal of relationism targets modern Western forms of individualism and liberalism that emphasize people's separateness or separability. Even while Sandel opposes individualism and liberalism, his advocacy of virtue ethics still rests on ancient Greek ideas of individual equality. Let's talk about this more later.

2.3 UTILITARIANISM

Q: Let's return to discussing Sandel's book *Justice* for a few minutes. He presents severe criticisms of utilitarianism.

136 | The Humanist Ethics of Li Zehou

Li: Theories of individualism and liberalism generally emerge and spread following the rise and development of capitalism. In ancient Greek and Roman law, as well as in Chinese tradition, there are very few examples of what we might call "individual rights." Utilitarianism is a type of contemporary liberalism that takes pleasure and pain as its basis. It opposes the holding of special rights and benefits by aristocrats, who are in the minority, and emphasizes achieving the greatest possible quantity of individual happiness amongst an entire population. One of the most famous advocates of utilitarianism is Jeremy Bentham, who takes the greatest happiness for the greatest number as his principle of justice. This has become very famous and is useful in practice. Bentham was a traditional British empiricist and was highly critical of popular notions of innate human rights, natural rights, and the social contract, which he criticized for being overly abstract and disconnected from reality. He relies instead on pleasure and pain as measures of good and bad, adding an empirical foundation that allows for a more secular, realistic, and practical form of individualism, and this served as a leading theory until John Rawls effectively dethroned utilitarianism in the 1970s. However, I think utilitarianism is reasonable in certain ways and can or even should still be used in political policymaking and the implementation of laws.

I also want to point out that the distinction I draw between ethics and morals is very important. It has to do with the differences among social systems, political functioning, individual actions, and psychological states. Many of the examples used by Sandel do not distinguish between these and are thus unclear. In government practice, utilitarianism can often prove quite appropriate, but this is not so for its use in determining standards for individual conduct.

Q: Why is that?

Li: All individuals exist within community. For the government, tasked with maintaining social existence, sacrificing individuals or a minority in order to protect the welfare of the majority is sometimes an unavoidable necessity. In such cases, this is not at all unjust. Bentham's theory begins from the perspective of what the government should do to ensure people's happiness and cannot be extended to become a moral standard for individual behavior. The famous "trolley car" discussions of utilitarianism, as a principle for determining whether to kill one person to save five others, are instances of such misapplication and a bit silly. Sandel's considerations of "utility" in determining the worth of human life, front teeth, and toes likewise misappropriate these ideas.

Q: But you have stated that "happiness" is not an ethical problem.

Li: Bentham's notion of "happiness" mainly refers to fundamental material aspects of the individual's feelings of pleasure and pain. I see these material things—clothing, nourishment, shelter, sex, physical health, long life, amusement—as presenting an ethical notion of happiness, one based on the bodily feelings of pleasure and pain. These things can be measured and compared. As I have said before, speaking summarily, being full makes people happier than being hungry, and dressing warmly makes people happier than freezing. These things are directly related to lived human existence and can provide certain objective standards.

Q: But isn't happiness more than just a bodily feeling or experience? Doesn't it include spiritual aspects?

Li: These aspects are especially troublesome, since they are difficult to measure and compare. As I've said before, once the basic needs of life are satisfied, it is difficult for people to agree on what happiness is or to determine which kinds of happiness should be more or less highly valued. Some people derive happiness from good food, clothing, and other material objects, while others enjoy particular adventurous experiences, spiritual endeavors, reading, or contemplation. So people have different feelings and make their own choices about what makes them happy. As I see it, statistics cannot measure different subjective feelings in an accurate "index of happiness." There can be no such index. This is to say, as there is no way to deduce the greatest amount of happiness for the greatest number of people beyond measuring material objects, the idea of "greatest happiness for the greatest number" can refer only to material aspects of life. While many of the spiritual aspects of happiness have nothing to do with satisfaction in material aspects of life, these fall under religion and aesthetics rather than ethics.

Q: In *Justice* Sandel notes that John Stuart Mill thinks there are greater and lesser kinds of happiness. Mill thinks that happiness cannot be completely quantified, whereas Bentham thinks it can.

Li: I strongly endorse Sandel's understanding of Bentham as more thoroughly utilitarian and Mill as somewhat straying from this. Mill was influenced by continental European thought, which makes him more than just a British Empiricist, and his emphasis on long-term or future benefit over immediate pleasure and pain, as well as freedom and dignity, are important developments. Even so, however, in order to clarify the issue, I still advocate the idea that only by limiting "the greatest happiness for the greatest number" to material aspects of life should it belong to political

138 | The Humanist Ethics of Li Zehou

philosophy. Showing this happiness to be not a contingent instance but rather a demand of historical necessity closely interrelated with human life and existence. This also closely interconnects judgments of fact with judgments of value, through their source in the continuous extension of human existence. That people seek happiness in terms of material life is a universally necessary fact, and it is also the universally necessary "justice" that people ought to seek.

Q: So Bentham's greatest happiness for the greatest number is still a valid principle?

Li: Let's contextualize the issue: During wartime many people are sacrificed, even innocent people—for example, in the firebombing of Dresden during World War II and in the dropping of nuclear bombs on Japan (interestingly, Sandel never discusses this extremely controversial example)—while in times of peace people are sometimes also sacrificed in dealing with natural disasters. In such cases, implementation of the principle of "the greatest happiness for the greatest number" is not at all unjust. However, these cases have to be considered and analyzed as historically particular and concrete. They cannot be abstracted and generalized. Sacrifice cannot be said to be always good or bad according to some abstract principle. Most importantly, as I just stated, we cannot take something like this as a principle of justice and then simply extend it to individual conduct. As situations and relations are unique, therefore duties, responsibilities, and conduct also differ greatly. We cannot and should not use an abstract principle of justice like "the greatest happiness for the greatest number" to judge or determine them. In the trolley car cases of whether to kill one to save five, Sandel sees a difference between the trolley conductor choosing a track that kills one person rather than five people and a bystander pushing a fat man in front of the trolly to stop it from killing five people. This is because the duties and responsibilities relevant to the trolley driver and to a bystander differ greatly. Society has norms regulating people's public behavior, and different jobs and careers have their particular rules of professional ethics as well. Applying these regulations in actual practice, however, requires accurately grasping and implementing them with regard to varying concrete situations. This implementation involves questions of the relation of principles (*jing* 經) to discernment (*quan* 權) in applying them with regard for the variations of actual circumstance. In war the killing and harming of innocent people is at times unavoidable. In contrast to Sandel's discussion of this in his

Appendix | 139

example of the Taliban in Afghanistan, Chinese tradition long ago put forth the idea of compassion for one's enemy being a form of weakness. War is at heart extremely cruel. Sunzi tells us that its "way" (*dao* 道) is one of sly craftiness. Overcoming one's enemies through such deceit and scheming lies outside the basic framework of general moral principles. Therein we must rely on a great variety of concrete situational specifics in making judgments. For instance, the mass killings of innocent civilians were egregious wrongs in the Nazis' genocide of Jewish populations and in the rape and murder committed by Japanese forces in the Nanjing Massacre. But the enormous civilian deaths of Hiroshima and Nagasaki were not. And so on. Of course, the ethics and morals of war is its own topic; but many theories of normative ethics and professional ethics must also investigate and evaluate how to deal concretely with various ethical and moral problems as they arise in the complex variety of actual daily conduct. Thus, Sandel's discussions of torture, conscription, refusal to bomb civilian homes, and General Lee's achievements of the American Civil War are like other examples such as the purchase of prison cells, buying a green card, and paying someone else to wait in line so as to receive quicker medical care in that they all involve particular situational considerations and require further concrete ethical analysis. Such issues cannot be resolved by discussing or relying on abstract principles of justice. Sandel addresses the question of whether military service should be bought and sold as in the market or whether it is a civic duty. This kind of issue needs to be dealt with differently in different countries, times, and circumstances (that is, whether under conditions of war or peace, what kind of combat is being considered, the conditions of that combat, and so forth). Such questions cannot be decided by an abstract principle. The way that Sandel's evaluations engage and shift among diverse approaches and standpoints in fact reflects precisely this.

2.4 LIBERALISM

Q: Sandel describes how liberalism takes the free choice and self-determination of the individual as its fundamental principle of justice, and uses this to object to utilitarianism's failure to adequately account for individual personhood.

Li: In *Justice* Sandel discusses two sorts of liberalism, egalitarian liberalism and libertarianism, and focuses a great deal of discussion on

140 | The Humanist Ethics of Li Zehou

Immanuel Kant and John Rawls. He grasps the gist of the issues, sticks close to actuality, and stays concise and clear. In these ways Sandel is highly successful.

Q: What do you think of liberalism?

Li: We should discuss Kant in detail later. He is most important.

Q: What I mean to ask is whether utilitarianism's focus on the many isn't more reasonable than liberalism's emphasis on the individual?

Li: No. Liberalism is a more advanced way of seeing things. It reflects the modern market economy as a fundamental arbiter of the circumstances of people's lives, and is much better suited to it. As a political theory, moreover, utilitarianism is itself a product of the conditions of modern social life that quantify people as individuals, and liberalism more clearly expresses the characteristically modern conceptions of individual rights and interests through emphasizing a social contract. It opposes utilitarianism's aggregation of human desires and highlights individual difference, diversity, and equality. Although things like the "veil of ignorance" and "atomic individuals" exist neither in history nor in reality—they are merely theoretical suppositions pronounced in liberal thought—still, liberalism, like the natural sciences, can posit preconditions that do not exist in actuality so as to conduct theoretical inference. As a historicist I of course do not endorse this kind of hypothetical reasoning, since it cannot truly help explain and address the roots and future trajectory of philosophical and ethical issues. But nevertheless, the reasoning built on these suppositions ultimately reflects and suits the needs of modern social life better than utilitarianism.

Utilitarianism has little regard for minorities and minority individuals. This can give rise to huge problems and tragedies. As Sandel points out, the banner of "greatest happiness for the greatest number" can be appropriated in service of severe religious persecution and genocide. Liberalism stresses that all people are ends in themselves and should not be used as mere instruments or means. It emphasizes individuals' freedom of choice and self-determination. This hugely elevates the value, status, and dignity of the individual, and liberates the individual from various forms of enslavement by past political and economic systems, traditional customs, and former ideologies. For example, in China today peasants are free to move from their villages in the countryside to work in the city, choosing their own occupations and selling their labor. Graduates are no longer forced to work for specific organizations in particular fields

Appendix | 141

but rather are free to choose their own career and even start their own business. Such individual rights are taken for granted today but were difficult to imagine under China's planned economy a few decades ago. Whether the planned economy was reasonable and just for its time is a separate question. In any case, communist China's Reform and Opening is a historically significant, major social change, and while it may involve more direct control of labor by capital, it is certainly a step towards the ideal of having people fulfill their natural talents and represents an overall positive development of society as a whole.

Q: It also brings about the freedom to work hard and still be poor, the freedom for college graduates to be unemployed, and so on. Aren't hardships like these bestowed precisely by the theories of justice based in the "natural human rights," "contractual principles," and "human equality" that devout liberals consider unquestionable?

Li: History advances in the midst of tragedy. The free sale of labor, fair competition in the market, and economic survival of the fittest hugely facilitate the development of social production and have greatly improved the lives of people of all classes. Overall, the benefits of a liberal market economy still vastly outweigh its harms.

Q: So we ought to thank these liberal thinkers?

Li: Just as we can say that Karl Marx "anticipated" the global economic integration of capitalism, we could also say that John Locke and Immanuel Kant, among others, "anticipated" the birth of modern free society. Liberal conceptions of justice are the basic principles of modern social morals. People follow them not because they are the products of a particular thinker, but rather mainly because these notions have the support of economic forces. These economic forces have made abstractly conceived ideas of "the atomic individual" and "natural human rights" something of a reality, increasingly incorporating the individual, the social contract, and public reason into the institutional order, behavioral norms, and moral standards of modern social life. This modern economy of free trade, fair exchange, commodity production, and the market, especially the free trade of labor that Marx discusses, are the foundation and origin of our lived reality, and it continues to spread and develop globally. Therefore, liberalism too will necessarily spread and develop around the world. Moreover, ideas can advance more quickly than actuality, and while these rational principles may be highly problematic today, they nevertheless stand as great contributions of the Enlightenment thinkers. That these

142 | The Humanist Ethics of Li Zehou

ideas continue to be passed onward and to spread geographically follows the direction and development of actual modern life. This is something communitarianism cannot combat.

I have written papers on the merits and demerits of liberalism, and we will discuss these pros and cons again below. In fact, while this dialogue is a response to Sandel, at the same time it also responds to liberalism.

2.5 ANTI-LIBERALISM

Q: Liberalism emphasizes notions of the individual, the self, freedom, equality, human rights, and democracy that are not only highly artificial, but also bring with them great inequalities. Total freedom and equality are simply fictions.

Li: That is why they have been denounced by so many different contemporary schools of thought, including Sandel's communitarianism and the so-called "new left." Freedom and equality all too often refer in substance to merely the free and fair exchange of goods. Sandel harshly criticizes the "market society" fostered by market economies in which everything has a price—and in which the damage and loss of morals is clear.

Q: Has liberalism been taken too far?

Li: Libertarians on the right have taken the principle of freedom to an extreme. Sandel provides numerous examples of this, such as their opposing heavy taxation of the wealthy. He shows that many people have the idea that money is earned through hard work, and think therefore it is unfair and unjust for those who earn more to pay a higher rate than the "lazy" or "dumb" people who earn less. Liberalism of this sort also opposes social welfare, compulsory health insurance, government-backed pensions or elderly care, and even laws requiring that people wear helmets on motorcycles and seatbelts in cars. It sees such requirements as impeding liberty and violating the individual's right to free choice. So such liberal thinkers also advocate freedom in things like selling blood and organs, surrogate pregnancy, suicide, and even selling one's own body to be cannibalized by others (all these are examples Sandel gives).

Q: This is a case of individual freedom, the "self," and "justice" being prioritized as supreme *a priori* rational principles, as you often put it.

Li: It separates these principles completely from concrete historical situation. Where do such principles come from? Kant says they are prod-

Appendix | 143

ucts of transcendental reason, Rawls argues from the "veil of ignorance," and many other thinkers have similar ideas.

Q: You stress that these principles come from the economic life of modern society, and state that with the large industrial production of commodities people have the freedom to buy and sell labor and goods at fair prices. These rational principles did not always exist in the past and are not produced contractually, nor are they *a priori*. Thus, the way Sandel criticizes and rejects particular principles does not truly get at their substance or foundation. Sandel operates only on the conceptual level.

Li: Here I am rather influenced by Karl Marx. Sandel's books put forth many examples in pointing out that consent between parties is not true "freedom" and that the social contract is not true "equality." In actual life there is often a lack of true agency in supposedly "free" and "equal" choices and agreements, a powerlessness that arises from economic inequality. This is thoroughly discussed by Marx and others. Marxists long ago pointed out the exploitation of surplus value in the sale of labor as a commodity, and that this is often given the guise of taking place under free and equal conditions, which reveals that a great deal of supposed liberty and equality is in fact fictitious and hypocritical. These are old problems of "formal justice" (justice as freedom and equality in political procedures) and "substantive justice" (justice as freedom and equality of economic and social position) that the new left likes to emphasize today.

Q: Sandel mentions that a CEO may make millions in annual income while teachers make thousands. With this degree of economic inequality, talking about the "justice" of mutual consent and individual free choice indeed seems a bit ridiculous.

Li: The most basic solution seems to be routing out economic inequality and striving for distributive justice. I think that the deepest and most thorough opposition to liberalism to this day has come from Marxist theories and Maoist practices. These are unsurpassed in being radically revolutionary and innovative—but they have also produced disastrous outcomes.

Q: Could you explain more?

Li: I've previously discussed the theoretical shortcomings of Marx. The idea of private ownership as the source of social ills lies at the heart of most forms of socialism and is directly opposed to liberalism's fundamental advocacy of the protection of private property, as in Locke. But Marx differs from other socialists in his economic theory. To put it succinctly, in the first chapter of *Capital*, Marx discusses the two-fold character of

144 | The Humanist Ethics of Li Zehou

labor, concrete labor and abstract labor. This forms the basis of his entire economic theory, as Marx himself emphasized, but it is also unfortunately the source of his main mistakes. From the notion of abstract labor Marx makes the logical inference of "socially necessary labor time," which lacks any empirical basis. Marx strongly criticized so-called "commodity fetishism," suggesting that today's market economy could be replaced by a planned economy in which the distribution of goods would first follow allocation according to people's labor time and then in the future move to allocation according to people's needs. This would supposedly solve problems of economic inequality along with related political challenges. On the world scale, true freedom and equality would be achieved by realizing a condition in which there are no countries, armies, governments, politicians, or police—that is, communism. Marx's idea of communism, at its root, rests on a flawed, Hegelian, purely logical inference regarding abstract labor, and I have thus adapted a term from Kant to call communism a "transcendental illusion." The transcendental illusion of communism can unite people and give them faith, passion, and courage, but as with other transcendental illusions it also can cause disaster. Mao Zedong insisted on this ideal and worked passionately to transform it into China's reality. In 1958 the Great Leap Forward attempted to carry out the ideal of public cafeterias in rural villages allowing people to "eat without paying money." Slogans like "Race toward Communism" were touted, and finally the Cultural Revolution aimed to further restrict "bourgeois power." However, we all know how these turned out.

2.6 MATERIAL INCENTIVE

Q: How exactly did they turn out?

Li: Here I'd like to mention a couple of articles that are often forgotten: Zhang Chunqiao's 张春桥 "On Over-all Dictatorship against the Bourgeoisie" and Yao Wenyuan's 姚文元 "On the Social Basis of Lin Biao's Anti-Party Clique," both published in early 1975, in *Red Flag* (*Hong qi* 红旗) and *People's Daily* (*Renmin ribao* 人民日報).[28] At that time the Cultural Revolution was already bankrupt, and Mao Zedong considered these essays very important. He even edited and published versions of them himself. These argued for the necessity of the Cultural Revolution, and organizations throughout China were instructed to study them. The articles quote several statements from Mao:

China is a socialist country and before Liberation was more or less capitalist. Currently it still employs the eight-grade wage scale, distribution according to work, and exchange based on currency. These are not much different than the old society; the only difference is the system of ownership.

Our country right now practices a commodity system, the wage system is unequal, there is an eight-grade wage scale, and so on. Only under the dictatorship of the proletariat can these be further restricted. So if people like Lin Biao took power, it would be very easy to implement a capitalist system.

Following Liu Shaoqi's line would only put material incentives and profit in command. It would not promote proletarian government, would use bonuses, and so on.

In other words, the revolution is not over.[29]

They called for continued revolution. The Cultural Revolution had started by denouncing the famous—specifically famous writers, performers, and professors—and high earning. It began in the arts and academia, and then turned toward the political realm. Mao stated that this cultural revolution should be repeated. He thought this would help eradicate the economic inequalities that were manufactured and upheld by establishment "capitalist roaders" through monetary and material inducements. Mao thought there was a capitalist class within the party itself and that this internal bourgeoise had its social roots in commodity production, the market economy, monetary exchange, the eight-grade wage scale, small-scale agricultural production, and so on.

Q: Mao's acuity is impressive.

Li: Marx and Mao were opposed to the market economy very early on. Following Mao, Zhang Chunqiao identified and questioned the idea of everything becoming a commodity long before Sandel. Interestingly, Sandel suggests that material incentives used by schools or parents to encourage and reward achievements (such as high grades) may actually interfere with the cultivation of moral character. Mao Zedong often spoke against such material incentives as well, and repeatedly emphasized that instead "politics"—which we can also understand as morals—should drive people. Similarly, criticisms of capitalism during the Cultural Revolution were really aimed at personal interests, which are, of course, related to the individual's desires for economic gains and material things. This is

146 | The Humanist Ethics of Li Zehou

an example of using morals to counter the market and eliminate desires, and it is much a much deeper analysis and criticism than Sandel's. The Cultural Revolution promoted moral ideals of altruism, most famously in the figure of Lei Feng 雷鋒, and denounced selfish pursuit of self-interest along with the "revisionary" (that is, capitalist) ideology founded in it. Such selfishness is of course connected to economic interests and material desires of individual self-preservation. These teachings used morals to counter the market and personal desires, and present a criticism much deeper than Sandel's.

Q: During Mao's time there was great controversy over hourly wages versus piece-rate earnings. Isn't the latter an example of material incentive? But then if people are paid hourly, they may not work hard. So in reality the material incentive of piece-rate earnings is much more effective for production than hourly wages.

Li: Thus Marx's *Communist Manifesto* fails to deal with the problem of people's natural desire to avoid labor; he instead avoids the issue by simply morally denouncing such desires. But rational moral doctrines and directives ultimately cannot fully resolve the needs of emotion and desire in actual human life. Following World War II, the British Labour Party overextended the country's welfare policies, and both productivity and quality of life suffered. The English lost much of their competitive edge over other countries. Lady Thatcher reversed this, opposing unions and lurching the country toward a new, neo-liberal right, and saw considerable success.

Q: In Mao's time we have examples of some of the highest leaders rising directly from the common workers and peasants and still retaining only their original wages, not even having enough money to host visits from friends during the holidays. Today this is utterly unimaginable.

Li: This is similar to the theoretical position of the Paris Commune, which both Marx and Lenin commended. Mao himself often longed for the old system in which the Red Army was not given wages but rather subsisted on type of provision system, and even for the later abolition of army ranks and titles. All teachers were to be uniformly designated "professors," with no hierarchy of associate and assistant professorships—and so forth. But how long could this type of thing last?

Q: In Cambodia this idea was more thoroughly implemented. Money was completely done away with and urban populations were sent to farm in the countryside so as to create equality. As a result, between one and three million people (around a quarter of the population) died. It seems that China's Cultural Revolution was likewise accompanied by slow production, the crumbling of professions, and difficult living conditions. The "equality" that resulted was one of ubiquitous national poverty. Trying to govern a nation according to morals brings about vast discontent. Thus, the nation rejoiced at the fall of the Gang of Four, and when Deng Xiaoping 鄧小平 decided that it would be best to first let a portion of the population prosper, China rapidly developed into a much wealthier nation overall.

Li: Money can promote social advancement. Sandel also mentions that certain services or privileges, such as priority mail, fast lanes on highways, or fast elevators to observation floors in skyscrapers, all of which cost extra and whose price is prohibitive for poorer people, do not engender feelings of moral unease despite their clear exhibition of economic inequality. Clearly, the crucial factors here lie in the concrete felt situations and holding to "proper measure," and not in some abstract rational principle of justice.

Q: During the Cultural Revolution people were often hurt or even killed in severe bicycle accidents. At first, the police would speak to the parties involved and then let everyone go under the idea that "moral teachings" should rule. This proved ineffective. Later, all they had to do was implement fines, allowing money to be the driving force, and such accidents quickly decreased.

Li: Just as we should fine someone for not wearing a helmet on a motorcycle despite this impinging on their individual right to free choice, here utilitarian considerations beat out individual liberty. Of course, however, this still ultimately protects people's rights and interests—those to life and safety.

2.7 The Tension between History and Morals

Q: Sandel mentions that Finland bases the amount of speeding fines on the offender's income, with a 2003 ticket reaching €170,000. Singapore likewise has many harsh fines, and social order there is better because of it. However, these methods can sometimes still be ineffective, such as when such fines are insignificant to people making millions of dollars. The government in Singapore has now found that having an offender's name or photo shown on the news or published in newspapers successfully reduces crime because the offender feels shame. This demonstrates the power of morals.

148 | The Humanist Ethics of Li Zehou

Li: It seems that achieving forms of total substantive equality, such as economic equality, is difficult to bring about. Everyone is different—people have unique talents, abilities, characters, personal histories, and educations—and this makes them unequal. But if total economic equality is impossible, it is not necessary either. We cannot approach issues of justice or moral duty through abstract ideals of equality. The world is principally characterized by diverse integration and endless variety, not by equalness. Here, the crucial element remains "proper measure" in dealing with the gap between rich and poor. The most important element of my theory of historical ontology is "proper measure."

Q: Do you think that moral degeneration is more prominent now due to the corrosive effects of money?

Li: Morality is very complex. Many different factors play a role in today's situation.

First, we can ask whether humankind as a whole is becoming less moral. I don't think this is the case. For thousands of years people have bemoaned a decline in morality from earlier times, and we also see the rejection of this view by many—in China, for example, beginning from the ancient philosopher Han Feizi forward. On the whole, both the social ethics and individual morality are advancing. We see this in liberalism's pronounced advocacy of individual freedom, human dignity, and autonomy, including especially the push for women's equal rights. These have tremendously improved and advanced social life. Overall, the level of social morality today far surpasses that of past eras.

Second, what appears in transitional periods of social advancement to be the prominence of "moral degeneration" is in fact simply progressive collapse of the old order and old morals during a period when modernity's new order and new morals have not yet been fully established. In such circumstances, people have lost reliable norms and standards by which to act. This creates conditions of great variety in moral behavior, some good and some bad. Especially due to the warping and even vulgarity of people's conduct that arises from decayed earlier ideas and institutions taking on new forms, the new is hard to accept and have faith in. This can lead people to lose their bearings of right and wrong, even to the point of feeling morality to be empty.

Q: What is this warping and vulgarity?

Li: Third, people in China today get extremely angry about the connection of power to money and the corruption of public officials.

Appendix | 149

These issues differ from the problems Sandel addresses in discussing the general encroachment on morals by markets. They are, rather, problems of institutionalized "feudal" privilege usurping the market and monopolizing trade, which creates what Marx called "extra-economic exploitation." These problems are more fundamental than the market itself, although they often arise in forms of market exchange. To a large extent the issue is that modern social morals have not yet been fully established in the legal system, and so privilege runs rampant. Today's problems result from there being no law to follow, laws not being followed, and laws not being effectively enforced or carried out. Most of Sandel's discussions deal with the market's infringement on morals in developed countries where modern social morals are already mostly backed by law. Since China faces both this third issue and the second matter of moral transition and disorientation, the situation is much more complex and more severe. The mixing of pre-modern and modern elements leaves moral standards in chaos and moral depravity particularly prominent. Thus, the applicability of the various examples Sandel gives to China should be analyzed and considered according to China's particular situation.

Q: You use "the antinomy between historicism and ethicism" to describe this?

Li: "Antinomy" is perhaps not the best word. Maybe "the tension between history and morals" is a better way to put it?

Q: In the '80s you discussed the Warring States period in China in a manner that seems very relevant today. You describe a situation of rapid material development and historical progression that includes large-scale expansion of production and consumption. Accompanying this, wealth, pleasure, and desires continuously accumulate and increase, as do naked acts of aggressive greed. You thus highlight the great amount of depravity and suffering brought on by cultural progression as well as the power that material desire has over people.[30]

Li: That's why, while recognizing the great benefits brought about by the market economy, we must also acknowledge the various problems, harms, and even disasters that can accompany or already have accompanied these. For this reason, we should attempt to ascertain and grasp the "proper measure" of various particular situations from a standpoint that takes into consideration this dimension of the tension between history and morals in order to provide guidance and norms for moral behavior. As I've written before, we ought to promote economic development in

150 | The Humanist Ethics of Li Zehou

so far as it improves people's lives, and yet at the same time we should remain affectively responsive to the suffering that remains in the world and retain a sense of benevolence toward others. We do this in order to allow historical tragedy and moral emotion to guide us in grasping and establishing "proper measure." This is what I call "political art" (*zhengzhi yishu* 政治藝術),[31] which allows for "conforming to emotions as well as reason" (*heqing heli* 合情合理). We cannot simply adopt strict utilitarian or liberal principles of justice. This is the approach we should assume in responding to the many various real-life issues Sandel discusses. From the practice of naming school buildings for large donors to the pervasiveness of advertisements in our schools and homes, from what gifts and wishes to give to how we give them, our assessment and treatment of the benefits and problems of particular practices cannot be determined along the lines of a single principle, but rather require the art of "proper measure." Sandel also states that these matters should be handled on a case-by-case basis. Fortunately, China has not yet reached the point at which the market governs all; yet, as I mentioned early on in our dialogue, we must take steps now to prevent and mitigate these issues.

Q: You talk about grasping "proper measure" as a way of "conforming to emotions as well as reason" and also as a matter of empathizing with or having compassion for weaker groups. Is this related to the emotio-rational structure?

Li: Yes, you could understand it this way. But the emotio-rational structure does not just refer to the individual's internal psychology; it also includes the external social order and norms.

Q: Doesn't John Rawls's "difference principle" present a theory of "justice as fairness" that emphasizes precisely helping disadvantaged groups?

Li: Rawls doesn't seem to really tell us where the "difference principle" comes from, does he? I think we might understand it as the philosophical elevation of Roosevelt's New Deal. Theoretically, we can also see it as originating in Kant's idea of "helping others." This sort of help differs from the libertarian's notion of helping via philanthropy or giving alms. From the anthropological perspective, it is a duty of living in a community. Without the "weak," there are no "strong," and in this inter-reliance of their objective existence lies the justness and responsibility of such "helping." The permeation of emotion into these relationships can help facilitate social harmony.

2.8 Similar but Not the Same

Q: Sandel talks a lot about John Rawls. What do you think of Rawls?

Li: I quite like Rawls. He discusses political philosophy and especially distributive justice. In *A Theory of Justice* Rawls proposes the difference principle.[32] In some sense this principle has unknowingly been carried out in China for the last thirty years. When China opened up to global trade the idea was to let some people get rich first so that eventually even those in the distant countryside or mountain villages would also benefit. If we understand free trade and fair exchange, under a market economy of large industrial production, as constituting *Theory*'s first principle of justice, and even as the basis of liberalism in general (Hayek's popularity in China at the time seems no accident), we may see China's Reform and Opening as a real-life example of the difference principle, part of Rawls's second principle of justice, in action. This offers a relatively good theory for affirming conditions that, despite economic inequality, in fact benefit all people. The next step is figuring out how to move toward fairer and more reasonable distributive justice and common prosperity. That requires a new theory. I've talked before about giving Rawls a Marxist foundation. As I see it, what makes Rawls's theory reasonable and pragmatic is its basis in modern economic life. There have been thousands of essays on Rawls, but very few have emphasized this point. With this foundation in modern economic life, we may integrate Chinese tradition with actual experience to construct free, fair, equal, and just political principles and institutions that surpass Rawls. However, this is a massive and extraordinarily complex issue requiring rigorous demonstrative reasoning and exceptionally innovative thought. I am capable merely of pointing out the possibility of such a theory.

Relatedly, since we are discussing ethics, I should mention I think very highly of Rawls's notion of "overlapping consensus," which happens to be a target of Sandel's criticism. We will discuss this a bit later.

Q: Let's sum up a few points before we go on. Sandel offers arguments against both utilitarianism and liberalism and pushes us to reconsider Aristotle's notions of the "common good," the "good life," and virtue ethics. You accept utilitarianism as well as leftist egalitarian liberalism, in which you see the principles of modern social morals. At the same time, you stress that we cannot directly apply these in an abstract and general manner, but rather ought to start from concrete lived and felt

152 | The Humanist Ethics of Li Zehou

situations. You also propose taking traditional Confucian teachings as religious morals to exert a "regulative and properly (limited) constitutive" function[33] here and thereby reduce the various harms brought about by modern social morals. In affirming pursuit of "the common good" or "the good life" as ends you say that you are "similar to but not the same as" Sandel. This is because China and the West alike pursue virtue ethics. However, China links state and family through seeing the good citizen as cultivated through being a good family member, which emphasizes the emotio-rational structure. The West separates family from state in differentiating between public and private, seeing reason as supreme. Thereby Chinese culture looks for harmony where the West strives for justice. You advocate a distinction between religious and social morals and the regulation of the latter by the former, whereas Sandel seems to conflate the two in a virtue monism.

Li: Some people have criticized Sandel's notions of "the common good" and "the good life" as being unclear as to their specific content. When I claim "harmony is higher than justice," it is because I believe harmony between people, harmony between mind and body, and harmony between human and nature consist in the "regulation and proper constitution" of modern social morals by the emotio-rational structure and relationality. This serves the continuous extension of human existence, which is the highest level and most fundamental aspect of "common good" and "good life"—where "ends" truly lie. It is higher than right and wrong, than fair and reasonable justice, but it cannot replace justice. Such harmony stands on a foundation of justice. This is why it is only "regulative and properly constitutive," and unable to determine or govern "justice." Harmony is a matter of transforming the people through virtue (education), whereas justice is a matter of governing by law.

Q: So you see humans' ultimate pursuit as lying in emotionality, in the felt relations and interactions of concrete human life, and not in reason?

Li: You could say that. In fact, this is precisely the direction in which I would like to move our discussion. For instance, Sandel suggests the possibility of understanding filial obligation of children to parents as a sort of reciprocal obligation,[34] which is also to look at it as a rational justice of fair exchange. In China, in contrast, filial piety is a matter of emotions. Confucius explains the traditional three-year mourning period after the death of a parent as reciprocation, a sort of requital for the parent's care in the child's first three years of life. But Confucius describes it

Appendix | 153

in terms of emotion rather than rational principle, ultimately responding to the question of whether it is acceptable to violate the ritual by asking, "Would you feel at ease about it?" (*Analects* 17.21). "Feeling at ease" (*an* 安) is an emotion of human psychology and not merely a rational duty. Confucius also emphasizes the need for respect in caring for one's parents: "Even hounds and horses are provided and cared for. Without respect, what is the difference?" (*Analects* 2.7). Emotional factors of harmony and respect are elevated above the fairness and reasonableness of obligations. This is "regulative and properly constitutive" of justice. I argued in "A Reevaluation of Confucius" for understanding humaneness (*ren*) as a "psychological principle," in which "psychology" is far greater than mere reason. This is precisely why it can be "regulative and properly constitutive." The *Analects* concerns itself with matters of relations (most of all that between parent and child), with special emphasis on emotions, rather than public reason. The *Great Learning* similarly tells us that public order follows from an orderly family. And Mencius stresses that compassionate government arises from a compassionate heart, emphasizing the value of such government lies in the people's emotional affirmation of it, again highlighting the crucial role of emotions.

2.9 Xunzi

Q: You mention Confucius and Mencius, but don't you more greatly admire Xunzi?

Li: Mencius presents an *a priori* philosophy of human nature and virtue, whereas Xunzi is an empiricist. My own theory of sedimentation (*jidianlun* 積澱論) explains the *a priori* as the accumulation and consolidation of human experience (what I refer to as "experience becoming *a priori*" [*jingyan bian xianyan* 經驗變先驗]).[35] This of course sides with Xunzi. Mencius discusses "emotions" (*qing*) in terms of an innate and *a priori* "heart-mind of compassion," and contemporary scholars such as Donald Munro interpret this as the feelings (*qing*) of natural biology. However, the type of "emotion" that Xunzi and I talk about are different from these conceptions. We understand emotion to be infused with reason.

Xunzi's discussion begins from the natural emotions and desires of our biological existence, which are related to basic human survival and the continuous extension of human existence. This is extremely important. Confucius roots "ritual regulations" in individual "humaneness," but historically speaking ritual regulations did not arise directly from the

154 | The Humanist Ethics of Li Zehou

emotions of individuals. Rather, they were gestated through the emotional experiences of shamanistic ceremonial practices, which involved participants' intense emotional engagement.[36] These profound shared emotional experiences far surpassed the individual's personal feelings, originating mainly from the lived and felt existence and situation of that particular group. I see Xunzi, who begins from the actual conditions of human communities and the basic desire for survival, as elaborating clearly and compellingly the earlier Confucian ideas that "rituals are generated from emotionality" and "rituals are such due to human emotionality," found in the Guodian bamboo slips.

Q: Please go on.

Li: The *Xunzi* is a very important book. Let's discuss it just a bit here. First of all, Xunzi begins by coupling inborn emotions (*qing*) with desires. Xunzi tells us,

> The *qing* of people is that for food they want meats and for clothes they want embroidered garments.
>
> When hungry they desire to eat, when cold they desire warmth, when tired they desire rest, they like what is beneficial and hate what is harmful. This is something people have from birth.[37]

For Xunzi, ritual begins with management of these material desires. People's natural desires lead them to seek their satisfaction, and if unchecked this pursuit creates strife, chaos, and ultimately poverty. Ritual, Xunzi tells us, was instituted by earlier kings to prevent such chaos and provide us with proper practices by which we can shape and satisfy our innate desires.

> From what did ritual arise? I say: Humans are born having desires. When they have desires but do not get the objects of their desire, then they cannot but seek some means of satisfaction. If there is no measure or limit to their seeking, then they cannot help but struggle with each other. If they struggle with each other then there will be chaos, and if there is chaos then they will be impoverished. The former kings hated such chaos, and so they established rituals and standards of rightness (*yi*) in order to divide things among people, to nurture their desires, and to satisfy their seeking.[38]

In establishing the necessity of ritual, Xunzi closely links inborn emotions to desires, primarily desires for the means of survival, clearly indicating how ritual arises from those material needs of communal survival that are deeply intertwined with people's emotions and desire. Ritual does not originate from "heavenly principle," "innate conscience" or "pure reason." Xunzi continues, "Thus, ritual is a means of nurture (*yang* 養)."[39] Nurturing what? Nurturing human life. It is a matter of the maintenance and continuous extension of human existence. It is in this "nurturing" that we establish the order, gradation, and distinctions of seniority, rank, status, worth, and value that constitute society. We should emphasize that what Xunzi describes here is not unique to China but rather is a universal part of ancient history that all primitive communities alike passed through. While the particular systems of order ("ritual") created in different cultures may vary greatly, they are alike in their fundamental role of maintaining communal survival. Confucius describes the differences in ritual among different systems in *Analects* 2.23.

Q: So it's really all about survival—your "philosophy of eating" (*chi-fan zhexue* 吃飯哲學)?

Li: Exactly. People need to survive. This is the most basic human need, but academics often overlook this simple piece of common sense. They prefer to talk only about more lofty abstract topics. In reality, human life is not just a matter of facts; it is one of value judgments, as well. There is no "value neutral" stance here. Humans live in certain periods of history, within particular communities. This is my materialism, and my materialist conception of history, which is also the foundation and starting point of my ethics.

Q: When Xunzi talks about ritual and music he seeks to establish rational order throughout society. But isn't he also trying to establish corresponding moral notions and emotions within individuals?

Li: This has to do with the relationship between human culture and human psychology. Confucians tend to concentrate on funerals, and they teach that people with different relationships to the deceased must dress and mourn differently. Those who were closest wear the most humble and crude clothing to show that they are the most upset. We see here the normativizing of emotion within particular manifestations of reason, and this constitutes a particular emotio-rational structure that spans the internal and external. Expressing one's sadness in the type of clothing one wears is not just about outward appearance. Rituals, clothing, and music all mold a person's emotions, and these emotions are in turn expressed

156 | The Humanist Ethics of Li Zehou

through the same material forms of action, dress, and song. This constitutes the interplay and unity between emotions and ideas that has been emphasized throughout Chinese tradition, as in its conception of *cheng* 誠 ("sincerity").

Q: So Xunzi's theory begins with humans in their natural state and focuses on how ritual and music can mold us into a socialized persons. He clearly sees natural human emotions and desires as well as the norms that reshape them as both extremely important. Socialized persons are not only rationally but also emotionally cultivated. Socialization thus strings together the external and internal aspects of people—that is, human culture and human nature (psychology).

Li: Traditional Chinese views of the world do not begin with "water" (as in ancient Greek philosophy) or "the Word" (as in the Bible). Instead, the cosmos and all things are seen as originating in relations between male and female. Mencius, for example, tells us the greatest human relationship is between husbands and wives (*Mencius* 5A2). Even the strong emphasis on "filial piety" (*xiao* 孝) in traditional Chinese thought, normally demanding obedience toward parents, allowed for marriage without the parents' approval when necessary (*Mencius* 4A26). This displays the prioritization of the desire and need to procreate. I see the opening statement of the *Zhongyong* 中庸 (Doctrine of the Mean), which tells us that human nature comes from heaven and became very important for later Confucians, as referring to people having an inborn constitution geared for natural survival.[40] "Relations" also arise from this. The *Book of Changes* (*Yizhuan* 易傳) tells us,

> Only after there were male and female were there husband and wife. Only after there were husband and wife were there parent and child. Only after there were parent and child were there sovereign and minister. Only after there were sovereign and minister were there high and low (superiors and subordinates). Only after there were high and low did ritual and rightness have places in which to operate.[41]

Clearly, the relationship of husband and wife is of utmost importance. China's "ritual education" produces its system of norms and its order of the "five relations" through relations based in natural emotions and desires between male and female, husbands and wives. Individuals are not equal, but exist in closely connected emotional relations with one another. And it is in such relations that humans achieve and experience meaning as moral persons with particular values and attitudes towards life. These are established not only rationally but also emotionally. This is the outlook of Chinese virtue ethics. It is not the same as Aristotle's virtue ethics, based in relationships among free and equal individuals. In *Historical Ontology* I note that many modern Chinese philosophers, including Liang Shuming and Feng Youlan 馮友蘭 (1895–1990), point out that the Western tradition lacks an account of humans as being internally constituted through relationships. Thomas Hobbes (1588–1679), who takes individual security as the basis for social contracts, in which members forgo certain rights in order to establish a government with supreme power, can be seen as the first modern liberal. A great variety of later thinkers from John Locke to Jean-Jacques Rousseau to Immanuel Kant viewed the individual as an independent unit and reason as fundamental. These notions, along with the idea of the social contract, have become foundational elements of liberalism. Although thinkers like Hegel and Marx have convincingly overturned these ideas, they remain highly influential to the point that communitarianism has now arisen to oppose liberalism by turning back to Aristotle's virtue ethics of equal individuals with no "internal" or constitutive relations or emotions.

Q: But many Western philosophers, such as Hume, also talk about sympathy and see it as the foundation and basic motivation for morals. In *A Theory of Justice*, John Rawls even discusses the emotional "sense" of justice as well as jealousy and envy. Doesn't this demonstrate an awareness of the importance of emotions?

Li: These are still very different. While Rawls does specifically discuss "the sense of justice," and Erin Cline has even published a book comparing this to Confucius, Mencius, and Xunzi,[42] they are in fact not alike. Rawls discusses how love between parents and children extends to social groups and then to a sense of social justice in a manner that is quite general and abstract. Not only does he give no account of the relation between the natural and social factors therein, he also establishes this on a rational foundation of mutual reciprocation. Such a conception of "love" thus seems rather indistinct. China's "five relations," on the other hand, involve various highly socialized human emotions which occur within diverse concrete social relationships. These are not general notions or intuitive capacities like empathy, which can be found in animals, and they are certainly quite different from a vaguely described sense of justice founded in individual equality. The five relations conceive of interpersonal

158 | The Humanist Ethics of Li Zehou

relationships, ethical order, and mutual responsibilities both rationally and as a matter of emotions. They consist in unequal relations between superiors and inferiors, parents and children, husbands and wives, older and younger siblings, and friends (which include distinctions of elder and younger, senior and junior). Here there is almost no conception of independent, equal, free individuals. There are only interactive relations. It is important, however, that within these unequal relationships there is a strong emphasis on "harmony." This "harmony" of course involves emotions, and only with this "harmony" can the long-term continuance of these relations be maintained. In *Historical Ontology* I quoted the "Li Yun" 禮運 chapter of the *Record of Ritual* (*Li ji* 禮記):

> What are human emotions? Happiness, anger, sorrow, fear, love, hate, and desire, these are the seven emotions; people are capable of these seven without having to learn them. What are human obligations? Parents' affection, children's filiality, older brothers' care, younger brothers' respect, husbands' proper conduct, wives' obedience, elders' gratitude, juniors' obedience, rulers' humaneness, ministers' loyalty. These are the ten human obligations.

This is very clear. That people are "capable of these seven without having to learn them" indicates they are physiological animal desires and feelings. To culture these biological feelings into the ten obligations is to rationalize, order, and standardize them, incorporating them into the sets of relations that constitute the emotio-rational structure. Both emotion and reason play roles here, and they structurally interconnect in diverse ways as regards different ethical relations. All of these involve differentiation and are unequal, yet although unequal they are relations of harmonious coexistence characterized by delight and warm emotional ties. This is entirely unlike the homogenous Greek notion of virtue ethics based in individual equality, and likewise differs from Rawls's sense of justice. Here emotions differ with different relations and cannot be summarily encompassed in a vague notion of "love." While the Confucians also discuss "love," the implications, content, and form of this emotion shift depending on its object. Loving one's parents differs from loving one's children, and love for a spouse differs from love for a friend. Expressions of love towards elders should have elements of respect, and elders should be tender in loving younger people. How can this all be captured in the

Appendix | 159

single term "love"? This makes love itself even more intricate, rich, and complex. Thus, social harmony can be idealized as a holistic happiness and achievement that arises from diversity, similar to music. Classical Confucianism advocated such an ideal in proposing a connection between music and governance.[43]

2.10 Emotional Harmony Is Higher than Rational Justice

Q: Doesn't ancient Greek philosophy also talk about harmony?

Li: That is a harmony of rational order, as in Pythagoras's likening of the movement of celestial bodies to music. There is no pronounced connection with emotions. In contrast, Confucian harmony, based in "ritual and music," lays heavy emphasis on its practical actualization through emotions. This involves not only rational order but also (or even more so) a logic of emotion. For example, fathers are meant to educate their children. This is a rational duty. However, at the same time Confucians also advocate "exchanging children" to be educated by other families, because otherwise the strictness necessary for effective education could create emotional distance between parents and children, which Mencius sees as extremely bad (4A18). Such distance is a matter not only of rational disagreement over right and wrong but also of emotional divergence and even of conflict resulting therefrom. Thus, we have on the one hand the importance of fulfilling one's fatherly duty (educating one's child), emphasized in the *Xunzi*, and on the other hand the importance of emotional harmony within the family, discussed in the *Analects*.

This dynamic generally holds for other relationships as well, even that of basic equality between friends. The *Analects* tells us we should look out for and encourage our friends, while the *Mencius* declares the "way" of friendship to be constructive criticism. Of course, we must be careful not to overdo such criticism, since doing so could potentially damage this valuable relationship. Moreover, the defining quality of friendship is trust (*xin* 信), which involves not only rational promises between equals but also emotions of faithful companionship. The Guodian bamboo slips similarly discuss trust's relation to emotions (as seen in *Xing zi ming chu* slips 40 and 51). Between rulers and ministers we likewise see a call for each to fulfill their respective duties as well as emphasis on the crucial emotional bond between them. As for relationships between siblings, Confucians do not see these as composed of two equal parties in the manner Aristotle describes. Rather, siblings require distinction and

160 | The Humanist Ethics of Li Zehou

corresponding arrangement between older and younger, along with the appropriate corresponding emotions and attitudes.

The diverse positions within human relations thus each include distinct and unequal emotional attitudes. Husbands and wives cannot be fully equal; it is often the case that one leads and the other follows. In ancient times, economic considerations often determined that the husband was in charge and took charge of external affairs while the wife cared for the home. Today things are sometimes opposite, and that is also fine. When it comes to the division of household affairs, what would we gain by coming up with clear set delineations of right and wrong? Do we need a conception of "justice" to govern these kinds of things, and lawyers to sort matters out for us? What is important for spouses is maintaining the family though caring for and loving each other—that is, emotional harmony. It is not possible to never argue, but couples can work through their disagreements. This happens when both parties preserve the stability and continuance of their relationship through emotional harmony. In this way people's diverse feelings are very specifically regulated and concretely manifest through various relationships, while these relationships in turn express themselves in that variety of specific human emotions. This is what makes human emotions intricate, complex, and rich, as mentioned above. It also promotes the development of human nature or psychology, which is the "humanization of nature."

Traditionally, social morals and religious morals were unified and inseparable, and reason and emotionality similarly so. However, times have changed. Due to modern changes in social and especially economic life, large families and clans (that is, China's patriarchal clan system) are gone, and the relationships of its traditional principles and doctrine have also disappeared or lost their political, ethical, and conceptual validity. Independent individual, contractual standards and public reason have become the fundamental principles of social order. People's fundamental "equality" is now emphasized, as we see in Rawls. However, don't people still live in and through various relationships of inequality, or at least non-equivalence, of older and younger, senior and junior, upper and lower, right and left, near and far, close and distant? People have now become free, equal, and independent individuals and are no longer governed by the norms of the past. Yet, in the emotional orientations of their actual interactions, don't people still employ the emotio-rational structures of the "seven emotions and ten obligations" discussed above? Today, institutionalized ethics may have been dissolved, but relational emotions continue to be part of our existence. Shouldn't we recognize this aspect of ethics?

Q: Do you want to use relationism to replace, or even reject, individualism?

Li: No. Just as the integration of emotion and reason is not a denial or rejection of reason but merely of the ultimate supremacy of reason, relationism is not a denial of modern individualism but rather merely opposes the libertarian view of individualism as supreme. Relationism, which is founded on emotio-rational structures, can serve as traditional Chinese religious morals and provide a regulative and properly constitutive principle for modern social morals' individualism. This seems better suited to China than the many other religions and ideologies that look to God, divine will, or socio-historical determinism. It also possesses a universality that allows it to be expanded and realized globally.

Q: In sum, you have basically returned to the distinction between mere reason and the emotio-rational structure.

Li: Philosophically, we find that, as Jinhua Jia 賈晉華 tells us, the *xian* 咸 hexagram of the *Zhou Book of Changes* (which represents the intermingling of male and female) is related and even identified with the Chinese character *gan* 感. *Gan* also denotes interpersonal emotional connectedness and even cosmic emotional responsiveness or resonance. This is the Confucian "emotional cosmology" (*youqing yuzhouguan* 有情宇宙觀) of China's shamanistic-historical tradition (*wu-shi chuantong* 巫史傳統): heaven, earth, and the myriad things all reside within specific and concrete circumstances of emotionally interactive relations. This differs hugely from the Western tradition's focus on logos, reason, language, and logic. I have previously published two passages that seem especially pertinent here:

> I was surprised to discover that the four famous virtues in Greece—namely, prudence, justice, wisdom, and courage—do not include a virtue of humaneness or love. That is, they do not include emotionality. With the exception of courage, the other three virtues are highly rational. In *After Virtue* Alasdair MacIntyre argues that wisdom is at the heart of virtue or moral character, which likewise emphasizes reason and rational judgment. This stubborn adherence to rationalist tradition in the West is strange to Chinese people. Of course the Greeks also talked about *eros* (desire) and believed it to be the basis of

162 | The Humanist Ethics of Li Zehou

wisdom, and Christianity talks about *agape*, but these are not the same as the Chinese rationalization of biologically based familial relations and emotions into the concepts of humaneness, kindness [the love superiors show to inferiors, including parents to children], and filial piety [which is the love inferiors show to superiors]. . . . The moral character and virtues that Chinese tradition discusses are very concrete and deeply emotional, but they also include cognitive, rational, and intellectual elements, and oppose blind or ignorant loyalty or subservience. Among the three major Chinese virtues (*san dade* 三達德) of wisdom, humaneness, and courage, humaneness is the most fundamental both practically and theoretically. The *Record of Ritual* records that Confucius was especially conscious of ritual regulations dealing with the dead and taught that treating the deceased as simply dead persons exhibited a lack of "humaneness," while treating the deceased the same as living persons showed lack of "wisdom." To navigate this, Confucius supported burying people with artificial imitations of objects (food, furniture, and so on). I find this deeply interesting. Humaneness and wisdom together compose the psychological forms of the "emotio-rational structure" on many different levels and in diverse proportions.[44]

Ruling through ritual is not the same as governance through punishment, and rule by people (*renzhi* 人治) is not the same as rule of law (*fazhi* 法治). . . . This not only emphasizes the objectivity of external laws but also stresses emotional identification and harmonious coherence in interpersonal relations based in kinship and blood ties. It is still important to consider how to best preserve certain aspects of this tradition, such as preference for private over legal resolution and for explanation over verdicts, within the political and social systems of modern rule of law. Of course, this is very difficult and may influence efficiency. But making inroads in this new direction is still worth to striving for. Perhaps, however, it may be too early to advocate moving in this direction.[45]

2.11 Is It too Soon?

Q: Why do you say it may be too early to advocate this?

Li: As I have been saying, I am wary of discussing "emotion as substance" too much these days. This is because we must have "rule of law," and only then should we discuss "rule by people"; we must have "justice," and only then should we discuss "harmony." Since we have yet to realize rule of law or justice, it is dangerous to push for rule by people and harmony. This goes back to my "theory of two morals." The foundation of modern social life is public reason, which involves social morals, a modern legal system, formal justice, and "the priority of the right over the good." The emotions and faith of religious morals can only serve regulative and properly constitutive functions; they cannot replace or determine modern public reason. Even if mastery of this "properly constitutive" function is crucial, the fundamental principle is that it cannot damage social morals, which are primary.

Q: Then why do you advocate "regulation" by emotion as substance and relationism?

Li: I very much admire Adam Smith's acute foresight in discussing the detrimental effects of "economic man" (the rational agent of free and equal exchange) on traditional morals in the early stages of commodity production and the market economy, which led him to advocate a conception of the moral person based in empathy and emotional connection. However, Smith's thought here still centered on "justice" and public reason. The many examples that Sandel engages with are little more than reaffirmations of Adam Smith's prescience. Today, traditional Chinese relations are disintegrating. The various bonds based in kinship that make up the traditional relations increasingly fade away. The past society of familiarity with one another is being replaced by a world of strangers concerned for themselves. Neighbors live in the same building for years, even on the same floor, and do not know one another at all.

Q: Can we return to those traditional relations?

Li: It would be very difficult. Life is based on social and economic advancements that cannot be rewound. However, China remains even now still characterized by relatively rich and highly developed emotional relationships and interpersonal warmth. Practices such as treating people to meals, gift giving, and in-person visits are still pervasive, as are gatherings of family and friends, especially for the holidays. People take great joy in these activities. Just look at China's Spring Festival, which sees a stunning number of people visiting family and friends. When people are upset, moreover, they find someone close to talk to rather than seeking a counselor or psychiatric help. These all show how strong emotional relations remain a prevalent part of Chinese society.

Q: So you think this tradition continues and can even be carried forward?

164 | The Humanist Ethics of Li Zehou

Li: Yes. Consider views on matters of criminal offence. In ancient China people believed you should make up for bad deeds with good ones. They also saw rational principles as unfeeling and inflexible, in contrast to emotions, which allow us to understand and forgive others. Chinese prisons provide capital offenders a final meal of rich food and drink, so that they may enjoy the last moments of their material life. In stark contrast, Western prisons offer a priest for spiritual repentance. Is the former clearly inferior to the latter? Not necessarily. Today Chinese law allows for adjustment of criminal punishment of those who have elderly parents dependent on them, so as not to leave the elderly with no family to care for them. There is also the stay of execution in certain verdicts of the death penalty, which allows for conversion to imprisonment for good behavior. This practice is superior to eliminating the death penalty, and avoids being caught between the two extremes of either giving or not giving the death penalty. It frees up a quite flexible space for prudent and practical adjustment between these two. Here, the foundation of justice is filled with humane emotion, yet still allows for appropriate punishment of those who ought to receive execution. Indeed, sometimes execution for certain crimes is socially necessary for the emotional response needed among the people. This accords with justice while also complying with the emotions of the people. As these issues all heavily involve relationality and human emotion, they seem generally quite difficult to regulate through principles of justice of public reason. Confucius and Confucianism talk about the interplay between abstract principles and their flexible application in actual practice (*jing* and *quan*), which also involves questions of how to manage "formal justice" and "substantive justice" in various concrete circumstances. This warrants further and more thorough discussion.

Q: The Chinese tradition sees emotional relations as based in the immediate family and developing outward from there toward the larger community. When Fei Xiaotong 費孝通 (1910–2005) asserts traditional China's "arrangement of graded order" (*chaxu geju* 差序格局) in his influential *From the Soil: The Foundation of Chinese Society* (*Xiangtu Zhongguo* 鄉土中國), doesn't he discuss the idea that ripples in water gradually fade the farther outward they move, and that thus such relational connectedness cannot be realized on a scale as vast as the Chinese nation?[46]

Li: Chinese tradition was not concerned with relations merely within one's own family clan. There were also the relations between clans, such as those of marriage, that linked them, along with the relations of classmates, of colleagues, of being from the same hometown, working in the same profession, studying under the same teacher, surviving the same hardships, and so on. These kinds of things connect people in the complex and tangled ways that make up the net of relationality that constitutes society as a whole. Here, diverse graded relationships, although marked by inequality, exist together in interpersonal harmony. Such a society differs greatly from one composed of bonds between atomic "equal" individuals. This is also the manner in which the virtue ethics of relationism differs from that of Aristotle and from Rawls's "sense of justice." The sense of justice is a facet of modern social morals. I have already mentioned that public virtue includes aspects of emotion (public reason is not merely a system of rational order but also requires emotional backing) but that these are not equivalent to the emotions of interpersonal relations. However, the emotions of our relations can overlap with, reinforce, and deepen the emotional aspects of public virtue. Of course, conflicts and opposition will also arise between them, and these issues require concrete analysis.

Q: Add to this the classical teachings that the virtue of humaneness consists in loving people, that we should be overflowing with love for people, and of universal fraternity as an ideal, and this becomes an extremely vast and deep web of emotions.[47]

Li: On the whole, Confucianism establishes an "emotional cosmology"—an outlook that affirms the material world and human life. Here, emotions analogically connect humans, in body and mind, to the natural world. In so doing, this outlook thereby affirms, emphasizes, and elevates people's natural needs, desires, and emotions. That is, it rationalizes them. It does not pursue spiritual transcendence or entrance to a heavenly kingdom. This presents us with many important theoretical and practical questions regarding our present and future, such as how to reestablish an emotional harmony of diverse relations in modern society's "world of alienation" and how the idea that "harmony is higher than justice" can serve a regulative and properly constitutive role in public reason's construction of modern social morals, laws, and norms.

Q: Can you expand on the details of this?

Li: I cannot. As mentioned before, ethical philosophy provides only the "outline" of certain ideas. Expanding on their details is a task belonging in parts to political philosophy, moral psychology, and philosophy of religion. This research should be undertaken by more specialists. And importantly, those aspects falling under political philosophy need to draw more heavily on actual experience, so as to provide more comprehensive particulars.

166 | The Humanist Ethics of Li Zehou

Q: So you only come up with questions?

Li: I believe it is important to put forward the right questions. In sum, my discussions of the emotio-rational structure and relationism simply aim to express disagreement with notions of *a priori* "reason" as well as why I reject vague notions of natural empathy (from Mencius's "heart-mind of compassion" to the theories of sympathy in Adam Smith and David Hume) and Rawls's "sense of justice" as explaining the origin and motivation of moral action.

Q: Mencius laughed at King Xuan of Qi for sympathizing with an ox brought out for sacrifice and so having it replaced with a sheep. He also tells us that a "gentleman" (morally cultivated person) keeps his distance from the butcher because he cannot bear to eat meat after hearing the cries of the butchered animal.

Li: Here we see that such "empathy" is unable to explain or resolve ethical or moral problems. This is because this kind of "empathy" is not clearly differentiated from animal instincts. Animals also display empathy, as well as altruistic instincts, even to the point of self-sacrifice. Do animals therefore have morality? Sociobiologists think so, but I disagree. Animals have morals no more than they have beliefs and religion. This is because they have no "emotio-rational structure." Ethics and morality are how humankind has established itself and are characterized by governance by reason. This is also the human culture and human psychology I discuss so often.

Q: This requires returning to the aspects of human psychology that inform your conception of the emotio-rational structure, including the distinctively human capacities, emotions, and conceptions of good and evil.

Li: We should keep in mind that I discuss human nature not as our natural tendencies but rather as our "humanized nature" (*renhua de ziran* 人化的自然). This is a matter of the emotio-rational structure. Externally, this emotio-rational structure expresses itself in human culture as the regulation of "justice" by circumstance and emotion. Internally, it expresses itself in human nature (human psychology) as the harmonious concord of distinctively human emotions, capacities, and conceptions of good and evil.

Section 3: Kant, Human Nature, and Good and Evil

3.1 HUMANS AS ENDS

Q: You see Kant as very important, and Sandel also talks a lot about Kant. What do you think of him?

Li: Kant is the foremost representative of deontological ethics, and any discussion of ethics must address him. However, his theory and its difficulties are complex, and I have my own rather unique views on them.

Q: What are your views?

Li: I fully separate Kant's second principle, that humans are ends, from his first and third (respectively "Act only in accordance with that maxim through which you can at the same time will that it become a universal law" and "The will of every rational being is a will giving universal law").[48] I see the idea of humans as ends as a product of its times and as possessing practical content: everyone is an end and not a mere means, and we cannot treat, use, or interact with others as merely instruments. This is a social ideal produced in society's historical development reaching a certain era.

The idea that humans are ends, like notions of inherent human rights and natural equality, is not an *a priori* principle we have had since ancient times. It is therefore also not equivalent to the free will capable of universal legislation. Under the ancient Greek institution of slavery, people were merely tools capable of speech. They were not ends. In times of war, soldiers are simply the pawns of their generals. They are not ends. In revolutionary movements, people are required to dutifully serve a larger vision, as components in a grand scheme. Again, they are not ends. Still today there are many instances in which humans are not ends. Humans serving as appendages of machines, tools of production, and dutiful servants are seen all over. However, there are two important points to be made here. First, things will not be like this forever. Rather, this is a necessary stage of historical progress. Technological development will allow robots to gradually replace humans in much monotonous, miserable, strenuous, mechanical, and uncreative labor, and progressively lessen instances of humans serving as tools throughout society. Second, since today humans are relatively independent, people can decide for themselves what job they want. They no longer need to be obedient tools or mere cogs in a machine.

Yet, because history is still progressing, people remain far from acquiring true individual independence and freedom. Kant took the conceptual consciousness of modern capitalist society and elevated it to an absolute mandate, and in so doing provided a lofty theoretical basis for later liberalism. He overthrew the entirety of previous history by highlighting the idea that the totality exists for the individual, which we see in contemporary declarations of human rights. Each of us has the right to pursue truly becoming "oneself," neither a tool of authority, of the group,

168 | The Humanist Ethics of Li Zehou

or of others, nor a slave to religion, institutions, customs, or ideology. Humans are free, equal, and independent individuals, and they have a right to autonomous choice and self-determination. Although this idea has the weakness of being ahistorical, it gives voice to the spirit of modern society. As the actuality and the ideal of present and future, it cannot be evaded, denied, or resisted. It therefore has an epoch-defining, eternal value for humankind. Sandel accurately homes in on Kant in carrying out his philosophical attack, and at the same time cannot help but continue to hold Kant in high esteem. The ethical and moral thought of this great Enlightenment thinker continues to shine radiantly even today. Building on earlier thinkers and inspiring later generations, Kant's philosophy is a core element of modern social morals. While modern social morals do not and cannot themselves fully realize the ideal of humans as ends, they are a major step in historical progress toward realizing this ideal.

3.2 Universal Laws

Q: What about the other two principles?

Li: I interpret them in a way that very few others share. I see Kant's three major critiques as aiming to deal with the question of "what makes humans human," especially in terms of human capacity. "Universal laws" and "autonomy of will" (or "free will") in actuality can be understood together as the single principle that humans possess free will capable of universal legislation.[49] As Kant says, "The categorical imperative is thus only a single one, and specifically this: *Act only in accordance with that maxim through which you can at the same time will that it become a universal law*."[50] What this actually reveals are the formal structures of moral action. It refers to the coercive mechanisms of internal psychology and not to the concrete content of particular social eras. In Kant's thought these maintain an internal connection to his second principle that humans are ends, in that free, equal, and independent humans should possess a "universally legislative" "free will" and this displays the dignity and force of individual character. However, the first and third principles are also importantly distinct from the second. And since the "free will" capable of "universal legislation" is merely a formal element of psychology, it finds great difficulty in providing itself substantial content and is thus exceedingly vague and unspecific. Hegel sternly criticized Kant's formalism for this very reason. Hegel replaces Kant's moral imperative with an ethics that has specific historical content and rejects the notion of an abstract "free will" capable of "universal legislation" in actual life. In fact, the notion that humans are ends is a matter of external human culture and political philosophy. The first and third principles, on the other hand, are matters of internal human nature and moral psychology. I understand Kant as erecting "capital-H 'Humanity'" on the dual internal and external aspects of human nature and human culture, respectively.

Q: Doesn't Kant describe not committing suicide, not lying, developing oneself, and helping others as four substantive principles demonstrative the two categories of perfect and imperfect duties,[51] which you refer to as "strong" and "weak" imperatives?

Li: Kant believes that these four examples can serve as universal laws because being otherwise would go against natural law and be self-contradictory. As I see it, in contrast, they can serve as ethical laws because they are duties or principles that any community relies on in order to continue its existence, and this in turn is why individuals should follow them. If people were to generally commit suicide, tell lies, fail to develop themselves, and not help others, then any community (and therefore humankind) would not continue to survive. That's why so many religions condemn suicide and lying and demand the individual's sincere accordance with such proscriptions as part of their basic teachings. However, in the complexity of actual life it is difficult or even impossible to fully abide by these rules. Is it moral to tell the truth to an enemy and put your companions in danger? In fact, it is not hard to find situations in which acts of lying and even suicide seem moral. Sandel's discussion of whether euthanasia or assisted suicide is moral examines a topic of intense contemporary controversy. Clearly, the logic of Kant's "universal legislation" is not directly applicable in actual life. The defense of the principle that "one should never lie" Sandel presents, through the examples of Kant's own life and President Clinton's nimble use of language, is quite a stretch.[52] While the proscription against lying is an ethical principle indispensable to society, as a moral imperative for individual behavior it has no universal necessity. These four examples, in fact, just so happen to primarily turn on questions of communal welfare rather than on the individual rights stressed in liberalism. Moreover, how these proscriptions are applied and realized remains dependent on concrete circumstance.

3.3 FREE WILL

Q: Then what is the significance of the notion of universal legislation with which Kant is so concerned?

170 | The Humanist Ethics of Li Zehou

Li: I see great significance in that it highlights the powerful psychological forms exhibited in people's carrying out moral duties. It helps us see that these are the distinctively human capacities that make humans human, and it indicates the central role of "free will" as a defining element of "human nature," or human psychology. It points us toward the emotio-rational structure unique to humans.

Q: Can you explain this in greater detail?

Li: Kant's conception tells us that when people act morally they affirm a certain conviction: the manner in which I am acting accords with a principle that all people should adopt, and all people should follow my example; thus, my behavior can be willed to be a universal law. In Chinese thought, such action is conceived of as "establishing one's heart and mind for the cosmos and establishing one's life for the vitality of the people."[53] It does not take into consideration my own wellbeing (the consequences of an action according to the particulars of my situation, including pleasure and pain, fortune and misfortune, safety and danger, benefit and harm, or life and death), but rather presents a model for behavior that must be followed as a rational absolute mandate (a "categorical imperative"). This highlights the unmatched force and magnificence of humans as rational beings and from this brings forth the immense strength of human life, which far surpasses that of other animal species. People are no longer simply animals that live to eat, drink, and enjoy other sensory pleasures; they are able to take rational control of themselves and overcome even the desire for live itself. The "free will," capable of disregarding pleasure and pain, fortune and misfortune, life and death, and other facets of empirical, sensory existence, makes up the ontological foundation that makes humans human. This is in fact what Confucius meant in putting forth the ideal of humaneness as overcoming the self to act in accordance with ritual regulations (*Analects* 12.1). The same teaching also appears in Mencius's discussion of "floodlike *qi*"[54] and description of the great man (*da zhangfu* 大丈夫) as "unable to be seduced by wealth and prestige, unable to be moved by poverty and low status, and unable to be bent by awe and military might"[55] (*Mencius* 2A2, 3B2). I call the psychological characteristics of this type of behavior the "solidification of reason" (*lixing ningju* 理性凝聚). In my view this is the true implication of Kant's first (universal legislation) and third (free will) principles. Kant's appreciation of the average person's ability to act in accordance with morals reflects this psychological "legislation" and the form of its psychological structures, and not the substantive content of human culture and society.

Kant's endless praise of the populace's role in the French Revolution is directed toward the psychological forms of their willingness to sacrifice themselves and not its concrete ethical content (excessive fervor for the revolutionary movement). The particular social content of ethics changes with the times, but the form of this psychological structure does not age.

Q: Is this the moral capacity distinctive to humans that you emphasize in *Ethics* (*Lunlixue gangyao* 倫理學綱要)?

Li: It is one component of the distinctively human capacities, which also includes epistemological and aesthetic capacities that likewise differ from those of animals. However, free will is the core human capacity. Both logically and practically speaking, ethics and morals have priority in relation to cognition. I differ from Kant in emphasizing that no human capacities are *a priori* or innate, but rather they belong to humans as products of history and education.

Q: In *Critique of Critical Philosophy* (*Pipan zhexue de pipan* 批判哲學的批判),[56] you emphasize that "education" (*jiaoyu* 教育), in the sense of the cultivation of human nature or psychology, is the core of all future academic subjects.

Li: In that book I discuss how one teaches a child not to lie and other proscriptions for the sake of cultivating a free will that can rationally overcome and control emotional aspects of themselves. This cultivates the individual to become more than an animal simply attracted to benefit and avoiding harm, afraid of pain and delighting in pleasure. The *Mencius* also argues that through difficulties and suffering, human psychology or nature is formed and fortified (6B35). The strict training of the Spartan forces is another instance of cultivating this unyielding "free will" of the "solidification of reason."

3.4 ETHICS AND MORALS

Q: Since it is a single psychological form, you are saying that the self-sacrifices of both terrorists and fire fighters on 9/11 are equivalent in terms of their individual morality being a matter of rational governance of emotions and their being rational beings. Terrorists also believe that their behavior is grounded in "free will" and should be "universally legislated," and that their self-sacrifice in holy war is worthy of respect and imitation.

Li: But the religious and ethical principles terrorists follow, as well as their concepts of good and evil, are horribly wrong. Furthermore, among these are many people, especially children and women, who have been

172 | The Humanist Ethics of Li Zehou

tricked into believing that their self-sacrifice will allow them to go to heaven and enjoy sensory pleasures and happiness. These are not cases of morality.

Q: Then you differentiate between ethics (accordance with and the inculcation of external conceptions of good and evil, through which reason arises from ritual regulations) and morality (the formal structures of internal psychology, in which emotions are determined by reason).

Li: Precisely. Although Hegel also differentiates between ethics and morals, he instead saw morality as merely a matter of abstract universal principles, fundamentally failing to pick up on and emphasize the importance of morality as the very specific forms of the individual's psychological structures. This fundamentally differs from me. Other later scholars have also drawn the distinction, but their understandings likewise differ fundamentally from my own. Sandel's analyses of many real-world examples do not clearly distinguish questions of ethics, which are related to institutions and bear on political action, legal trials, and policies, from matters of morality, which bear on individual behavior and psychology. Of course, any absolute distinction between them may be difficult, but the distinction itself remains extremely necessary. Conflating political action and individual action makes clear discussion of ethical and moral issues very difficult.

Ethics concerns external institutions, customs, order, norms, and standards. Morality concerns the psychological characteristics and individual actions that accord with and enact those institutions, customs, order, norms and standards. The difference can be seen, for example, in the various psychological orientations of Lawrence Kohlberg's three levels of moral development (pre-conventional morality, conventional morality, and post-conventional morality). Ethics and conceptions of good and evil change with the times and vary among societies. This is supported by a great many documents and much cultural theory, and Sandel also agrees. Certain things accepted in the past are now rejected, and what is celebrated here and now may be criticized and scorned in other places and times. We have seen such difference, for example, in ideas about whether women should remarry or remain chaste, receive education, and cover their skin in public. There are great divergences in the expression of morality in individual psychology and action, as well, as seen in the fact that Kohlberg's three levels exist not only in children but among adults as well. Yet, the fact that morality ought principally to be expressed in action means that following shared laws can also be regarded as moral conduct.

Appendix | 173

This point is generally recognized, although such accordance with conventions does not constitute morality in a strict Kantian sense. According to Kant's standard, only conduct that can be conceptually expanded as universal law, and not choices that take into account personal wellbeing and benefit nor those that merely abide by standards or institutions, can be considered moral. All other action is merely behavior that follows general, conditional hypothetical imperatives. The absolute nature of the psychological forms of Kantian universal laws is characteristic of the rational structures of all of humankind, from ancient to modern and East to West. This is because morality constitutes the most important part of individual psychological substance (*xinli benti* 心理本體), which is what makes humans human and what makes possible the continuous existence of groups and humankind. This, in fact, is precisely the absolute aspect of human moral psychology sedimented within the relativity of ethics and culture. I accept plurality and relativity in aspects of both ethics and morality, but I oppose relativism.

In summary, I see Kant's first and third principles as principally describing aspects of human nature. They concern moral psychology, not a political philosophy attempting to universally legislate all of humankind. In fact, no such philosophy is possible. Even Rawls ultimately revised his Kantian theory of justice, ridding it of metaphysics and falling back on a conception of "overlapping consensus."

3.5 The Four Arrows

Q: This seems to relate back to three of your ideas, namely that emotionality is the developmental foundation of ritual, that reason develops from ritual while also influencing it, and that reason dominates emotions. This can be expressed with the "four arrows" of figure A.2.

Li: This presents my historical materialism and diverges from the logic of many political philosophies that move exclusively from "reason" (thought, concepts) to "ritual regulations" (institutions, order). "Emotionality" here includes human emotions and desires, but is not limited to these. It refers more broadly to the circumstance (*qingjing* 情境) of the living existence of the entire community, which is interrelated with individual emotions and desires. The later mention of "emotion" in this

Emotionality ⟶ Ritual Regulations ⇠------⇢ Reason ⟶ Emotion

Figure A.2.

174 | The Humanist Ethics of Li Zehou

model refers to individual emotions and desires, but as the entirety of one's mental state, not merely as feelings.

Among the four items of this model there are four arrows representing relationships. The first moves from emotionality to ritual regulations and was discussed already in relation to Xunzi. The second arrow moves from ritual regulations to reason, which was also discussed earlier as the transformation of external ethical norms, customs, order, institutions, and standards into concepts of right and wrong and good and evil within the individual. This involves rational, cognitive knowledge. In this process, religious leaders and philosophers often elevate reason from the empirical to the *a priori* and transcendent in the form of orders or principles from God, innate conscience, pure reason, the true nature of the cosmos, and so on. The third arrow, pointing from reason to emotion, principally denotes cultivation of the will through the solidification of reason—the governance of emotions by reason. Here reason controls and cultivates emotions and desires through identification with concepts of good and evil, thereby governing behavior. Because of this, the distinctively human capacity of the "free will" is precisely the capacity to consciously act according to one's conceptions of good and evil. It is a capacity for self-coercion.

Q: These three arrows diagram the complex relations of emotions and reason. It seems you want to avoid simply collapsing the source and motivation for ethics and morals into either reason or emotions, regardless of their form as external principles of heaven, internal moral conscience, or inborn biological emotions and desires.

Li: I continually emphasize the importance of history and education throughout my work. Ritual regulations are produced through the historical lived existence of emotionality and instilled into individuals as reason (concepts of good and evil) through education, which allows the free will to govern emotions. Thus we have Kant's "practical reason." At the same time, the impulsive forces of emotions facilitate and actualize this.

What needs to be made clear here is that conceptions of good and evil are not the "free will" of the solidification of reason but rather the concrete rational ideas which are the content of this "free will." Ritual regulations, which originated through practices of shamanism, include formal aspects of the emotio-rational structure, as will power, while also possessing the content of concrete notions of good and evil. Therefore "reason" here has two major connotations: the solidification of reason (as the will) and the construction of reason (knowledge, as conceptions of good and evil). The movement from ritual to reason cultivates these two aspects of individual reason.

Q: If people's internal conceptions of good and evil come from external sources such as ritual regulations, order, and institutions, how can there be the divergence, opposition, and conflict we find between new and old versions of these conceptions? Why would we advocate the promotion of new morals and rejection of the old?

Li: This is precisely the progressive and anticipatory nature of concepts. Once ritual regulations have entered reason's conceptual scheme of cognitive knowledge, reason itself becomes relatively independent. Because people's lives are in a constant state of change, their thought and conduct have aspects of obeying and identifying with ritual as well as aspects of rejecting, challenging, and opposing ritual. This includes reinterpreting, revising, and altering regulations. This dynamic quality of concepts can be quite pronounced. New concepts have their origin both in actual human life and in their own logic of conceptual transformation and development. They are entirely able to break through the established norms and requirements of rituals. Therefore, the move from ritual to reason does not involve any sort of mechanistic or deterministic outlook. Ideas can precede the arrival of a new order, new institutions, or new norms (that is, new "ritual regulations"), and can contribute to the destruction or change of old ones. In this way the relationship between rituals and reason is also bidirectional. This is the significance of the fourth dashed arrow that moves in the opposite direction between the two, from reason to ritual regulations. The other relationships also have aspects that move in this opposite direction, but these are not nearly as important as that which occurs between ritual and reason.

3.6 The Emotions of Individual Psychology

Q: But you also say that human nature, as moral psychology, includes emotions, and that Hume can be used to correct some of Kant's oversights.

Li: The distinctively human capacity, emotions, and conceptions of good and evil are three components of my understanding of human moral psychology. Human capacity (free will) and conceptions of good and evil (rational knowledge) come together in actual conduct. They are what motivates moral action. But in addition to free will and conceptions of good and evil, the impulsive force of emotions is also very important. These are the emotions governed by reason in our model of "four arrows."

176 | The Humanist Ethics of Li Zehou

We should keep in mind that this governance involves not only reason's control, suppression, and even extinguishing of desires (although this is its principal aspect), but also the cultivation, development, and even catharsis of certain emotions and desires, as well. This engages emotions as a tremendous impulsive force facilitating the realization of rational behavior.

Q: It seems that Sandel discusses this very little.

Li: Sandel talks mostly about political philosophy and so does not need to deal with issues of moral or individual psychology. I on the other hand emphasize human nature and so must look closely at these. But as I have explained many times, I am not engaging in empirical psychology, but rather putting forth a philosophical perspective. My ethics is a philosophy that contains elements of both political philosophy and moral psychology, but is certainly not either of these in themselves. I specialize in neither, and therefore the discussions herein of utilitarianism, liberalism, and moral psychology are put only in simple, broad strokes. Rawls similarly describes certain aspects of moral psychology in *A Theory of Justice*. Here I mean simply to put forward the conception of "reason's governance of emotions."

Q: Do both our distinctively human capacity and our emotions require cultivation?

Li: Emotions have their basis in natural physiology, and of course animals also have emotions. Moreover, as these are produced through the long and brutal struggle for survival of each species' history, the natural emotions of biological species include both "good" sentiments and actions such as sympathy, altruism, and cooperation and "evil" ones like selfishness, cruelty, murder, and viciousness. During China's Cultural Revolution many middle- and high-school students committed acts of extreme cruelty and viciousness. Moreover, it is commonplace for terrorists, mercenaries, and even regular soldiers to become trigger-happy and take pleasure in killing. These are instances of particular circumstances in which misdirected conceptions of good and evil lead to the unleashing of certain animal instincts. Such misguided notions of good and evil and wicked elements of society can result in people becoming more savage and crueler than animals. This falls under Kant's idea of "radical evil." Thus, cultivating "good" animal instincts and removing, controlling, or repressing bad ones occur principally through proper rational recognition of good and evil and the solidification of reason's power (the free will) to control certain basic instincts. Here notions of "good" and "evil" are spoken of in reference to communal life and the survival of humankind.

Fostering fundamental instincts of love and repugnance into impulsive emotional forces in carrying out rational commands is the process of moral cultivation of "what makes humans human." In its opposition to empiricism, Kant's practical reason excludes all factors of sensible experience from the drive to follow moral imperatives. It is therefore unable to attend to this point and requires supplemental thought.

3.7 THE UNIFICATION OF MENCIUS AND XUNZI IN CONFUCIUS

Q: You are saying that the interference of reason can make natural human emotions evil as well as good.

Li: Taking pleasure in the misfortune of others, self-deception, and cruelty come from animal instincts originally oriented toward the need of survival. When driven by reason, these can develop in humans to heights and levels of complexity far beyond what animals could ever achieve. For instance, animals do not commit mass murder simply for pleasure. Likewise, "good" animal instincts like sympathy, compassion, and cooperation can develop in humans to levels such as universal love. In fact, the study of social biology is quite valuable in exploring the possibility of tracing human moral action back to its physiological animal origin. However, assuming that moral action can be directly boiled down to animal instincts would be a major error. Humans each have their own DNA and are thus naturally endowed with differences, and yet people often develop similarly when they share like experiences. Our neurons themselves are inborn, but the particular connections and structural forms between them develop in diverse ways through experience and education. Thus, *a posteriori* education is a crucial formative factor of psychology.

Here, the thought of Mencius, who claims that human nature is inherently good but must be cultivated, can be unified with that of Xunzi, who argues that human nature is inherently bad and goodness is therefore reliant on human artifice. The two are united through Confucius's emphasis on learning. In the *Analects* we find Confucius's teachings to include "Human nature is similar, but practices and customs differ" (17.2). He also claims that people "arise through poetry, are established through ritual, and achieve themselves through music" (8.8). This can also be understood as inclusive of David Hume's and Adam Smith's notions of sympathy. So it is neither Mencius's idea of innate goodness nor Christianity's original sin, nor even Hume's or social biology's notions of natural instincts, that truly accounts for the origin of morality. Rather, *learning and education*

178 | The Humanist Ethics of Li Zehou

are morality's real source. According to Ludwig Wittgenstein's notion of "rules of the game," the rules of language come from actual life, not individual minds. Individual psychology is thus formed through cultivation by social norms. When children learn language, they are really learning behavioral norms of social life, or the "rules of the game." This is why Wittgenstein rejects psychologism and individualism. In terms of ethics, this is my model of "four arrows." Both "emotionality" as interconnected emotional circumstance and the individual's personal experience of cultivated "emotions" have essentially social aspects.

Q: Your discussion here of emotions and desires, including your citation of the *Xunzi*, seems mostly oriented toward the fundamental material needs of human survival. Yet people also have many higher-level desires, such as those for fame, status, wealth, success, pursuit of truth, and so forth, in addition to many aesthetic desires. How do you explain these?

Li: "High-level" and "low-level" desires are related to one another in complex ways, both direct and indirect. For the most part, higher-level desires arise only when lower-level ones have been adequately satisfied. The latter provide a foundation for the former, and often permeate into them. This can be seen in the relationship between sex and love, as well as between feeding oneself and wealth, fame, status, and success. One has to analyze particular situations to assess these links. In our discussion of utilitarianism earlier we already talked about higher-level and lower-level happiness.

Q: Are there moral desires? Mencius tells us, "What is desirable may be called good" (*Mencius* 7B25).

Li: This mention of desires in terms of "what is desirable" is unrelated to physiological needs. It refers rather to conscious moral aspirations and knowledge, to the "rightness of ritual" (*liyi* 禮義) that we psychologically consolidate—that is, concepts of good and bad. Similar to Kant's "What may I hope?,"[57] such moral "desires" are no longer connected to the desires of basic natural needs (needs of survival). We see here that if higher-level and lower-level desires are confused and not properly distinguished we become unable to discuss these issues clearly. There are many complexities within the emotio-rational structure.

Q: Your main idea throughout this work is the emotio-rational structure.

Li: Moral emotions are important here as well. For example, rational ideas and conceptions of good and evil permeate emotions such as respect, reverence, self-assurance, self-abasement, self-respect, self-blame, shame, sympathy, anger, envy, hate, and jealousness. The structures of the relationships between each of these emotions and the rational elements of psychology differ, and the forms they take are extremely complex. These should be investigated by the various specific academic areas that deal with their particulars, such as philosophy of mind, moral psychology, child psychology, and brain science. However, simply from child psychology we see clearly the general process model of "ritual" (external guidance, norms, and punishments) → "reason" (rational ideas and cognition, conceptions of good and evil, and the dominating force of the solidification of reason) → "emotions" (making happy wrongdoers into remorseful ones).

In ancient China the terms *li* 禮 ("ritual") and *yue* 樂 ("music") were spoken of together. Ritual came from shamanistic ceremonies, taboos, totems, and so on, which included music and involved hierarchical distinctions that then became the patterns for rational knowledge (conceptions of good and evil and of right and wrong). However, through music and ceremonies this also directly shaped emotions, which despite their natural physiological basis are distinctly human. The classical Confucian *Record of Ritual* tells of a gentleman feeling a chill sadness in the autumn. This is not a biological sensation due to the cold but rather an emotion regarding human relations. It refers to cultivated emotions that are not directly connected to natural physiological desires (the sorrow is not due to the cold), and these assist reason in driving moral behavior. The influence of reason refines and enriches emotions so that they develop from mere physiological instincts to become "human emotions." There are many levels and categories of emotions and desires. Western philosophers list and describe a good number of them, some of which are emotions that are completely disconnected from desires. These include, for example, the satisfaction associated with wisdom, the pleasure accompanying morality, and aesthetic enjoyment. Already disconnected from physiological pleasure and pain as well as from desires for basic needs, these emotions are permeated by reason to form a certain sort of emotio-rational structure. As we discussed earlier regarding utilitarian happiness, there are different levels of pleasure.

Q: Just now you discussed the cultivation and repression of "good" and "evil" animal instincts, respectively. However, children's books often include tricksters as their protagonists as well as examples of unruly and stubborn children to whom kids often take a liking. What do you think of this?

Li: This is a question for specialists in child psychology. My thoughts are that these characters help enrich children's imaginations and exercise their proactive judgment. This satisfies and cultivates children's

180 | The Humanist Ethics of Li Zehou

psychologies more fully than simple moral instruction. These negative examples, moreover, are usually restricted by context and not fully affirmed, generally serving the ultimate means of a didactically positive ending. The vast majority of children's stories present very clear moral categorization of characters and actions: good and bad are quite well defined in the wolf and the rabbit or the fox and the hen. Children enjoy identifying the good guy and the bad guy, a process through which their emotions and reason acquire moral orientation, which is also the formation of the emotio-rational structure of moral psychology.

Q: What you are telling us, then, is that this all serves to cultivate cognitive and emotional identification of good and bad.

Li: However, when children grow up and enter into social life, they find that situations are often much more complicated than these stories. Mo Yan tells us, "There is a hazy expanse in each person's heart in which right and wrong and good and bad are difficult to set clearly."[58] In actual life, all people find themselves at times in various open expanses in which good and bad or right and wrong are deeply intertangled and very hard to distinguish or "set clearly." Moreover, it is not the case that good people are without serious faults or that bad people have no goodness in them. Fyodor Dostoevsky's novels describe the intertwining of good and evil in ways that are extraordinarily powerful and moving. Similar issues of moral complexity appear in Confucian works, which point out difficult or even painful decisions we must make when facing moral dilemmas. Choosing between social justice and familial loyalty, for example, appears in the *Analects'* well-known story of a sheep-stealing father (13.18). The issue of futility comes up when Confucius advocates carrying out moral action even when we know it has no practical effectiveness, while in another passage he states that if he finds he cannot succeed in carrying out the "Way" he will take to a raft and float away on the high seas (*Analects* 14.38, 5.7). However, children are unable to comprehend this complexity of actual life. They have biological instincts that run contrary to social restrictions and therefore still first need to cultivate clear moral ideas and emotions. Continuing to take the proscription against lying as an example, we all know that adults sometimes lie, but we still need to teach children to never do so because they are not yet able to fully manage in which particular situations it may be necessary or good to lie.

Q: Indeed, it is not easy to navigate the moral dilemmas of actual life.

Li: Jean-Paul Sartre, when discussing existentialist free choice, was once asked, "If someone had to choose between sacrificing their life to oppose the Nazis, or going along with them in order to take care of their aging mother, what should they do?" Sartre himself gives no answer. In China this falls under the traditional idea that often times one can only be fully loyal *or* filial, but not both. Today, when the tension between history and morals is tremendous, the divergence and contradiction between "public virtue" and "private virtue" (for example, situations in which one must choose to either uphold contractual stipulations or carry out an act of friendship) has made moral dilemmas both more prevalent and more pronounced. Among these we find conflicts between the market and morals that prove very difficult to resolve. Sandel's book gives many examples of the loss of morality at the hands of the market. For example, when fines for bad behavior become simply payment allowing for that behavior, we see a loss of moral emotion in those performing the once taboo act. Sandel describes how once daycares started fining Israeli parents for being late to pick up their children, the parents began arriving late more frequently.[59] Apparently, they thought that since they were paying extra they were off the hook for keeping the teacher late, and no longer felt as guilty. And yet, being fined is indeed equivalent to paying for something. When the fine was later discontinued the parents continued to be late. What should be done? And what happened after? Sandel does not say.

Q: It seems that moral emotions are even more complex than the distinctive human capacity?

Li: I have stated that admiration for choosing death over surrender is a type of moral emotion, but this is a nuanced, complex issue. We generally do not feel admiration toward people who sacrifice their lives out of blind obedience. More likely, we may feel pity for them. And toward those who have committed heinous acts and only then chosen death over surrender, we feel disgust. For example, we feel sad compassion for the ignorant children of the Hitler Youth, who marched toward death in naiveté. Toward Nazi leaders, on the other hand, we feel revulsion even when they are defended as loyally fulfilling their duty (which can be seen as an instance of the categorical imperative). This is because they have trampled over the fundamental human emotions and concepts of good and evil that have been historically accumulated by humankind.

3.8 It Doesn't Work the Other Way Around

Q: You have talked a lot about the close connection between emotions and conceptions of good and evil. What do you think of reversing this and following Hume with certain additions of Kant's thought,

182 | The Humanist Ethics of Li Zehou

seeing emotions as moral motivation and reason as their servant or instrument?

Li: This does not work. Such a view proves more or less equivalent to that of sociobiology. As I've said already, animals also have emotions such as sympathy, anger, and love. These feelings are determined by natural causal laws of biological existence, and differ entirely from the moral character of human "free will" (consciously disregarding consequences of benefit or harm, individual pleasure and pain, and even one's own death). Such an outlook discounts "what makes humans human," the emotio-rational structure. I continue to uphold Kant on this point. Much of the emotivism and intuitionism popular recently in the West celebrates Hume. However, even instantaneous moral intuitions are still cultivated by education (in its broad sense), including non-conscious rational elements. This is still a type of emotio-rational structure. I discussed this at length in the 1950s in my work on aesthetic intuition.

Q: Sociobiologist and defender of liberalism Friedrich Hayek argues that animals altruistically sacrifice themselves just like humans.

Li: Such "altruistic" self-sacrifice by animals is also instinctual and not an act of free will. Hayek actually rejects social biology in thinking that only by ridding ourselves of such original altruistic instincts can we become free individuals (that is, humans). Hayek emphasizes spontaneous social order and the free competition of individuals while denouncing rational constructs and welfare policies. Some have called him a social Darwinist, as he advocates ideas of survival of the fittest. Hayek has been very influential in China. However, Sandel rarely mentions him. If we simplify things and say that Rawls carries forward Kant's principle of helping others, then perhaps we can say that Hayek builds on Kant's principle of developing oneself? Both Rawls and Hayek are major thinkers, and we could say that they represent the leftist and rightist schools of liberal thought (although Hayek refuses to call himself libertarian). Of course, sweeping these two both under the fold of Kant, especially considering Hayek's opposition to rational constructs, may be a bit of a stretch. I am probably a little too fond of Kant.

Q: Even though you greatly admire Kant, you still want to supplement or correct his thought with the notion of "emotion as substance," which is based in traditional Chinese thought. Neither leftist nor rightist schools of liberalism, including Rawls and Hayek, emphasize emotions. They talk principally about rational conceptions of justice. To this day they still stress the atomic individual, individual rights, free choice, and even the rational calculation of effects in the market to determine what is just, which is reflected in Sandel's references to many contemporary economists in his book.

Li: Many political philosophers after Kant leave emotions without any significant place in their theories. However, I do not see a strong notion of the atomic individual in Kant. His later work on history and politics, moreover, can be seen as in direct communication with Hegel and Marx. Allen Wood even labels Kant's thought "proto-Marxism." In his book *Kant's Ethical Thought* he has a section titled "Kant's historical materialism."[60] While Wood admits that Kant's thought does not include ideas of class struggle or the abolition of private ownership, he still argues for similarities with Marx. Wood writes,

> Along with Marx, Kant understands the basis of history as the development of people's socially productive powers, their collective capacities to produce their means of subsistence in distinctive ways that vary with historical conditions. Through history these capacities change and grow, and human history therefore passes through different stages, which correspond to the dominant mode of productive activity. Along with Marx, Kant also views history as a scene not only of conflict and strife but of deepening inequality and oppression. And as in Marx's theory of history, the root of this conflict is a struggle between groups of people with antagonistic economic interests, where the different groups represent different stages in humanity's economic development.[61]

Like Wood, I see Kant's later writings as ultimately moving towards collectivism, not individualism. In other words, I would argue that Kant offers a study of humanity, not individual persons. Absolute reason's supposed transcendence of humanity is, in fact, its integration into the totality of humankind. It is a kind of historical anthropology. The notion of the atomic individual was promoted by later liberalism and does not accord with Kant's own thought. While in some ways Kant inherited and developed on Locke and Rousseau, his thought differs significantly from theirs. Similarly, my inheritance of Kant diverges greatly from that of various forms of liberalism. I find my way back to Kant through the theories of

184 | The Humanist Ethics of Li Zehou

Hegel and Marx. Kant replaces God with pure reason, Hegel takes God to be the dialectical movement of human spirit (*Geist*), and Marx turns this into the history of material production.

Q: Sandel places Kant in line with the European and American tradition of liberalism represented by John Stuart Mill. Many others, including yourself, have even referred to him as the pinnacle of modern liberalism.

Li: That's true. However, throughout my book on Kant, *Critique of Critical Philosophy*, I discuss Kant as connected to and in line with Hegel and Marx. There I make clear that I see Kant as a crucial pivot from the individualism of thinkers like Locke and Rousseau to the collectivist outlooks of Hegel and Marx. Kant elevates notions of the *a priori* and pure reason rather than the atomic individual or social contract theory, and aims to replace theological notions of God with the former, not the latter. The "human" in Kant's question "what is the human" should be understood in terms of the historical movement from the collective to the individual. It is not a suppositional, isolated, unchanging, absolute atomic individual. This is why I think Rawls's use of the "veil of ignorance" is a one-sided take on Kant. In the real world there is no such thing as a completely independent, pure self stripped of all aims and relationships. When I take the transformative and innovative approach of looking at Kant through Hegel and Marx, it does not negate Kant's own thought but rather provides a critical new way by which to understand Kant. In the appendix to the sixth edition of *Critique of Critical Philosophy*, I stated,

> At the beginning of modernization two hundred years ago, it was necessary to break free of the domination of the religion and theology of the Middle Ages in order to establish modern social morals. Kant offered an equally sacred notion of pure reason to replace God and the independent and autonomous free will to resist the pre-modern submission to authority. This paved the way for the individual freedom required of modernization. However, since Nietzsche famously touted that "God is dead," modernization has increasingly revealed its more negative aspects. Liberalism and individualism opened the door for postmodern nihilism. Despite the persistence of many scholars on trivial investigations of Kantian theories of the transcendental, the individual, and reason, an intellectual turn is all but unavoidable. John Rawls, in his *Lectures on the*

History of Moral Philosophy, describes Kant's Kingdom of Ends as a republic of permanent peace. Paul Guyer argues that the highest good for Kant is happiness for humanity, not just for the individual. Roger Sullivan argues that "because the moral law appears to us as sacred as if it were God's will, reverence for that law, Kant wrote, leads us to religion, which he defined as the performance of our duties as conscientiously as if they were divine commands."[62] The first edition of *Critique of Critical Philosophy* argues that in Kant's third *Critique*, God is simply a subjective human belief. God (like all "transcendental" or "*a priori*" notions) in fact revolves around humans, and the continuous extension of human existence is more fundamental. This all moves toward to the question "what is the human" and the anthropological outlook of "taking people as the root" (*yi ren wei ben* 以人為本) (taking the continuous extension of human existence as fundamental). This anthropological outlook is historical. Kant's understanding of history was that when viewed in terms of individual subjects it is a muddled disarray, but when viewed as a whole we find among the conduct of these free wills a long gradual process of development marked by patterns of regularity. This is the "hidden plan of nature." He tells us that the greatest problem nature forces humans to solve is that of establishing civil society of universal rule of law, which will allow for an everlasting peace of allied republics. Kant points out that sooner or later it will be each people's commercial spirit and monetary benefit, not individual morals, that will be the motivating force that brings about the end of war and realization of peace. All of this can be directly linked to today's actuality. Clearly, moving from the *a priori* toward experience, from the individual toward humankind, and from pure reason severed from experience and happiness toward the ontology of humankind, toward historical progress, toward world peace and the flourishing of the collective (and primarily flourishing in aspects of the material existence of humankind)—this constitutes a new "direction" alternative to traditional study of Kant. Over three decades ago in [the first edition of] *Critique of Critical Philosophy* I embarked on this new anthropological direction, emphasizing Marx's concept of "the humanization of nature" and proposing the

186 | The Humanist Ethics of Li Zehou

> use and manufacture of tools to explain how "the question of
> how knowledge is possible ought to be answered through the
> question of how humankind is possible."[63]

Maybe I'm getting off topic here, but when we talk about individual freedom and contractual principles, it is only by continuously addressing the
importance of this foundation in anthropology and economic life that we
can take into account the historical fact and extended processes of movement from the communal existence toward existing for the individual.
This connects back to our discussions of Xunzi, emotion and desire, and
the integration of emotion and reason.

Q: Can you talk about the case of "The Queen vs. Dudley and Stephens" (1884), which Sandel discusses at length?[64]

Li: Sandel placed this case as the opening chapter in organizing
Justice: A Reader.[65] Simply put, the idea that humans are ends would
consider it most moral for the four people in this case to all die together
of starvation rather than killing and eating someone. This would realize the psychological forms of self-sacrifice in establishing and following
what we could "universally legislate" in the exercise of "free will." Viewed
in terms of actual circumstance, the killing of one person so that the
other three survive, although far less commendable, is still forgivable and
understandable. We are generally unwilling to await death helplessly and
would want to live a few days longer in hope of rescue. Moreover, the
victim was close to death anyway. I suppose it would have been best to
wait for the victim to die naturally before consuming him. Then it would
not have been a criminal matter. If the courts did not decide that the
sailors in "The Queen vs. Dudley and Stephens" case were guilty and
should be executed then that might imply that it would be reasonable
to go on to kill everyone else on the boat. Eventually the Queen's Bench
Division pardoned the two men, reducing their sentence to six months
in jail. (The third sailor had served as state's witness.) The decision for
this reduced sentence did not rely on a rational utilitarian principle (such
as that the death of one is preferable to the deaths of four) but rather
was a product of consideration for the specific circumstances, of "human
sentiment," in which there must have been a large element of emotion. (I
haven't researched this case; this is my conjecture.) In my article "On the
Integration of Confucianism and Legalism" (*Shuo Ru-Fa hu yong* 說儒法
互用),[66] I point out that the Han dynasty scholar Dong Zhongshu 董仲
舒 (179–104 BCE) opposed instituting a law that punishes harming one's

Appendix | 187

father with a death penalty on the basis that consideration of emotional and situational aspects of particular human life is essential in such cases.[67] The crucial point here lies in how emotional factors enter into rational judgment, considerations, and decisions, as well as in how the traditional Confucian concept of "discernment" (*quan*) is able to perform a "regulative and properly constitutive" function, going beyond strict abstract rules or principles (*jing*) but not abandoning the moral "Way."

Q: Can "conformance with emotions" (*heqing* 合情) be rationally described or expressed?

Li: To borrow a phrase from Chairman Mao, there is no love or hate without cause or reason. Emotional aspects of human existence can certainly be described and examined through rational analysis. At the same time, through factual description and explanation, emotions can not only affect but also even convince people of things. That is to say, emotions have causes and reasons, and "conformance" to them also has a certain rationally understandable pattern. However, at times these patterns of emotionality pass beyond the original scope of established principles of law while nevertheless according with public sentiment and will. In China the need to take particular circumstances (including emotions) into consideration when dealing with situations is widely promoted, and people often do not see it necessary to adhere firmly to established principles for doing things. Confucius talked about ritual throughout his life, and yet while he repeatedly criticized Guan Zhong 管仲 for "not knowing ritual," Confucius nevertheless lauded his overall virtue (*ren* 仁) (*Analects* 3.22, 14.16–17). This is a classic illustration of how we might carry out "discernment" (not adhering blindly to the established rules of ritual) through "conformance with emotions." Here we find that reason is not simply a matter of knowing "ritual regulations" (as established social norms and laws), but is connected with patterns of emotional relation, as well.

3.9 CONCEPTIONS OF GOOD AND EVIL

Q: In addition to including capacities and emotions, you also see conceptions of good and evil as principal elements of human psychology. These conceptions are part of the changing (historically specific) ethics of human culture, so how can they have entered into the "absolute" aspects of internal moral human nature or psychology?

Li: We have already discussed these conceptions a good deal. It is precisely because they are part of the ethics of human culture, which is

188 | The Humanist Ethics of Li Zehou

external and changing, that the internal structures of human psychology, especially the distinctively human capacity, are not simply empty containers. Our free will, which arises through the solidification of reason, must possess concrete content in order to be able to produce concrete behavior. The capacity itself is potentially independent of these evolving conceptions of good and evil, but without these concepts it is equivalent to a quiver of arrows without a bow. The arrows have only potentiality in themselves. All willful action must contain concrete content, and ethics is the study of people's concrete actions.

Q: If conceptions of good and evil are subject to change how can we say that they are part of universal human nature (psychology)?

Li: This is why we must emphasize (and in fact have already discussed above) that while conceptions of good and evil change over time and differ among societies, they also advance within the continuous accumulation of social development and advancement of human life. We see this, for instance, where taking care of elders has replaced the idea of killing them and where funerary objects have replaced the burial of living humans to accompany the dead. After all, foot binding has ended, and romantic love has become more accepted. Additionally, with the gradual homogenization of material life and market economies, many conceptions of good and evil are also gradually becoming similar. This is occurring through the sedimentation of absolutes in various pairs of values ("goods" and "evils"), which results from continual improvements and enrichment in many areas of life, including food, clothing, housing, transportation, sexual liberation, health, and entertainment, as well as increase in fundamental spiritual enjoyment and happiness. For instance, most of the world now despises the Taliban's conceptions of what is good and evil concerning women. People's ethical views have an increasing amount in common. In this way, the conceptions of good and evil produced through the accumulation of human history move from human culture to human psychology to become a part of shared human nature (psychology), permeating into our distinctive human capacity and emotions.

Q: Is this description of changing and accumulating conceptions of good and evil opposed to both ethical absolutism and ethical relativism?

Li: I continue to support the idea that social advancement results in ethical and moral advancement. Relativism recognizes the variability of conceptions of good and evil based on society, but does not adequately take into account the importance of the accumulative nature of history. Primitive peoples hunted other humans, and, at the time, both the hunters and the hunted thought of this as just the way things were. This custom was reasonable and brought no emotional distress. At that time, it was just. What about today? The ruins of ancient Rome show areas where people battled and were often eaten by animals. At first the masses found great pleasure in watching the mauling of early Christians. Later, when Christianity became the state religion, the same stands were filled with cheering Christians who supposedly held a doctrine of love. Would this be possible today? During the early Qing dynasty whole families were killed as punishment for the crimes of a single member. Would this be tolerated today? Once, Chinese girls of their own accord asked for their feet to be bound. Does this still happen today? Both institutions of social ethics and individual moral psychology have changed. Many traditional concepts and emotions have been abandoned. Both our understanding of the laws of nature and our inner consciences have shifted.

Social advancement leads to the transformation of concepts, and this transformation of concepts in turn results in changing emotions. The ethics and morals of all humankind are advancing. In the late 1970s and early '80s, why were jeans and long hair such controversial issues in China? Wasn't it that these involved not only ideas (bourgeois liberalization, the transgression of customs and social mores) but also emotions (favor or disgust, fondness or contempt)? Common conceptions of good and evil, like the emotions of like and dislike, generally accumulate within conflict. Reasonable concepts and positive emotions can only be affirmed, reinforced, broadened, and deepened in being carried forward and engaged in conflict. In this way people build up absolutes within opposition, which results in the growth of human nature, or human psychology. So why, as Sandel asks, should events for the revival of Nazism be forbidden but not events opposing racial segregation? Sandel uses this question to express his opposition to liberalism's "neutrality," which has difficulty dealing with such issues.

The basis for this problem with neutrality arises from the increasingly universal and commonly accepted conceptions of good and evil formed through the historical accumulation of humankind. That is, shared ideas continue to arise from the empirical lessons accumulated through the continuous extension of human existence. Friedrich Engels (1820–1895) said that the liberation of women is a measure of the liberation of humanity. The way that cultures and religions in and beyond China have treated women is a most clear-cut illustration that the abuse, suppression, and unfairness that women face is still common but will, sooner or later,

190 | The Humanist Ethics of Li Zehou

change. There is no ethical relativism here. Rather, this is precisely the extension of the tendency of moral human psychology toward good and away from evil.

This also accords with the continuous extension of the existence of the integrated totality of the material life of humankind. It even exhibits the cultivation and development of individual emotional psychology as well as the advancement and improvement of shared emotionality—the two extremes of my model of "four arrows." The movement back and forth between emotions within the individual and shared emotional circumstance forms a positive cycle of interaction that can be seen as a dialectic between human nature and human culture. This is historical progress. Clearly, many liberal principles arise not from the theoretical suppositions of Kant and Rawls, but rather from social life and the experience of humankind. Kant and others abstract this as the universal certainty of *a priori* reason, innate human rights, and the atomic individual. Even though such a standpoint is untenable, these ideas hugely elevate the position of humans and encourage people to work hard to realize certain ideals, which has positive effects on history and actual life.

3.10 WHAT CAI YUANPEI TELLS US

Q: It seems as though concepts of good and evil, human emotions, and human capacities (free will) make up three major elements of your "moral psychology," which refers to the internal psychological structures of the individual.

Li: I'd like to borrow on the *History of Chinese Ethics* (*Zhongguo lunlixue shi* 中國倫理學史) by Cai Yuanpei 蔡元培 (1868–1940). He argues that in order for people to achieve moral virtue they must first have wisdom, which implies the ability to differentiate between good and bad. Furthermore, they must like what is good and dislike what is bad in order to implement their understanding, which means that emotions are also important to actual practice. Even with these emotions, however, people may encounter obstacles and find themselves hesitating. Thus, will is essential as well. Cai's identification here of wisdom, emotions, and will as central to moral virtue (*de* 德) corresponds to the promotion of wisdom, humaneness, and courage as the three major virtues (*san dade* 三達德) of classical Confucianism. "Courage" as a virtue here refers not necessarily to physical acts of boldness, but rather to the courage to be firm and persistent through one's free will. It is the courage of Mencius's description of going against thousands when one knows one is right (*Mencius* 2A2). Likewise, it is also the power to act under the rule of rational principals, as with Kant's "categorical imperative."

Q: At the beginning of the interview, you said that the distinctively human capacities can be separated into three groups: knowledge (the internal construction of reason), the will (the solidification of reason), and aesthetics (the melting of reason). Here you are talking about the moral action of free will, which includes the three virtues of wisdom, humaneness, and courage. If wisdom can be related to knowledge, and courage to free will and human capacity, then does humaneness represent the aesthetic melting of reason?

Li: No. Humaneness here is empathy and the emotions of human psychology. It is important that I clarify that when Confucius tells us "overcoming oneself and returning to ritual is humaneness," he is talking about humaneness not as one of the three major virtues but rather as the culmination of all three together. Here we find the free will of "overcoming oneself" to be the highest level of Confucius's many descriptions of humaneness in the *Analects*. Confucius's alternative description of humaneness as "loving others" is more in line with the conception of humaneness as one of (and not the culmination of) the three major virtues. As those familiar with the *Analects* know, we can understand these different levels on which Confucius discusses humaneness as corresponding to the various levels of cultivation of the disciples he is addressing.

3.11 SUPREME GOODNESS

Q: If you think that conceptions of good and evil change due to the times and society, then why do you talk about a "supreme goodness" (*zhi shan* 至善)? And what is the significance of your description of the continuous extension of human existence and practical activity of the whole of humankind as this supreme goodness?

Li: This gives "goodness" as well as ethics and morals an objective and real ultimate grounding. I believe that conceptions of good and evil ultimately cannot be separated from the living existence and concrete life of humankind. This is in line with the Chinese tradition, as when the *Book of Changes* states, "The reciprocal process of *yin* and *yang* is called the way (*dao* 道); that which allows the way to continue to operate is human goodness."[68] I therefore disagree with ethical theories that ascribe "supreme goodness" to deities, *a priori* reason, or natural teleology. I'm

192 | The Humanist Ethics of Li Zehou

also opposed to explanations of "goodness" as individual intuition or the ineffable. This is a philosophical issue of anthropological historical ontology. It is precisely what the Chinese tradition promotes in telling us "the Way begins in emotionality" and "rituals are generated from emotionality." This strongly affirms the material existential activity of the continuous extension of the existence of the natural world and humankind on an emotional level. This is the "emotional cosmology" of the Chinese tradition that I discussed earlier in *On Traditional Chinese Intellectual History*.

It is important to note that there is indeed a question about the relationship between the concept of "goodness" and the divine here. People often see moral goodness as a sort of spirit, soul, or idea associated with the divine that transcends and has priority to actual social life. Such views see divine support as necessary to giving morals the power of absoluteness for people, and do not accept the idea that moral goodness lies in and comes from life itself. When Sandel talks about the "common good" he reveals flickers of religious morals and the shadow of Christianity. His advocacy of "republican virtue" has a Christian background, as does his promotion of freedom rooted in civic virtue in place of liberalism's focus on volitional freedom.[69] The absence of these religious elements would seem to leave a lack of absoluteness. We find the shadow of the divine at the root of many academic theories in the West, which generally believe that only divine transcendence of humankind has true certainty and absoluteness. Even Kant's "pure reason" also transcends humankind. Because all norms, conventions, and laws of the human world are changing and relative, they therefore cannot be trusted. These academic theories ignore the importance of the certainty and absoluteness sedimented by humankind through millennia of experience, history, and education. Viewed in terms of anthropological historical ontology, there is absoluteness in the notion of "supreme goodness" as the preservation of human existence. As it serves as original fundamental value (or ontological value, *benti jiazhi* 本體價值), it does not require connection to divine intention, the will of Heaven, or God. This is basically my "metaphysics." I fill the blank space left by "the death of God" with "the continuous extension of human existence."

Q: Doesn't taking the continuous extension of human existence as "supreme goodness" repress the value of the individual?

Li: This question is very important. In the '90s I pointed out that in the past individuals existed for the community, and in many ways today we still see ways in which individuals exist for the community, such as in war. However, in everyday life this has already changed and ought to continue to change. Especially in terms of ethics, we cannot talk about society without considering the individual, and thus liberalism has made important contributions to this area of human history. So when I discuss this concept of "supreme goodness," I stress that we should be very careful to guard against the suppression, smothering, or harming of the individual in the name of nations, ethnic groups, religions, social classes, or ideologies, including "humankind." Here we see clearly how liberalism is much more advanced than utilitarianism.

Q: Sandel talks repeatedly about gay marriage. Given what you have just said, are we then unable to oppose gay marriage on the grounds of even "the continuous extension of human existence" as the "supreme good"?

Li: The opposition to homosexuality and gay marriage in America is based in religious doctrine (divine command). Gay love has inborn physiological causes, and homosexuals after all do not make up a portion of the population large enough that this practice would harm the overall continuous extension of human existence. So there are no grounds to oppose it.

Q: Your position here is utilitarian and not liberalism's prioritization of the protection of individual rights over consideration of the "overall" situation.

Li: That's incorrect. My position is both. The "overall" situation sometimes also requires consideration. That is why I say that in certain particular situations utilitarianism and the idea of "unified" desires are more appropriate than advocacy of liberalism. However, only in those particular situations.

Q: Sandel has said that according to liberalism one should be free to decide for oneself matters regarding one's own body. Thus, gay marriage, communal marriage, not marrying, and polygamy should all be allowed.

Li: I think this is still a type of abstract thinking. The forms of marriage vary in accordance with society, the times, culture, and tradition. Communal marriage (ancient societies), monogamy (Christianity), multiple wives (Islam), concubinage (traditional China), and multiple husbands (certain ethnic minorities, such as the Mosuo in southwestern China) all have roots in their economic and religious cultural traditions. What is right or wrong, proper or improper cannot be universally determined by the abstract principle that people should decide for themselves.

Q: What about the future? It has become common now for couples to live together without getting married.

194 | The Humanist Ethics of Li Zehou

Li: I don't know. It seems very likely that many different forms of marriage will exist side by side in the future. Many thinkers, from Plato (427–347 BCE) and Engels to Kang Youwei 康有為 (1858–1927) and Mao Zedong, have put forth thought opposed to traditional family structures, including theories about bringing up children publicly and getting rid of the nuclear family, but I don't agree with these ideas. Even if the future brings more open, complex, and various manifestations of love, our emotional connections to our family, especially that of motherly love, are strongly backed by animal instincts. There are women today who do not want children, but not very many. Therefore, it may be neither possible nor necessary to get rid of the family unit, which seems to be the best method of raising children. Relationships between parents and children are not merely rational but also emotional. To first save one's own drowning child is not a rational responsibility, as Sandel examines it, but rather arises from emotion. Sandel examines the complex issues of surrogate pregnancy at some length, but he never highlights emotions in that discussion. Yet emotions play a tremendously important role among family members.

Q: What do you think about genetic engineering? Sandel's book *A Case against Perfection: Ethics in the Age of Genetic Engineering*[70] specifically addresses this topic.

Li: Many people oppose genetic engineering. Often they believe that embryonic cells are human life, and that we therefore should not violate "nature" or God by artificially copying them. Like opposition to fetal abortion, this position arises from religious morals. Such religious morals are not native to China, and so China has no such anti-abortion movement. However, in actuality these ideas hinder important developments of biotechnology. Today's world is, in fact, the product of the humanization of nature. Grains, fruits, and animals have all become products of human cultivation, and yet this doesn't violate "nature." Zhuangzi long ago opposed riding horses and driving cattle, claiming that such acts infringe upon nature. Yet, without these, how could we have human civilization? Without today's advanced technology, how would we have modern lifestyles and long life expectancies? This is why historical ontology emphasizes and gives ontological priority to manufacturing, from the first making of tools to today's high-tech production.

Contemporary technology will also bring about harm and even disasters, but humans will ultimately overcome these, as has already been evidenced by history. London's transformation from its smoggy past and the cleanup of the Thames are good examples of this. The air pollution in China today will see a similar future. We should take this same perspective toward genetic engineering, as well. "Techno-social substance" has always been the foundation of any society, and it will remain the core of the "continuous extension of human existence." It is true that today's high-tech developments could erase all of humanity, and therefore continually reminding ourselves of this and warning against it indeed have great value. However, the value of warning against the dangers of technology does not make technology itself bad. Sandel holds similar views on this point and ultimately concludes that genetic research benefits medical care.

Q: Sandel and Kant believe free will (what you call the "solidification of reason") is unable to be explained and verified through neurocognitive science (the brain science you often refer to).

Li: This is a big question, and one that philosophy has struggled with for a long time. At stake here is the issue of body-mind dualism. As a materialist, I believe in body-mind monism, as I have explained previously in discussing epistemology and "replacing religion with aesthetic education" (*meiyu dai zongjiao* 美育代宗教). However, in Kant's time, people believed that the world of reason (free will) could be independent and separate from the sensory world, and thus it is not at all strange that they would think we cannot explain reason with the same science that explains the phenomenological world. However, since today we see free will as a psychological state, it is therefore related to the neurons through which this psychological state emerges. And due to this relationship to neurology, brain science will be able to provide certain explanations of free will in the future, even revealing the neurological activity that makes humans distinct from other species of animals through laboratory studies and experiments. This I expect will affirm the existence of complex neurological channels and structures formed through historical sedimentation and individual education.

Such conclusions of brain science wouldn't at all detract from the "freedom" of free will. Free will has its own fundamental causal laws of neurological physiology, and can therefore be investigated by science. Free will is no different from noumena of the phenomenological world. It is not mystical and granted by heaven nor *a priori* and unknowable. I reinterpret the Chinese tradition's lack of a personal God as "the mysticality of reason" (*lixing de shenmi* 理性的神秘), which is also the notion that

196 | The Humanist Ethics of Li Zehou

the thing-in-itself cannot be known.[71] Yet I certainly do not see free will as an unknowable thing-in-itself. When I discuss the thing-in-itself, I am referring to why the universe in its entirety exists.

3.12 The *Three Character Classic* and Civic Education

Q: Of course, this also brings up questions about what type of ethical norms (traditional religious morals or modern social morals) should be adopted in education today.

Li: Modern social morals should remain paramount. Again I'd like to quote from my work *How Can Chinese Philosophy Go on Stage?*:

> Q: Is civic education more important than the *Three Character Classic (Sanzi Jing* 三字經)?[72]
>
> Li: Yes, just as it is more important than reading the Koran or Bible. Civic education indoctrinates one with the behavioral norms and ethical order that must be adhered to in modern society along with the reasons behind these. They cultivate children from early youth to recognize the importance of reason, adherence to public order, protection of public property, clarification of the boundaries of rights, and distinguishing public from private, while also giving them such concepts as freedom, equality, autonomy, human rights. After attaining these, children then read the *Three Character Classic* and other traditional classics, which teach filial piety toward one's parents, respect for one's teachers, generational order, industry, studiousness, respect for the elderly, goodwill toward the young, understanding of history, the importance of experience, and so on. This allows for an integration of the content of civic education with more traditional teachings and facilitates harmony between emotions and reason. While there are unavoidable differences and even conflicts between the two, some of these can be managed by creating new interpretations. For example, the emphasis on the relationship between kings and ministers in many classical Chinese texts can be construed in modern times as discussing the decision-making role of higher-ups in relation to the role of those below in carrying out these plans, wherein we can see each side as maintaining independence, equality, and freedom of character and identity. A boss can

fire someone, but an employee can also quit. This is based in modern social morals while also according with classical Confucian ideas about reciprocal duty or responsibility among kings and ministers. It rejects later ideas that arose under autocratic governance demanding unconditional subservience and adherence to one's ruler, especially the emperor. However, there are also irreconcilable differences between the classical texts and civic education, and in these cases right and wrong should be determined clearly in accordance with suitability to modern social life.

Accordance with, promotion of, and devotion to "public virtue" (modern social morals) are greatly needed among Chinese people today. On this foundation, individuals can still freely choose the beliefs of their "private virtue" (religious morals) and find meaning and values for their lives in the teachings of Buddhism, Christianity, Islam, Confucianism, and even Communism (as a political religion).

Q: Civic education seems to focus only on rational principles. Does it not include aspects of emotion and faith?

Li: Yes, it does. When you are in line and someone cuts in, don't you naturally feel upset about it? When you are in a rush and have to cut in line, don't you feel sorry about it? "Public virtue" (modern social morals) also demands support of the ancillary force of emotions. The most upsetting aspect of Chinese society today is the way that privilege disrupts, destroys, and transcends procedural justice. People's special identities and positions allow them to not wait in line, to plow through red lights, to get government positions, and to make a lot of money. The particular republican civic virtues Sandel discusses in *Democracy's Discontent*—fidelity, economic independence, honesty, industry, moderation, discipline, piety, self-control, respect for authority and tradition, resolve, courage, love of country, enthusiasm for the common good—are largely matters of public virtue and modern social morals. Like the virtues of ancient Greece, these differ from those of Chinese tradition's emphasis on humane love.

3.13 VALUE NEUTRALITY

Q: I want to ask again about liberalism's advocacy of justice in terms of value neutrality, individual rights, social contracts, freedom and equality, and so on. Are these also moral principles? Sandel sees Rawls's requirement that these values be decoupled from religion, tradition, and

198 | The Humanist Ethics of Li Zehou

metaphysics as a type of amoral politics. Sandel emphasizes that Rawls's "overlapping consensus" and value neutrality cannot serve as aims of human life. He stresses that there should be higher values and moral spirit guiding government and sees the infringement of the market on morals as ultimately rooted in value neutrality. This is a major theme of Sandel's works. And yet, you strongly support Rawls's decoupling of the right from the good, identifying it with your own advocacy of "modern social morals." These morals do not require connection to any religion, doctrine, tradition, ideology, or metaphysics. They are grounded in contemporary economic life, as you describe above.

Li: That is why I disagree with Sandel's criticism. I think that Sandel doesn't attach enough importance to the history of developed countries and the reality that developing countries must first break free of their medieval institutions. Sandel says that America's founding fathers were opposed to manufacture and industry, instead promoting agriculture and republican institutions motivated moral reasons. But the actuality of it is that two hundred years later America became the largest industrial manufacturer in the world. This economic development was not a product of the moral consciousness of America's founding fathers. Sandel also suggests that in the debate over abolition, arguments in favor of slavery were beaten out by moral concerns. In reality, economic forces were the fundamental cause of the ultimate victory of abolitionist theories favoring a system of employment over slavery.

This is representative of Sandel's arguments in general. Sandel and the broader communitarian opposition to liberalism on the surface seem similar to Hegel's rejection of Kant, using actual communities to reject abstract conceptions of the independent and isolated self or individual. Unfortunately, however, Sandel and other communitarians lack Hegel's historical sense of concrete universals. They fail to recognize the important shift from Hegel to Marx and don't see that liberalism is historically rooted in modern economic life. Therefore, the liberal individual freedom and value neutrality they oppose are in fact pressing necessities for many nations in breaking free from the economic and political institutions of their traditional societies (such as primitive tribalism, slavery, and serfdom, as well as religious and cultural autocracy and privilege). Value neutrality, prioritization of rights, and individual freedom are the "common good" or "virtue ethics" strongly needed for social development by certain countries and regions in moving beyond their medieval institutions. What is needed now is to affirm and reinforce such ethics, as at present we lack even formalistic rule of law, equality, human rights, and freedom of expression in China.

The struggle towards these ideas itself is a type of virtue and moral good. Without rule of law, privilege runs rampant, the people are trampled upon, and the individual is crushed. After 1949 with the establishment of the People's Republic of China, many powerful leaders said, "Laws will tie our hands and feet." They rejected rule of law and emphasized "rule by people," but in fact this became rule by particular individuals. The injustices committed by the "people's courts" during the Cultural Revolution involved a conflation of the roles of the police, prosecutors, and the court. There was no legal procedure. That is why I have been advocating rule of law, and have hardly mentioned democracy, for over two decades.

In 1995 I put forward my theory of "the four orders" (*si shunxu* 四順序) in which I placed democratic government last (and was harshly criticized for it). China can have neither democracy along the lines of the classical Greek model Sandel promotes, in which the entire citizenry actively participates, nor modern liberal democracy of equal individual suffrage, competition among multiple political parties, and direct presidential elections. Either of these could easily devolve into various forms of autocratic tyranny. Every citizen has the right to participate in government, but the method, procedure, and level of such participation cannot be reduplicated according to some fixed model. Only in consideration of present actual circumstances can things be gradually improved, with Chinese society treading its own unique path through the accumulation of experience.

In sum, I see principles of justice such as individual rights and value neutrality as the moral content of modern rule of law. These principles of justice and their ability to function effectively in actual life do not in fact come from concepts or theories. They do not come from John Stuart Mill, Immanuel Kant, and John Rawls, nor from Karl Marx, but rather from the economic life of modern people. These principles are also the moral "good" that positively impacts and supports modern life. In this context, "the right" is also "the good," and "freedom" does not conflict with "virtue." Freedom itself is virtuous (in terms of public virtue) and is now a component of the common good and the good life. These have become the moral principles that ought to guide not only political and economic institutions but also personal conduct.

Although people in developed countries may sometimes view these as obvious and self-evident rules of government or standards of behavior, and not necessarily attach moral significance to them, for the peoples of other countries and regions these are often objects of great struggle and even objects of "ultimate concern," moral identity, and a sense of spiritual

200 | The Humanist Ethics of Li Zehou

belonging. This is also true of the value neutrality that Sandel criticizes so harshly. These moral principles are often arrived at only with great hardship and through tremendous tragedies caused by traditional values' domination of people's lives. Principles of justice such as individual rights and value neutrality are important means of breaking beyond traditional institutions that integrate politics and religion. Indeed, people can demand value neutrality independent of any belief in religion. Today the pursuit of neutrality seems commonplace, but it was first attained with immense hardship—not unlike today's Islamic feminists, whose struggle is as great as that of those who sacrifice themselves for their religion.

Sandel claims that value neutrality will result in the spread of fundamentalism. However, isn't the lack of value neutrality that occurs in conflating religious and social morals even more closely related to the spread of fundamentalism? The Taliban's values are certainly not neutral. They even find it necessary to destroy ancient Buddhist carvings. Thus, today it is quite reasonable to take the right as the good (modern social morals), disconnected from traditional religious beliefs, culture, and customs. It is precisely due to suppression and restriction by these earlier beliefs, customs, and morals that the struggle for freedom, equality, human rights, and democracy has been carried forward across generations. Through the global unification of economic life this continues to become increasingly pronounced. From Sandel's questions and illustrative examples we see that the same ideas of "value neutrality" and "procedural justice" that America has developed to unhealthy excess also remain ideals and goals that many places have yet to achieve.

The cause of the difference here is that in some cultures social life has already been modernized whereas in others it has yet to be modernized. The latter severely and broadly lack procedural concepts and neutral standpoints. The customs, concepts, institutions, and theories of their various traditions and revolutions continuously infringe on, restrict, and interfere with individual freedoms and rights—from courts to schools, society to individuals, and practice to thought. Because of this, while recognizing the various harms and excesses that liberalism has brought in developed countries and thus agreeing with Sandel's emphasis on the market's damaging effects on morals, I am unable to support the idea of the good having priority to the right or various other positions that advocate prioritizing the Bible, Koran, or *Three Character Classic* over civic education.

Chinese tradition emphasizes "transforming the people through virtue (education)" (*yi de hua min* 以德化民). During the Han dynasty many officials sought to increase people's virtue through proper social customs, which shows the conflation of religious and social morals at that time. Today on the other hand we must first theoretically distinguish the two types of morals. In this way we can then discuss how religious morals may be "regulative and properly constitutive" for modern social morals, which allows us to emphasize rule of law as the foundation for "transforming the people through virtue." We cannot simply "rule by virtue" (*yi de zhi guo* 以德治國).

Q: What do you really think of communitarians like Sandel?

Li: First, as I stated over a decade ago, I do not agree with communitarianism or Sandel. Overall, even in America communitarianism could not possibly replace liberalism; it can only serve as a complement or corrective to it, views that help mitigate certain problems. The modern social morals I discuss are overall very close to liberalism. In addition to freedom, equality, independence, human rights, and democracy, they also include tolerance, compromise, cooperation, mutual respect, equality of opportunity, and value neutrality. These are all founded on the public reason of modern society. It is my view that we should recognize these as morals but distinguish them from religious morals, which are suffused with particular emotions and beliefs and involve the pursuit of "the good." The critiques of liberalism found in Sandel and other communitarians, in contrast, do not see these principles as a substantive morality.

Second, I also value religious morals as "regulative and properly constitutive" for modern social morals. I advocate the use of the "emotio-rational structure" drawn from traditional Chinese thought to correct liberal public reason, especially its overemphasis on formal and procedural justice, the atomic individual, and absolute free choice. My "theory of two morals" allows for the infusion of "substantive justice" in certain situations. This infusion is also "regulative and proper constitutive," and can be approached in a variety of ways: through history, lived and felt circumstance, concrete relations, the emotio-rational structure, proper measure (*du*), discernment (*quan*), and so forth.

So to summarize, I advocate guiding society through virtue rather than utility, free choice, or the market. On this point Sandel and I align. However, as I stated at the outset, China and America differ in their levels of social development as well as their cultural traditions. They therefore

202 | The Humanist Ethics of Li Zehou

also differ in how they should view markets and morals, as well as in their versions of virtue ethics, with Aristotle and Christianity on the one side and traditional Chinese virtue ethics on the other. Herein there is divergence especially on questions of acceptance or rejection of the "two types of morals."

Q: Sandel talks about abortion a lot. What do you think of this?

Li: Many religions oppose abortion. Even Confucianism has the notion that the greatest violation of filial piety is not having progeny and thus failing to carry forward one's (parents') bloodline. This often supported the practice of taking multiple wives or concubines. However, the manner in which modern social morals take the individual as moral subject grants women basic rights of procreation and abortion, so that we ought to denounce religious doctrines that see a fetus as equivalent to an infant. This is not a noncommittal, "value neutral" position. It is not mere formal justice, but rather a position of "substantive" moral commitment.

Q: Isn't there a contradiction between being pro-choice and your position advocating the "continuous extension of human existence"? This can be seen, for example, in the demand for procreation you just mentioned is supported by Confucian thought. Many religious doctrines seem to align with this aspect of your thought better than "modern social morals" do.

Li: The "continuous extension of human existence" is historical. It is not a fixed doctrine antecedent to the empirical. Ancient people had relatively short lives, and the death rate of children was extremely high, so there were practical reasons for and contextual appropriateness in opposing abortion. Today the situation is entirely different, and acts of abortion are no longer relevant to the "continuous extension of human existence."

Q: Do people have the right to commit suicide?

Li: The notion of the atomic individual and many forms of liberalism see people as having the right to do as they like with their own bodies, which gives them the right to commit suicide. As Sandel points out, according to Kant's proposal that humans are ends, people cannot treat their bodies as mere objects, and therefore they have no right to commit suicide. But neither Sandel nor Kant fully addresses why we should see people as ends in themselves. They analyze this simply as an *a priori* and self-evident universal truth.

From the perspective of Confucian relationism, humans are relational beings. That people are raised and cared for by their families and communities leaves them with duties and responsibilities to these relations and even their "species" (humankind). People do not belong to themselves alone. The very first passage of the *Classic of Filial Piety* (*Xiao jing* 孝經) tells us that since our bodies are received from our parents, we are not allowed to harm them. If even harming one's body is denounced, how could suicide possibly be allowed? I often say that before committing suicide young people should ask themselves, "Is this the right or fair way to treat my parents, who put such effort into bringing me up?"

But this is not to say that suicide is never allowable under any circumstances. I have mentioned assisted suicide (especially when someone is in great pain), euthanasia, and other historical examples where prolonging life may not be the best option. My position here merely involves relationism and "emotion as substance" being "regulative and properly constitutive" for individualism's claim that one has the right to governance of one's own body. They are not determinative. They are neither the absolute abstract rules of religious doctrine (thou shalt not kill thyself) nor those of liberalism (that one ought to be allowed to commit suicide). Sandel also acknowledges that here empathy may overpower people's duty to preserve life.[73] Duties have various types and levels, such as those of citizenship and those of religious faith, those toward friends and family, and those toward humankind. These differ greatly from one another and cannot be carried out or managed in uniform ways.

Q: So then in what ways are people (individuals) ends in themselves?

Li: As the whole of humankind is composed of individual people, the full development of the individual should be the totality's ultimate aim, toward which it aspires and for which it struggles in its historical progress.

3.14 THE PRIORITY OF THE RIGHT OVER THE GOOD

Q: Unlike the targets of much of Sandel's criticism, you do not seem to see "the priority of the right over the good" in terms of the right being separable and independent of the good. Can you clarify your response regarding this?

Li: First, my historical ontology understands "the priority of the right over the good" as being a product of history. It does not come from a transcendental subjective self (as Kant would have it). This priority is a universal rule demanded of, affirmed by, and carried out in modern

204 | The Humanist Ethics of Li Zehou

social life, and was arrived at through the continuous extension of human existence. The modern production of commercial goods by big industry, the free sale of labor, fair trade, and the market economy form the basis for this emphasis on free choice and individual rights.

Second, even though what is "right" today is equivalent to what is "good," I still stress that these two concepts need to be distinguished from one another. This is because in many countries and regions what is "right" differs importantly from conceptions of "the good" in existing religion, tradition, culture, and ideologies. In fact, the two are often quite at odds with each other. What is "right" is the public reason that ought to be accorded with in modern social life. Therefore, the best attitude to take toward both rational and irrational emotional belief in religious and ideological conceptions of goodness is often to maintain a silent distance. This is a reason for value neutrality. Sandel also says that rights do not necessarily have to rely on any one group's traditional or present conception of "good."

Third, in actual life, such emphasis on individual rights is not easily distinguished from traditional religious, cultural, or ideological conceptions of the good. In reality, it is very hard to fully realize value neutrality. As Sandel tells us, when people advocate women's rights (such as the right to abortion) they adopt a religious stance (such as opposition to Catholicism) even if their views themselves are unconnected to religious faith. The libertarians who stress absolute individual rights and free choice also oppose the free sale of children and votes. The emotions of various rational and irrational religious and ideological beliefs still either directly or indirectly permeate, influence, and function through public reason, formal justice, procedural justice, and value neutrality. This incites a variety of disputes, debates, and even severe conflicts, as seen with issues of abortion, gay marriage, and euthanasia in America. Rawls's theory of "overlapping consensus" on the right, decoupled from diverse conceptions of the good, is an important "ideal" theory that works to distance individual rights from the severe religious disputes and conflicts over conceptions of the good. Following global economic integration, the public reason of individual liberty and equal human rights will continue to spread, and in so doing will continue to seek "overlapping consensus" as a principle of modern political life that various religions, cultures, and traditions can all accept. This will promote value neutrality and is exceptionally important. As for the many examples of problems arising from value neutrality that Sandel gives, these can be dealt with through making judgments and decisions according to what is rationally and emotionally appropriate according to particular situations.

Fourth, I published "A Record of Philosophical Inquiry" (*Zhexue tanxun lu* 哲學探尋錄) in 1994, within a year of Rawls publishing *Political Liberalism*.[74] In that work I put forth the distinction of religious morals ("goodness," emotions, beliefs) from modern social morals (human rights, public reason) and thereafter emphasized the need to first differentiate the two from one another so that the former can provide the regulative and properly constitutive principle for the latter in the form of permeation, influence, and function, but not determination. On this point I also write that many things that bring benefit also have negative effects, producing loss as well as gain, and that this cannot be avoided. The important thing here is "proper measure," which involves dealing with situations differently according to their particular circumstances.

Rawls's theory of "overlapping consensus" is a passive method that attempts to avoid the problem of conflicting religious beliefs, but my theory of regulation is one of proactive delimitation. Their point of divergence lies in that Rawls does not explicate what makes "overlapping consensus" possible, whereas I argue that it is possible because people have in common that they live within the modern economic order. These theories are, however, alike in seeing rights as having precedence over the good. Rawls requires that rights be decoupled from the good, which is similar to my emphasis on the priority of distinguishing religious from social morals. Like Rawls's position, my prioritization of this distinction attempted to avoid the so-called clash of tradition and modernization that was being hotly discussed at the time.

Both positions reserve judgment regarding whether traditional morals are "right" or "wrong." At the same time, I also believe that we cannot completely decouple rights from conceptions of the good, and I therefore emphasize the need for careful investigation and analysis of traditional morals to identify where they go wrong. This allows us to carry forward that which is valuable and leave behind that which is not, striving to make religious morals regulative and properly constitutive but not determinative, that is, not valued to the point of challenging or replacing rights. In this way we can avoid again subordinating modern individual rights to traditional conceptions of the good and the re-enslavement of the individual to the community. However, it is not easy to say what concrete measures we can take to control this. That is why I call this a matter of "political art."

206 | The Humanist Ethics of Li Zehou

We've already discussed what kinds of political rallies or activities should be allowed. Similarly, we might ask whether freedom of religious belief means that someone should be free to believe in malevolent and harmful doctrines. How do we differentiate between good or acceptable religious teachings and evil or harmful ones? In terms of welfare, what level of material assistance is appropriate, or should we oppose it altogether? Should military service be voluntary or compulsory? If we have freedom of the press, should this include pornography? In these and many other cases, we face the challenge of measuring and balancing benefit and harm as well as questions of how to coordinate or harmonize formal and substantial justice when they conflict. In such cases, even small errors of judgment can have severe consequences.

Figuring out the proper limits of speech or action can be quite challenging, and must be taken on piecemeal. This type of political art can only be experienced, created, and mastered within particular concrete situations. It is not something that can be solved directly with the *a priori* principles or theoretical presuppositions of a bookish academic. Moreover, it should be emphasized again that any "regulation and proper constitution" or permeation, influence, and functioning of substantive justice within formal justice must occur on the basis of first differentiating between religious and social morals (the good and the right). Today China needs first of all to establish "public morals"—freedom, equality, human rights, and democratic political life—in order to break free of various traditions and ideologies of the past. In terms of assuring "the good life" for people today, rule of law is better than rule by people, having procedures is better than not having them, and civic education is more valuable than the *Three Character Classic*.

The only problem lies in how to bring back human emotions so as to alleviate the emotional vapidity and coldness of human relationships brought by mechanistic public reason, formal justice, the market economy, fair trade, and the atomic individual. Relationism could still be useful, not as a set of traditional rules but from the perspective of "emotion as substance." It could be very beneficial in preventing an expanding division between rich and poor and the fixed separation of social classes. This is why in the beginning of this dialogue I raised the topic of the "emotio-rational structure." It is also why above, in discussing conflicts between public and private virtue or between adhering to contractual stipulations and being a good friend, I emphasize the importance of compromise and arbitration on a personal rather than a legal level—the possibility of give and take on both sides leading to win-win outcomes. Of course, in many situations legal recourse may still be necessary. We might consider, for example, the way individual marriages are now free and independent—not to be determined by traditional ideas or practices such as arranged marriage—and yet children generally may seek out their parents' thoughts on such matters. Here thriving emotional connections are in no way impaired by public virtue.

Q: Your proposal of the "regulative and properly constitutive" function of religious morals is very important. Could you talk about it a little bit more?

Li: First, I borrowed the language of being "regulative and properly constitutive" from Kant's epistemology, in which the regulative is opposed to the constitutive. I would like to emphasize that whether borrowing the terms is suitable or not is its own special topic; however, there is no space to discuss this here. Second, "properly" in this conception always means limited. Third, the relationship between these two, the regulative and the constitutive, is historically concrete. This principle is the core of my "theory of two morals." It is historical, ideal, and emotional.

By historical I mean, first, the circumstantial quality of history. This recognizes the particular nature of specific eras and societies, so that all ethics and morals are determined by concrete historical circumstance. Modern social morals are clearly not composed of *a priori* principles but rather are a product of history. Second, the progressive nature of history means that for humankind as a whole advancement in terms of material life is followed by advancement of ethics and morals. Third, history is accumulative. As discussed above, the sedimentation of certain common conceptions of good and evil as well as corresponding emotions occurs through the history and education of humankind. We therefore can gradually come to possess common ethical criteria and moral standards. These three main aspects of historicism, as circumstantial, progressive, and accumulative, on the one hand clearly admit a quality of relativity in ethics, while on the other hand they also oppose the elevation of this relativity to a sort of sacred or absolute truth. Indeed, it clearly rejects ethical relativism, and even more strongly dismisses situationism.

By ideal, I refer mainly to using paradigmatic cases to measure the future gain and loss, benefit and harm, of actions. I do not support the liberal conception of "the end of history,"[75] which takes capitalism as its ultimate aim. Rather, I believe we can aspire toward a distant social ideal without a specifically delineated path by which it must be arrived at. We

208 | The Humanist Ethics of Li Zehou

can see such a notion in the "Origin and Development of Ritual" ("Li yun" 禮運) chapter of the *Record of Ritual*. We see one as well as in Kang Youwei's *Book of Great Unity* (*Da tong shu* 大同書), which despite severe shortcomings shows no lack of imagination in setting forth an ideal that hardly hopes to be realized. These works draw out social ideals without drawing out the ideal society.

We have already discussed emotions a great deal and I won't repeat myself. "Relationism" in modern times is also emotional. From these qualities—the historical, ideal, and emotional—we can consider how religious morals may be regulative and properly constitutive for modern social morals. Of course, the concrete issues here are extremely complex, and there remains a vast and often unclear distance between "proper constitution" and "determination." This makes it even more important that we rely on the accumulation of actual experience in putting forth various reasons for moral demarcation as well as in gradually formulating these as rules. Here we must rely on empiricism rather than *a priori* theories. As "proper measure" can only be mastered within actual practice, it is characterized by particularity rather than the generality of abstract principles. We must move from the particular to the general, not vice versa.

Sandel tells us he cannot fully answer the question of what kind of political discourse can guide us toward "the good life."[76] In comparison with the several points Sandel draws as the ultimate conclusions of *Justice*, my "theory of two morals" and position that "harmony is higher than justice" may seem more abstract but in fact are more concrete as well as more general.

3.15 THE WAY OF THE "INNER SAGE AND EXTERNAL KING"

Q: Can you repeat again what you mean by the difference between being "regulative and properly constitutive" and being "determinative"?

Li: It means that we cannot fundamentally harm individual rights. In today's times, individual existence is the foundation of the existence of the totality. Individual rights cannot be infringed on in this aspect, as even Sandel, who opposes liberalism, admits. But this presents difficulty, and it involves quite a long historical process. To quote again from the appendix to the sixth edition of *Critique of Critical Philosophy*:

> Marx states, "The free development of each is the condition for
> the free development of all" (*Communist Manifesto*). But he also

states, "The relatively high-level development of character can only be attained through the historical process of sacrificing individuals. . . . The benefit of the race must always rely on the benefit of sacrificing individuals to broaden its own path" (*Theories of Surplus Value*). Kant tells us that history "grants the entire primeval nature of the human species its universal civil condition of full development" while also stating that achieving this goal involves "asocial sociality," "resistance," "conflict," "war," "vanity," "greed," and "desire for power," which of course involve sacrifice (of the individual self). This is a long historical process. On this point, Kant, Hegel, and Marx are similar. However, Hegel and Marx see this as an ironclad objective law (Hegel's so-called identification of history with logic), whereas Kant sees this as an inspirational teleological concept rather than one of scientific knowledge. In comparing them I find Kant more accurate.[77]

Q: Earlier we discussed your position that "harmony is higher than justice," and now you are also advocating "the priority of the right over the good." Isn't there some contradiction here?

Li: These ideas of "priority" and "being higher" do not necessarily contradict one another. The idea of "the priority of the right over the good" is the foundation of modern life. The notion that "harmony is higher than justice" provides the regulative and properly constitutive principle for this same modern life. The two at times diverge greatly and even find themselves in conflict. Coordinating and integrating the two requires great political art. It even more importantly necessitates a very arduous historical process. The liberalism that I endorse (in which the totality exists for the individual and individual rights have priority) is an aspect of my historicism. That is, it is a requirement or product of the historical development of a certain period. In this way liberalism is part of historicism, and history does not end with capitalist society and liberalism. This both emphasizes justice and takes the idea that "harmony is higher than justice" from China's "emotional cosmology" as regulative in order to move toward a more ideal future. This transcends liberalism.

Q: It looks like you still hold the views you expressed over a decade ago in *Historical Ontology*.

Li: That's true. My views generally change very little. In *Historical Ontology* I emphasize the difference between religious and social morals and argue for the former's "regulative and properly constitutive" function.

210 | The Humanist Ethics of Li Zehou

I express my agreement with Kant's and Rawls's theories of justice in terms of social morals. I stand behind the idea that individualism and contractual principles will necessarily rise from a foundation of modern commercial production, fair trade, and the free sale of labor. This is the modern version of "external kingliness." However, under the regulative function of China's "emotion as substance," as traditional religious morals that value heaven, earth, country (nation), parents (ancestors), and teachers (history), China can tread a path that does not follow the West and its supreme elevation of reason. In *Reading the Analects Today* I wrote,

> Through transformative creation, religious morals (the "inner sageliness") can serve as the individual's pursuit of meaning and higher realms of life. This can occur in religion, philosophy, poetry, and art. Through transformative creation, social morals ("external kingliness") can serve as China's form of modern politics. This emphasizes integrating interpersonal harmony, communal relationships, social ideals, the integration of emotions and reason, education and cultivation, and compromise into the modern political construction of a democratic system in order to set out on a future path of a certain degree of originality. . . . For Chinese people, valuing heaven, earth, country, parents, and teachers could serve as moral and extra-moral emotional identification with natural cosmology, homeland, parents and spouses, siblings and friends, and teachers and classmates as well as cultural tradition.[78]

This is also the path of "harmony being higher than justice." It is not that harmony will replace justice, but rather that harmony will "regulate" justice. This is also the "new Way of inner sageliness and outer kingliness" of "Western substance, Chinese application" (*Xi ti Zhong yong* 西體中用).

Q: Is this "new Way of inner sageliness and outer kingliness" related to the idea of constant cyclical interaction and a unified "Way" between the individual emotional psychology and shared emotional life discussed above in your model of "four arrows"? That is, is it related to the mutual interaction between rational cultivation of individual emotions and desires and the construction of harmonious relationship within the community?

Li: Yes, you could say that. The "new Way of inner sageliness and outer kingliness" is related to my emphasis on education and the cultivation of human psychology, and to my proposal that this cultivation develops the future of culture. It is also related to my emphasis on brain science. Chinese ethics traditionally focus strongly on personal cultivation. From Confucius, Mencius, and Xunzi in the classical period to the neo-Confucians of the Song and Ming dynasties, we see constant emphasis on self-cultivation. This was originally a requirement of rulers that arose from the ancient shamanistic tradition (the "magical" charisma or virtue of the shaman ruler evolved into the idea of the sage king). Later, it developed into the integrated religious, ethical, and political demands of "ritual education" (*lijiao* 禮教) on members of the upper governing classes of scholar-officials (*shidafu* 士大夫). However, the "inner sageliness" of the ruler never succeeded in directly translating or developing into "outer kingliness."

Here, the outlook of "emotion as substance" was restricted within the framework of a cosmology of *yinyang* and the five elements, as with Dong Zhongshu's view of humaneness as the heart-mind of "heaven" (or of the cosmos). This emotionalized the cosmos, drawing Confucianism into Legalism and melding ritual and law, and holding China's political and religious institutions together for two millennia. Today's need for a new conception of inner sageliness and outer kingliness is also the need for a renewed and reformed integration of Confucianism and legal institutions. This should involve the permeation of "emotion as substance" into the modern institutions of constitutional rule of law and liberal democracy. Externally, this focuses on building communal harmony and interpersonal goodwill on the basis of individual rights; internally, it stresses the cultivation of human emotions.

In the early '90s I wrote the short essay "The Century's New Dream" (Shiji xin meng 世紀新夢) in which I state that, while in the twentieth century people had dreamed of social utopia, perhaps in the next century people would strive toward a dream of cultivating human nature (psychology). I wrote, "The day that history ends, the unfolding of education begins." That is why I put forth the notion of the "emotio-rational structure" in *Reading the Analects Today*, first published around the same time, which I continue to emphasize here. These ideas seek to answer the question of how to establish healthy, well-rounded human psychology to increase social harmony and the cultivation of individual emotions. Cultivated desires are neither prone to indulgent excess nor requiring restriction. They value feelings of affection, self-cultivation, self-discipline, autonomy, empathy, and treating others well. Human relations thereby become more harmonious and cooperative, and both suffering and happiness are shared among members of society. Benefits here include improve-

212 | The Humanist Ethics of Li Zehou

ment of the circumstances, especially the emotional circumstances, of society as a whole. Only in this way can "the good life" and "the common good" be achieved.

This "new Way of inner sageliness and outer kingliness" is the path of Chinese virtue ethics. Virtue ethics involve questions of "what to do" and "how to be." The subtitle of Sandel's *Justice*—which directly asks, "What's the right thing to do?"—focuses on the former and can be seen as the principal question addressed by utilitarianism's notion of the greatest happiness for the greatest number, liberalism's advocacy of self-choice, Kant's "categorical imperative," and Rawls's "original position." These theories do not focus on the question of "what sort of person to be." The contemporary outpouring of support for Aristotle's and others' conceptions of virtue ethics in the West can be seen to arise from discontent with these theories as well as the market's present dominance over daily life and promotion of material desires. Thus, if Chinese tradition generates transformative creation (*zhuanhuanxing chuangzao* 轉化性創造) in a timely manner, it may be possible to bestow the idea of "the Way of inner sageliness and outer kingliness" with universal significance. Of course, this would still require actual exemplification of this, the possibility of which is all too distant from the present. As early Confucianism tells us, our burden is indeed heavy, the path long, and our prospects hazy.

3.16 CONFUCIUS PLUS KANT

Q: A review of the English translation of *The Chinese Aesthetic Tradition* (*Huaxia meixue* 華夏美學) reads, "Li's vision is inspiring, and if such a thing as 'world philosophy' is possible it will owe much to both Confucius and Kant."[79] When the editors of *China Reading Weekly* (*Zhonghua dushu bao* 中華讀書報) published a version of this review translated into Chinese, they added the title of "A Dialogue between Confucius and Kant." What do you think about this?

Li: In *The Chinese Aesthetic Tradition* I do not directly state this idea, but I do imply it. My "theory of two morals" and even today's discussion are very much about adding Kant and Confucius. My emphasis on the individual rights of modern social morals is connected to Kant, and my focus on the "emotio-rational structure" of religious morals comes from Confucius.

Q: Mou Zongsan 牟宗三 (1909–1995) also discussed Confucius and Kant. How do your views differ from his?

Li: Mou talks about Kant from a metaphysical perspective drawn from neo-Confucian theories of the heart-mind and human nature. He concentrates on ideas of "immanent transcendence" and "intellectual intuition," which are in fact mystical experiences. These notions are not well aligned with Kant. I have criticized Mou many times in this aspect, for instance in "On the Four Stages of Confucianism" (Shuo Ruxue si qi 說儒學四期),[80] and I don't want to repeat myself here. As I said above, I discuss Kant through the lens of Hegel's and Marx's ideas of historical process and material life. This differs significantly from many others who develop on Kant, including Rawls and Mou Zongsan.

Q: We have to finish soon. Can you summarize your views on liberalism and communitarianism once more?

Li: These "isms" are, in themselves, very complex. I would have a hard time fully addressing them even without the limitations we have here. I've talked a bit about communitarianism already. I quite like that Sandel addresses the severe problems of "market societies." Although the role of the market in China is not fully developed enough for this to be an issue, the lack of religiosity in China makes it more susceptible to the market's negative influence on morality. This makes it important for China to recognize that we must avoid moving toward a society in which the market is seen as a universally positive force and equated with the common good. In this regard, the issues that Sandel brings up have great value and should be taken into consideration. However, I am unable to accept the basic arguments put forth by Sandel and communitarianism in general, as they can easily lead us back to control and governance of the individual by tradition, customs, and ideologies, where "morals" serve as instruments of government's interests.

In contrast, liberalism such as that of Rawls's "difference principle," "overlapping consensus," and "the priority of the right to the good" is exactly what China needs today. But China should also be careful to avoid being overwhelmed by immensely rational economic and political mechanisms. This is the importance of the corrective value of traditional Chinese notions such as "the Way begins in emotionality" and relationism, which can be "regulative and properly constitutive" for these rational mechanisms.

Sandel engages with many real-life examples in exploring important questions such as whether politics is a means to an end or an end of itself, whether each person should participate in politics, whether we should advocate positive or negative liberty, and whether government is

214 | The Humanist Ethics of Li Zehou

a necessary evil or agent of good. However, he does not—and is unable to—give answers to these questions. It seems they cannot be subsumed under single principles but rather must still be considered in light of concrete circumstance. Overall, I agree with the characterization of my thought as pursuing a world philosophy that incorporates Kant's philosophy with Confucius's. In terms of their fundamental theories, I don't agree with either communitarianism or liberalism.

Q: At present the most popular movements are associated with the new left, communitarianism, and new conservativism, which includes people like Leo Strauss and Carl Schmitt. We can see these all as opposed to Kant. They seem to pursue some kind of divine law or tradition with which to reestablish government over the people and save the world. They therefore oppose the Enlightenment, reason, and the social contract. However, you tell us that Chinese tradition views humans rather than the divine, action rather than the word, happiness rather than sin, pragmatic reason rather than *a priori* reason, and emotionality rather than spirituality as most fundamental.

Therefore, through "the empirical for humankind becoming *a priori* for the individual, history constructing reason, and psychology becoming ontologically fundamental (or psychology becoming substance, *benti* 本體)" this tradition can not only be connected with Kant's thought but also incorporate aspects of modern social morals that value the individual subject, contractual principles, and public reason. Adding regulation by "emotion as substance" and relationism, along with replacing the supremacy of reason with the "emotio-rational structure," gives us the new, modern, and universalizable path of the "new Way of inner sageliness and outer kingliness."

Li: Yes. I have said before that Kant strove to move from the divine to the human, but nowadays it is popular to search for the divine through the human. Regardless of the strength of this trend and its influence within Chinese academia, I will stick with Mao's teaching to bravely stand against popular currents. Young scholars in China seem to have three common weaknesses: nationalism, populism, and mysticism. That these are often clothed in Western notions makes things even more difficult to correct.

Q: You discuss both the Chinese and Western traditions, and your work builds on the thought of John Locke (1632–1704) and Alexis de Tocqueville (1805–1859) in addition to, of course, Kant. Yet you are suspicious and even disapprove of radical thinkers. Today in China very few people criticize Nietzsche, and yet you have done so repeatedly.

Li: Here I would like to refer to a statement I made not long ago:

I think it's necessary to lay out the thought of a few theorists before getting to Nietzsche.

First is Rousseau. He talks about the general will, and his ideas gave rise to later notions of Jacobinism and autocratic democracy.

Second is Marx. He told us class struggle is the motivation for historical development, but that society must rely on cooperation, negotiation, and compromise between classes if it is to continue to exist. Marx and Engels both agreed that societies with slaves were much more inhumane than earlier more primitive ones, but that this was a necessary step in history. This is why I have consistently emphasized that historicism and ethicism are often at odds with one another. It is worthwhile to conduct deeper studies on this tension, examining under what concrete circumstances historicism or ethicism takes the upper hand, while at the same time considering "proper measure" in the relationship between the two. For example, with China's sudden growth in the 1980s many people were supportive of the new factories being built, despite the harm from the factories' pollution, because they needed the jobs the factories provided. Marx, however, is mistaken in taking class struggle as what drives historical development. Of course, I admit that class conflict is a problem even now, otherwise why would so many people have committed suicide at Foxconn?[81] However, in terms of overall theory, we should stress harmony and compromise between classes. Zhuangzi opposed all alienation resulting from civilization. He denounced even the use of the simplest of machines, arguing that mechanistic activities lead to a mechanistic heart-mind. With such a view, people might as well simply return to the animal world. Moreover, if humans have evolved from animals, we might ask why animals would evolve into humans. I believe that humankind itself is the agent of its own creation.

In *Capital* Marx argues for a two-fold character of labor. In his theory, abstract labor leads to socially necessary labor time, which leads to distribution according to labor and finally to distribution according to need and Communism. This has logical plausibility but no foundation in the empirical. Kant

216 | The Humanist Ethics of Li Zehou

says that such transcendental illusions are untenable, although like religion, they are also able to inspire and motivate people, as seen in Christianity and Islam.

Third is Nietzsche. Many groups on the left think Nietzsche is some kind of sage and won't stand for a word to be said against him, but I have resisted this trend. His thought leads to Nazism. His contempt for the masses was stark and overt, and thus Hitler was similarly stark in proclaiming his ethnicity superior and the Jewish people vile. Today people talk quite a bit about Martin Heidegger (1889–1976) and Carl Schmitt (1888–1985), who represent the rightist tendency of Nietzschean thought and lean toward fascism. Doesn't Schmitt discuss the eternal struggle between God and evil? We also have Michel Foucault (1926–1984) and Gilles Deleuze (1925–1995), who carried forward the leftist tendency of Nietzschean thought, which tends toward anarchism. These are the disastrous effects of Nietzsche's thought.[82]

This account is neither entirely accurate nor comprehensive, and I am not at all satisfied with it. However, its main points are more or less adequate, and so I leave it at that.

Conclusion

Q: Since you've said that Confucianism can serve as traditional religious morals and thus guide modern social morals, what do you think of the many scholars who proselytize Confucianism as a religion?

Li: As everyone knows, I have never supported the establishment of Confucianism as a religion. Why? Simply put, it depreciates Confucianism's universal values.

Q: How so?

Li: Confucianism arose out of early shamanistic ritual ceremony. It possesses religious aspects oriented toward "ultimate concern" and the pursuit of happiness through spiritual and moral cultivation of character. However, it is not itself a religion. There is no personal god, no Kingdom of Heaven or Western Paradise, and no specific religious organization or ceremonies, which make it very different from major religions such as Christianity, Islam, Judaism, and Hinduism. Those who advocate religious Confucianism seek to establish a religious platform comparable to these religions on which to promote the Confucian classics. However, as I see it, Confucianism has already long been rooted in the values, customs, psychology, modes of emotional expression, and outlook on life of the Chinese people.[83] It continues to exist as the living emotio-rational structure of Chinese people. Above I noted that human relationships and the emotions integral to them hold special importance in Chinese society to this day. Feelings of intimacy are important to relations between family members, those of obligation and loyalty are important to friendship, and individual modesty is stressed. Here modesty is not just for the sake of politeness. It recognizes a single person's limitations and shortcomings, in the sense of Confucius's stress on the importance of reflecting on oneself (*Analects* 1.4). This differs from the unconditional prostration and self-abasement one is expected to show before God. Various religions talk about saving one's soul, but Confucianism is about cultivating the moral character of one's embodied living existence. This cultivation involves the humanization of nature that forms "what makes humans human," and is inseparable from the physical body. In fact, Confucianism presents a fairly accurate account of human history, in which it offers ordered cultural evolution rather than that God created humans. It also optimistically investigates and strives to influence future human events— that is, fate. Confucianism's investigations into the origins and future of humanity are more universal than comparable aspects of major world religions, which often teach that their followers are chosen people and the world will end in a final day of judgment. Confucianism looks at the workings of "the Way" in everyday situations and relationships. It has helped alleviate internal worries and external hardships through millennia of the continuous extension of living existence of billions of people's diligence, courage, self-improvement, tenacity, and resilience. Today and in the future, it can likewise exert global influence through the healthy and flourishing worldviews and values of over a billion Chinese people. This continuous extension of existence along with these attitudes and values are the fundamental spirit of Confucianism. Confucianism has much more to offer than simply a religion that competes with other world religions.

Q: Let's sum things up. In "The Century's New Dream" and a dialogue with professors from Sun Yat-Sen University (1995) you've stated, "There is no need to completely repeat the West's process of modernization. Rather, we can strive to forge our own path. This is my general

218 | The Humanist Ethics of Li Zehou

view." In "Neither Slander nor Praise, Neither Left nor Right" (*Bu fei bu yang, fei zuo fei you* 不誹不揚 非左非右)[84] (1998) you write,

> For more than a decade, although I haven't always expressed it directly, what has actually held a central position in my thought and essays is generally the issue of "transformative creation." This is also related to the question of how China can forge its own path of modernization economically, politically, and culturally. For a country and population as enormous as China, the value and significance of truly creating a new path of development that is neither the past's socialism nor today's capitalism would be incalculable. It would also be a contribution to humankind of the greatest order. Furthermore, in today's world China is perhaps the only country that still realistically has such potential, and this potential lies only in the next three decades or so. Therefore, I believe that certain intellectuals in Chinese humanities have a responsibility to take this issue under consideration.

Do you still hold these views?

Li: Absolutely. These views haven't changed at all, as they are directly connected with my philosophy. I cannot say much more than this in regard to the broader field of ethics, as it would touch upon issues of specialized research, especially in political philosophy (external human culture) and moral psychology (internal human psychology or nature). But in general, I believe that within the contemporary trend of anti-rationalism China should bring forth a reconstructed rationality—not "*a priori* reason" but rather "pragmatic reason." We likewise should reconstruct our culture in a way that does not pursue a commercial culture of material desires nor restricts desires as a culture of shame. Rather, we should promote harmonious relations and balanced views of emotion and reason in a culture of optimism and delight. This ethical investigation into a "Chinese path" that combines individual and social elements into a "Way of inner sageliness and outer kingliness" aims to promote the practical realization of transformative creation. In 1998 I proposed a window of opportunity of three decades, and half of that has already passed. China has certainly already begun to "walk its own path," and is doing so at an unprecedented pace. Its economic development has captured the world's attention, and social changes and progress have been tremendous. Yet politically and culturally, this new path remains largely untrodden. Therefore, on the whole we still need at least three decades. I cannot foretell the future, but I would like to reiterate that a few decades, while no more than a flash in the course of human history, to an individual person can be an entire life. Chinese people, especially those in charge, ought to have this respect for historical responsibility. This is also the essence of ethics.

Q: Looking back it, your response to Sandel here is very much an explication of your own philosophy.

Li: This is true. I did say at the outset that we would have to discuss my own philosophy.

Notes

Introduction

1. Li Zehou, *Lunlixue gangyao* 倫理學綱要 (Ethics) (Beijing: Renmin Ribao chubanshe, 2010).

2. Li Zehou, *Zhexue gangyao* 哲學綱要 (Outline of a philosophy) (Beijing: Peking University Press, 2011).

3. As *A Theory of Anthropo-Historical Ontology* (*Renleixue lishi bentilun* 人類學歷史本體論) by Qingdao Publishing in 2016 and again by People's Literature Publishing House in 2019, with the writings on ethics expanded and reconfigured in these later editions.

4. Most importantly in the essays, comments, dialogues, and discussions compiled in *Further Discussions of Ethics* (*Lunlixue gangyao xupian* 倫理學綱要續篇) (SDX Joint Publishing, 2017) and *A New Sketch of Ethics* (*Lunlixue xinshuo shuyao* 倫理學新說述要) (World Publishing, 2019).

5. The most recent Global Influence data (2016) ranks Li Zehou as the most influential Chinese philosopher within China, and third most influential globally. web.archive.org/web/20200928213107/http://www.globalinfluence.world/en/leader/zehou-li/ (accessed December 28, 2021).

6. This was the central question I took up in reviewing the original Chinese publication of *Response*, in Robert A. Carleo III, review of *Huiying Sangdeer ji qita*, *Philosophy East and West* 66, no. 3 (2016): 1027–29. See also Paul J. D'Ambrosio, "Approaches to Global Ethics: Michael Sandel's Justice and Li Zehou's Harmony," *Philosophy East and West* 66, no. 3 (2016): 720–38; Paul J. D'Ambrosio, "Li Zehou's 'Harmony Is Higher Than Justice': Context and a Collaborative Future," *Asian Studies* 8, no. 1 (2020): 142–44.

7. Strikingly, Li never mentions Sandel's *Liberalism and the Limits of Justice* (Cambridge: Cambridge University Press, 1998 [1982]), which like Li's *Response* forms a robust and sustained attack on modern liberalism's philosophical indi-

222 | Notes to Introduction

vidualism and rationalism, specifically as put forth by Immanuel Kant and John Rawls. In fact, Li discusses every one of Sandel's publications up to the time of writing except for *LLJ*.

8. Li Zehou and Liu Yuedi 劉悅笛, "Cong 'qing benti' fansi zhengzhi zhexue" 從「情本體」反思政治哲學 (Reflecting on political philosophy from 'emotion as substance'), *Kaifang shidai* 4 (2014): 194–215; "'Qing benti' shi shijiede" 「情本體」是世界的 ('Emotion as substance' belongs to the world), *Tansuo yu zhengming* 4 (2014): 4–9; "Guanyu 'qing benti' de Zhongguo zhexue duihua lu" 關於「情本體」的中國哲學對話錄 (Dialogue on Chinese philosophy's 'emotion as substance'), *Wen shi zhe* 3 (2014): 18–29; "Li Zehou, Liu Yuedi 2017 nian zhexue duitan lu" 李澤厚、劉悅笛 2017 年哲學對談錄 (Li Zehou and Liu Yuedi's 2017 philosophical dialogue), *Shehui kexuejia* 7 (2017): 39–48; "Lunlixue zatan: Li Zehou, Liu Yuedi 2018 nian duitan lu" 倫理學雜談——李澤厚、劉悅笛2018年對談錄 (Thought rambling on ethics: A dialogue between Li Zehou and Liu Yuedi), *Hunan shifan daxue shehui kexue xuebao* 5 (2018): 1–17.

9. Roger T. Ames and Jinhua Jia, eds., *Li Zehou and Confucian Philosophy* (Honolulu: University of Hawai'i Press, 2015); Rošker, Jana S. ed., *Ethics and the Beauty of Human Becoming—Special Issue Dedicated to Li Zehou on His 90th Birthday*, *Asian Studies* 8, no. 1 (2020). Compare with the articles of the special issue of *Philosophy East and West* 49, no. 2 (1999) on "'Subjectality' 主體性: Li Zehou and His Critical Analysis of Chinese Thought." The previous bent of scholarship arched toward Li's aesthetics, as is apparent from a quick review of early Anglophone publications: Woei Lien Chong, "History as the Realization of Beauty: Li Zehou's Aesthetic Marxism," *Contemporary Chinese Thought* 31, no. 2 (1999): 3–19; John Zijiang Ding, "Li Zehou: Chinese Aesthetics from a Post-Marxist and Confucian Perspective," in *Contemporary Chinese Philosophy*, ed. Chung-Ying Cheng and Nicholas Bunnin (Malden, MA: Blackwell, 2002), 246–59; Sandra A. Wawrytko "Sedimentation in Chinese Aesthetics and Epistemology: A Buddhist Expansion of Confucian Philosophy," *Journal of Chinese Philosophy* 40, no. 3/4 (2013): 473–92. This is also reflected in the three first monograph translations, *The Path of Beauty* (*Mei de licheng* 美的歷程) (1981), trans. Gong Lizeng (Hong Kong: Oxford University Press, 1994); *Four Essays on Aesthetics* (*Meixue si jiang* 美學四講) (1989), trans. Zehou Li and Jane Cauvel (Lanham, MD: Lexington Books, 2006); *The Chinese Aesthetic Tradition* (*Huaxia meixue* 華夏美學) (1988), trans. Maija Bell Samei (Honolulu: University of Hawai'i Press, 2010); and in the collection of essays by Li published in *Contemporary Chinese Thought* 31, no. 2 (1999), guest ed. Woei Lien Chong. This focus on aesthetics is true of earlier translation of Li's work into other languages, as well, including Korean, Japanese, and German.

10. Ames and Jia, *Li Zehou and Confucian Philosophy*, 1–17; Jana S. Rošker, *Following His Own Path: Li Zehou and Contemporary Chinese Philosophy* (Albany:

Notes to Introduction | 223

State University of New York Press, 2019), 1–46; Jana S. Rošker, *Becoming Human: Li Zehou's Ethics* (Leiden: Brill, 2020), viii–xiv; Li Zehou, *A History of Classical Chinese Thought*, trans. Andrew Lambert (New York: Routledge, 2020), x–xxviii; Li Zehou, *The Origins of Chinese Thought: From Shamanism to Ritual Regulations and Humaneness*, trans. Robert A. Carleo III (Leiden: Brill, 2018), 1–10; "Li Zehou," *Biographical Dictionary of the People's Republic of China*, ed. Yuwu Song (London: McFarland & Company, 2013), 190.

11. Derek Parfit "What We could Rationally Will," The Tanner Lectures on Human Values 2002 (available at tannerlectures.utah.edu/_documents/a-to-z/p/parfit_2002.pdf), 310–12; Thomas M. Scanlon, *Being Realistic about Reasons* (Oxford: Oxford University Press, 2014), 5–7, 86–90.

12. On the distinction between the contemporary rationalism of "reasons" and Kant's conception of reason, see Thomas M. Scanlon, "How I Am Not a Kantian," in Derek Parfit, *On What Matters*, vol. 2, ed. Samuel Scheffler (Oxford: Oxford University Press, 2011), 116–39. Scanlon points out that "Kant seems not to appeal at all, or at least not in a fundamental way, to reasons or their relative strength" (119). Rather, "in Kant's view it is only if one takes the Categorical Imperative as the fundamental principle of practical reasoning that one can see oneself as *deciding* what to do rather than merely being determined by one's inclinations" (117), which makes seeing oneself as a rational agent equivalent to the exercise of free will. This latter view is, in slightly modified form, the sort of rationalism that Li Zehou proposes.

13. For more detailed discussion of the relation between Kant and Li's conceptions of reason and the will, see Robert A. Carleo III, "Is Free Will Confucian? Li Zehou's Confucian Revision of the Kantian Will," *Philosophy East and West* 70, no. 1 (2020): 63–83.

14. Jonathan Haidt, "The Emotional Dog and Its Rational Tail: A Social Intuitionist Approach to Moral Judgment," *Psychological Review* 108 (2001): 814–34.

15. Terry Horgan and Mark Timmons, "Morphological Rationalism and the Psychology of Moral Judgment," *Ethical Theory and Moral Practice* 10 (2007): 280.

16. Li, *Zhexue gangyao*, 6.

17. Li, *Zhexue gangyao*, 6.

18. As where he writes, "For example, during wartime or revolution it is hard for every individual to be an 'end.' It may often be more moral to require that individuals self-consciously act as instruments, means, or pieces of a larger picture or project serving the needs or interests of the people, their nation, or the revolution." Li, *Zhexue gangyao*, 6.

19. Li, *Zhexue gangyao*, 6.

20. Li, *The Origins of Chinese Thought*, 176.

21. Li, *Zhexue gangyao*, 11.

22. Quoted in Li, *Zhexue gangyao*, 9.

224 | Notes to On Ethics

On Ethics

1. Translator's note: These comments aim to clarify the author's position following these symposium discussions, which here held at East China Normal University on May 21 and 27, 2014, and published in *Shenme shi daode? Li Zehou lunlixue taolunban shilu* 什麼是道德?——李澤厚倫理學討論班實錄 (What is morality? Recorded discussions of Li Zehou's ethics) (Shanghai: Huadong shifan daxue chuban she, 2015).

2. Li Zehou, *Lishi bentilun* 歷史本體論 (Historical ontology) (Beijing: SDX Joint Publishing, 2002).

3. Translator's note: See Li's clarification of his distinction between "ethics" and "morality" below, under "The Terminological Distinction between Ethics and Morality."

4. Translator's note: "What is morality" was the main theme under discussion at the East China Normal University symposiums Li is here discussing; as noted above, those discussions are published under precisely that name, *What is Morality? (Shenme shi daode* 什麼是道德?).

5. Translator's note: For Li's discussion of these cases at East China Normal University, see especially Li, *Shenme shi daode?*, 9–52. This has direct roots in Michael Sandel's book *Justice: What's the Right Thing to Do?* (New York: Farrar, Straus and Giroux, 2009), and Li's *Huiying Sangdeer ji qita* 回應桑德爾及其他 (A response to Michael Sandel and other matters) (Hong Kong: Oxford University Press, 2014), English translation below.

6. Translator's note: Some readers may notice that among contemporary Anglo-American moral theorists the opposite associations are common—ethics referring to personal values and morality referring to social norms about how to treat one another—and so may feel this requires some explanation. The inversion of those associations in Li Zehou and many other Chinese theorists' writing is largely a matter of conventional translation. The Chinese terms *daode* and *lunli* are generally translated "morality" and "ethics" as a matter of convention. The semantic content of these Chinese terms, however, places *daode* closer to *ethos/ethikos* in emphasizing a quality of personal character and *lunli* closer to morality in emphasizing regulations of human roles and relations. I have slightly adjusted the original text here so that Li expresses this himself.

7. Christopher Boehm, *Moral Origins: The Evolution of Virtue, Altruism, and Shame* (New York: Basic Books, 2012).

8. Boehm, *Moral Origins*, 176, 108.

9. These include the notions that a human emotional affinity for equality and opposition to hierarchical institutions evolved naturally, that equal sharing of prey facilitated people's survival and thereby produced morality, and that red cheeks express internal shame, which I believe are unfounded. Of course, I most

Notes to On Ethics | 225

strongly oppose Boehm's complete conflation of human morality with the so-called "morality" of primates and other animals.

10. Boehm, *Moral Origins*, 317.

11. Boehm, *Moral Origins*, 312.

12. Boehm, *Moral Origins*, 17.

13. Boehm, *Moral Origins*, 203.

14. *Pipan zhexue de pipan: Kangde shuping* 批判哲學的批判：康德述評 (Critique of critical philosophy: a new approach to Kant) (Beijing: Renmin chubanshe, 1979). The English version of this title is published as *A New Approach to Kant: A Confucian-Marxist's Viewpoint*, trans. Christopher Ahn and Jeanne Haizhen Allen (Singapore: Springer, 2018).

15. *Analects* 8.8. For an alternative reading of this line, see Roger T. Ames and Henry Rosemont, Jr., trans., *The Analects of Confucius: A Philosophical Translation* (New York: Ballantine Books, 1998), 122.

16. *Analects* 3.21; translation follows D. C. Lau, trans., *The Analects*, 2nd ed. (Hong Kong: Chinese University of Hong Kong Press, 1992), 25. On this point, see also Wang Guowei 王国维, *Yin-Zhou zhidu lun* 殷周制度論 and the more contemporary Lin Gang 林岗, *Koushu yu antou* 口述與案頭.

17. *Analects* 3.21.

18. Boehm, *Moral Origins*, 6; quoting Charles Darwin, *The Descent of Man, and Selection in Relation to Sex* (Princeton, NJ: Princeton University Press, 1982 (1871)), 71–72.

19. *Mengzi* 6A6; translation follows Bryan W. Van Norden, trans., *Mengzi: With Selections from Traditional Commentaries* (Indianapolis: Hackett, 2008), 149, with alterations.

20. *Mengzi* 2A6; translation follows D. C. Lau, trans., *Mencius: A Bilingual Edition*, rev. ed. (Hong Kong: Chinese University of Hong Kong Press, 2003).

21. *Mengzi* 2A6.

22. Hai Rui 海瑞 writes, "*ge jun xin, ding guo shi*" 格君心, 定國是 (*Zhi an shu* 治安疏).

23. For a recent statement of Li's conception of the dualistic nature of aesthetic sensibility, see Li Zehou, *Cong meixue liangchongxing dao qing benti* 從美感兩重性到情本體 (From the dualistic nature of aesthetic sensibility to emotion as substance) (Jinan: Shandong wenyi chubanshe, 2019).

24. John M. Doris and the Moral Psychology Research Group, *The Moral Psychology Handbook* (Oxford: Oxford University Press: 2010).

25. Translator's note: *Ethics* (*Lunlixue gangyao* 倫理學綱要) (2010) comprises essays from 1999 forward and forms the first part of Li's tripartite *Outline of a Philosophy* (*Zhexue gangyao* 哲學綱要 [Beijing: Beijing daxue chubanshe, 2011]), followed by collected writings on *Epistemology* and *Ontology*. This comprehensive statement of Li's philosophy has been republished in revised and expanded

226 | Notes to On Ethics

editions as *A Theory of Anthropo-Historical Ontology* (*Renleixue lishi bentilun* 人類學歷史本體論) by Qingdao Publishing in 2016 and by People's Literature Publishing House in 2019.

26. Translator's note: The political institutions of the Qin dynasty are generally associated with Legalist ideas and ideals, major proponents of which were direct students of Xunzi.

27. See Li Zehou, *Zhongguo gudai sixiang shilun* 中國古代思想史論 (On traditional Chinese intellectual history) (Beijing: SDX Joint Publishing, 2008 (1985)) and *Zhongguo jindai sixiang shilun* 中國近代思想史論 (On modern Chinese intellectual history) (Beijing: SDX Joint Publishing, 2008 (1979)).

28. In Li Zehou, *Jimao wu shuo* 己卯五說 (Five essays from 1999) (Beijing: Zhongguo dianying chubanshe, 1999); English translation in Li Zehou, *The Origins of Chinese Thought: From Shamanism to Ritual Regulations and Humaneness*, trans. R. A. Carleo III (Leiden: Brill, 2018), 11–53.

29. *Shang shu* 尚書, *Zhou shu* 周書 (Book of Zhou), "Tai shi zhong" 泰誓中 (Great Declaration II) 2, trans. James Legge. All translations from James Legge are taken from the Chinese Text Project, at ctext.org.

30. "Xi ci xia" 系辭下 1.

31. "Xi ci shang" 系辭上 5.

32. *Zhongyong*, trans. Wing-Tsit Chan, *A Source Book in Chinese Philosophy* (Princeton, NJ: Princeton University Press, 1963), 108.

33. Commentary to the Qian 乾 hexagram in the *Book of Changes*, *Zhouyi zhengyi* 周易正義, *Shisanjing zhushu zhengliben* 十三經注疏 整理本 (Beijing: Beijing daxue chubanshe, 2000), vol. 1, 11a.

34. See "Xin yi lun 'Ru-Fa huyong'" 新一輪「儒法互用」 ("A new phase of 'Integrating Confucianism and Legalism'") (1999), in Li's *Lunlixue gangyao* 倫理學綱要 (Ethics) (Beijing: Renmin Ribao chubanshe, 2010).

35. Translator's note: The distinction of "modern social morals" and "traditional religious morals" is the core of Li's "theory of two morals" (*liang de lun* 兩德論). Li argues that we ought to prioritize the "social morals" associated with Enlightenment humanism and modern liberal tradition while also seeking to allow the values and ideas of "traditional religious morals" to permeate and support modern social morals, where possible. See "The Theory of Two Morals," chapter 2 of *Ethics*, in Li, *Zhexue gangyao* 哲學綱要 (Outline of a Philosophy) (Beijing: Peking University Press, 2011), 13–38; "Guanyu 'liang de lun'" 關於"兩德論" (On my "theory of two morals"), in Li, *Renleixue lishi bentilun* 人類學歷史本體論 (The anthropo-historical ontology: An outline of my philosophy) (Beijing: Renmin wenxue chubanshe, 2019), 268–76; the entries on "Modern social morals," "Religious morals," and "Theory of two morals" in Paul J. D'Ambrosio, Robert A. Carleo III, and Andrew Lambert, "On Li Zehou's Philosophy: An Introduction by Three Translators," *Philosophy East and West* 66, no. 4 (2016): 1062–66; Paul D'Ambrosio, "Li Zehou's 'Harmony Is Higher Than Justice': Context and a Col-

Notes to On Ethics | 227

laborative Future," *Asian Studies* 8, no. 1 (2020): 127–46; and "Li Zehou's Theory of Two Morals" in Robert Anthony Carleo III, "Confucian Post-Liberalism," *Asian Studies* 8, no. 1 (2020): 155–60. Li discusses the two morals at length throughout *Response*, as well; see below, *Response*, §1.1, §2.11, §3.12–15.

36. The 2008 version of this text is collected in Li, *Zhexue gangyao*, 364–95; on mysticality, see especially 376–82. It is also printed as "Guanyu 'meiyu dai zongjiao' de zatan dawen" 關於「美育代宗教」的雜談答問) (Assorted discussions and dialogue on aesthetic edification replacing religion) in *Shiyong lixing yu legan wenhua* 實用理性與樂感文化 (Pragmatic reason and a culture of optimism) (Bejing: SDX Joint Publishing, 2008), 297–343; on mysticality, see especially 315–24.

37. Translator's note: Refers to the *Zhongyong*, one of the core Four Books canonized in Neo-Confucian teachings, which discusses that which is "prior to the arousal of pleasure, anger, sorrow, and joy," *xi nu ai le zhi wei fa* 喜怒哀樂之未發.

38. Dr. Robin Carhart-Harris, quoted in James Griffiths, "This Is Your Brain on LSD, Literally," CNN, April 13, 2016, edition.cnn.com/2016/04/12/health/lsd-brain-imaging/.

39. See Li Zehou, *Renleixue lishi bentilun* 人類學歷史本體論 (Anthropological-historical ontology) (Tianjin: Tianjin shehui kexue yuan chubanshe, 2008). [Translator's note: Readers may be interested to note that Li also describes the mysticality of rationality as the idea that "why the universe in its entirety exists" cannot be known, and so while we will eventually be able to give full scientific and causal explanation of brain processes, this will not ultimately answer questions of practical reason (*Response*, §3.11).]

40. Translator's note: In the original Chinese, Li here uses the term "higher than" (*gaoyu* 高於) (a term he himself elsewhere notes the ambiguity of). I have translated this as a matter of priority to highlight important and unique parts of Li's thought, but that is only part of the original idea. Li also means to say that practical reason is superior to speculative reason, in virtue of this priority and fundamentality. (Here "higher than" may be taken as shorthand for the more elaborate "higher than, superior to, and prior to" Li uses shortly below to describe this same relation.) Speculative reason is derivative, in some sense, of practical reason, although it also operates independently of—and seems to in turn reshape—practical reason.

41. "Xi ci shang" 12; trans. Richard John Lynn, *The Classic of the Changes: A New Translation of the I Ching as Interpreted by Wang Bi* (New York: Columbia University Press, 1994), 68.

42. This phrase is taken from Martin Heidegger ("Letter on Humanism," in *Basic Writings*, ed. D. F. Krell (London: Routledge, 1978), 217). Li discusses this line often (e.g., Li, *The Origins of Chinese Thought*, 226, and below in "History, Ethics, and Metaphysics"), and devotes an entire section to it in outlining his ontology (Li, *Zhexue gangyao*, 364–74).

228 | Notes to On Ethics

43. Translator's note: These "lines," which represent constitutive influence between the collectively held social norms of "ritual regulations" and their internalization as "rational principle" in individual psychology, constitute the basics of this general scheme of ethics. The earlier versions of Li's table are merely these two elements, flanked on either side by "emotion" (*qing* 情) (to be understood on the one side as concrete, sensible experience, which is fundamentally constitutive of social existence, and on the other side as the emotions integrated with reason in the "emotio-rational structure" of individual human psychology.) See *Response*, §2.1–2.2, §3.5, in this volume, and my short discussion of this in the Introductory.

44. Translator's note: Li proposes "emotion as substance" (*qing benti* 情本體) to characterize the religious morals of Chinese tradition, which sees the emotions and relations of human life as fundamentally constitutive of reality. See "On Emotion as Substance," chapter 3 of *Ethics*, in Li, *Zhexue gangyao*, 39–63; the entry in D'Ambrosio et al., "On Li Zehou's Philosophy," 1061; and *Response*, §1.3.

45. Translator's note: In these passages, Liang Shuming (like Li, but perhaps even more strongly than Li) uses the term "emotion" (*qing* 情) to refer to emotional connections with other people. Liang contrasts emotions with desires, which are selfish, and states that whereas our emotional connections to other people (*qing*) are the source of all virtue, because they push us to consider others in determining our actions, desires are the source of all problems, because in following them we consider only ourselves and not others. See "Ci qi zhongdian guohe zai," §5 of chapter 5 of Liang's *Zhongguo wenhua yaoyi* 中國文化要義 (The essence of Chinese culture) (Taipei: Taiwan Commercial Press, 2013 [1949]).

46. *Jia you bi zhou, xiang zhi qian jin* 家有敝帚，享之千金; a traditional Chinese phrase for cherishing one's things even if of little value.

47. In Li, *The Origins of Chinese Thought*, 211–28; original Chinese published as "Chuni Ruxue shenceng jiegou shuo" 初擬儒學深層結構說 (Preliminary remarks on the deep structures of Confucianism), in Li Minghui 李明輝, ed., *Rujia sixiang de xiandai quanshi* 儒家思想的現代詮釋 (Taipei: Zhongyang yanjiuyuan zhongguo wen zhe yanjiusuo, 1997), 59–78.

48. The long passage that follows is also published in Li, *The Origins of Chinese Thought*, 215–20; translated from the Chinese version in *You wu dao li, shi li gui ren* 由巫到禮 釋禮歸仁 (From shamanism to ritual regulations and humaneness) (Beijing: SDX Joint Publishing, 2015), pp. 175–80.

49. Originally from Li Zehou, "Guanyu Rujia yu 'xiandai Xin Rujia'" 關於儒家與"現代新儒家" (On Confucianism and "Modern New Confucianism"), in *Zou wo ziji de lu* 走我自己的路 (Walking my own path) (Taipei: Fengyun shidai chubanshe, 1990), 237–38.

50. "Xi ci shang" 5; trans. Richard John Lynn, *The Classic of the Changes*, 53.

51. *Analects* 7.21, 11.12; translation follows D. C. Lau.

52. *Analects* 3.12; trans. D. C. Lau.

53. *Analects* 14.38; trans. D. C. Lau.

Notes to On Ethics | 229

54. *Analects* 9.28; translation adapted from D. C. Lau, a metaphor for the resilience and perseverance of the cultivated person being shown through hardship.

55. "Xi ci xia" 1; trans. Richard John Lynn, *The Classic of the Changes*, 77.

56. "Xi ci shang" 5; trans. Richard John Lynn, *The Classic of the Changes*, 54.

57. Commentary for Qian 乾 and Kun 坤 hexagrams; trans. Richard John Lynn, *The Classic of the Changes*, 144.

58. *Analects* 17.2; translation follows D. C. Lau.

59. *Analects* 17.21; trans. James Legge.

60. *Analects* 2.7; translation follows D. C. Lau with alterations.

61. *Analects* 17.9; trans. D. C. Lau.

62. *Analects* 1.2; translation follows D. C. Lau with alterations.

63. *Analects* 8.8; trans. D. C. Lau, with emendations according to Li Zehou, *Lunyu jindu* 論語今讀 (Reading the Analects today) (Beijing: SDX Joint Publishing, 2008).

64. Translator's note: This rendering of *an shen li ming* follows Li's own English gloss on the phrase (see Li, *Zhexue gangyao*, 125).

65. In Chinese, *Shen zai jianghu, xin cun weique* 身在江湖, 心存魏闕 and *Guanhuai mo guo chao zhong shi, xiushou nan zuo bi shang guan* 關懷莫過朝中事, 袖手難做壁上觀.

66. From a 1953 letter, in *Albert Einstein: The Human Side*, ed. Helen Dukas and Banesh Hoffman (Princeton, NJ: Princeton University Press, 1981), 39.

67. Translator's note: Drawing history into metaphysics is the main concern of the dialogue concluding this volume, "History, Ethics, and Metaphysics." (Li also claims that discussion to top off his oeuvre on ethics *in toto*.) There he relates the idea that history enters metaphysics to other aspects of his philosophy, and elaborates on its basic proposition: that through culture and experience humans inherit and continuously co-create metaphysical ideas, that these ideas in fact *constitute* our metaphysics, and that metaphysics itself is thereby a product of historical human life.

68. Yan Fu, *Lun shubian zhi ji* 論世變之亟, in *Yan Fu ji* 嚴復集 (Beijing: Zhonghua shuju, 1986), vol. 1, 2.

69. *Analects* 9.26; trans. James Legge.

70. On Li's theory of two morals, see above, note 35.

71. Li Zehou, *Shiji xin meng* 世紀新夢 (Dream of a new century) (Hefei: Anhui wenyi chubanshe, 1998).

72. In Li Zehou, *Jimao wu shuo*.

73. English translation in *Li Zehou and Confucian Philosophy*, ed. Roger T. Ames and Jinhua Jia (Honolulu: University of Hawai'i Press, 2015), 18–30; original Chinese published as "Da Gaogeng san wen" 答高更三問, in *Zhonghua dushu bao* 中华讀書报, November 4, 2015; appears also in Li, *Renleixue lishi bentilun* (2016), 3–14.

74. "Di si tigang" 第四提綱 (1989), originally published in *Xueshu yuekan* 學術月刊 (1994) 10; reprinted in Li, *Renleixue lishi bentilun* (2016), 618–22.

230 | Notes to Further Comments on Ethics

75. The Chinese version of this text was originally published in *Tansuo yu zhengming* 探索與爭鳴, vol. 9, 2016.

Further Comments on Ethics

1. See Yu Zhenhua 郁振華, "Zai lun daode de nengli zhi zhi: Ping Huang Yong jiaoshou de liangzhi quanshi" 再論道德的能力之知——評黃勇教授的良知詮釋 (Revisiting moral knowing how: An evaluation of Huang Yong's explication of moral conscience), *Xueshu yuekan* 學術月刊 (*Academic Monthly*), December 2016.

2. *Lunlixue gangyao* 倫理學綱要 (Ethics) (2010), the first part of Li's *Zhexue gangyao* 哲學綱要 (Outline of a philosophy) (Beijing: Beijing daxue chubanshe, 2011); revised and expanded in *Renleixue lishi bentilun* 人類學歷史本體論 (A theory of anthropo-historical ontology) (Qingdao: Qingdao Publishing, 2016; Beijing: Renmin wenxue chubanshe, 2019).

3. Translator's note: See also the discussion of this below, in "History, Ethics, and Metaphysics," under "Moral Conscience Is Not Merely Cognition."

4. I continue to endorse the classical distinction between these three as cognition (*zhi* 知), emotion (*qing* 情), and conation (*yi* 意).

5. Translator's note: Li Zehou differentiates "subjectivity" (*zhuguanxing* 主觀性), primarily epistemological, from "subjectality" (*zhutixing* 主體性), principally ontological. See Li Zehou, "Subjectivity and 'Subjectality': A Response," *Philosophy East and West* 49, no. 2 (1999): 174–83; and Li Zehou, "A Supplementary Explanation of Subjectivity," *Contemporary Chinese Thought* 31, no. 2 (1999): 26–31.

6. *Mencius* 7A15 states, "That which people are capable of without learning is their genuine capability. That which they know without pondering is their genuine knowledge" (Bryan W. Van Norden, trans., *Mengzi: With Selections from Traditional Commentaries* (Indianapolis: Hackett, 2008), 174). "Genuine" translates *liang* 良. Van Norden notes, "here, 'genuine' marks the contrast between what is 'ingenuous' or 'original' as opposed to what is 'artificial' or 'acquired'" (Van Norden, *Mengzi*, 174).

7. See the *Great Learning* (*Daxue* 大學): "What is meant by 'making the will sincere' is allowing no self-deception, as when we hate a hateful odor or love a lovely sight" (translation combines Wing-Tsit Chan (*A Source Book in Chinese Philosophy* [Princeton, NJ: Princeton University Press, 1963], 89) and Bryan Van Norden (Justin Tiwald and Bryan W. Van Norden, eds., *Readings in Later Chinese Philosophy: Han Dynasty to the 10th Century* [Indianapolis: Hackett, 2014], 191). See also §5 and §229 of Wang Yang-Ming, *Instructions for Practical Living and Other Confucian Writings*, trans. Wing-Tsit Chan (New York: Columbia University Press, 1963), 9–12, 202.

8. See *Analects* 12.1 and 17.2.

9. "*Qi shanzhe wei ye*" 其善者偽也, a major theme repeated throughout "Human Nature Is Bad" (*Xing e* 性惡), chapter 23 of the *Xunzi*. Eric L. Hutton

Notes to Further Comments on Ethics | 231

astutely translates this line, "[People's] goodness is a matter of deliberate effort" (Hutton, *Xunzi: The Complete Text*. [Princeton, NJ]: Princeton University Press, 2014], 248).

10. See Wang, *Instructions for Practical Living and Other Confucian Writings*, §313, 239–40; §320, 250.

11. See Zhu Xi's commentary on the *Great Learning*, in Tiwald and Van Norden, *Readings in Later Chinese Philosophy*, 189.

12. Translation follows Bryan W. Van Norden in Tiwald and Van Norden, *Readings in Later Chinese Philosophy*.

13. As seen in Dong's teachings of "innate nature being humane and emotions being avaricious" (*xing ren qing tan* 性仁情貪) and "the three qualities of innate nature" (*xing sanpin* 性三品), which hold that the common people have merely the capacity for good and that it is the ruler's responsibility to foster this potential through education and other means. See the "True Nature" (Shi xing 實性) and "An In-Depth Investigation into Names and Designations" (Shencha minghao 深察名號) chapters of *Luxuriant Dew of the Spring and Autumn Annals* (*Chunqiu fanlu* 春秋繁露); English translation of the latter can be found in Tiwald and Van Norden, *Readings in Later Chinese Philosophy*.

14. Humaneness, rightness, propriety, and wisdom (*ren yi li zhi* 仁義禮智); see *Mencius* 2A6.

15. Happiness, anger, sadness, pleasure, love, disgust, and desire (*xi nu ai le ai wu yu* 喜怒哀樂愛惡欲).

16. Identified with Cheng Yi 程頤 and Zhu Xi, also identified as the Neo-Confucian "School of Principle" (*lixue* 理學).

17. See Li Zehou, "Song-Ming lixue zhuiqiu chaoyan de shibai" 宋明理學追求超驗的失敗 (The failure of Song-Ming Neo-Confucianism's pursuit of transcendence), in *Shiyong lixing yu legan wenhua* 實用理性與樂感文化 (Pragmatic reason and a culture of optimism) (Beijing: SDX Joint Publishing, 2008), 60–65.

18. *Mencius* 2A6; translation of these terms follows Van Norden, *Mengzi*, 46–47.

19. For greater explication of this position, see Li Zehou, *Zhongguo gudai sixiang shilun* 中國古代思想史論 (On traditional Chinese intellectual history) (Beijing: SDX Joint Publishing, 2008 (1985)), especially "Legan wenhua" 樂感文化 (Culture of optimism), 323–33; in English as Li Zehou, *A History of Classical Chinese Thought*, trans. Andrew Lambert (New York: Routledge, 2020), especially "A Culture Characterized by Sensitivity to Delight," 317–34.

20. Commentary to the Qian hexagram, *Zhouyi zhengyi*, vol. 1, 11a.

21. *Analects* 8.8.

22. I advocate returning to classical Confucianism, and oppose Song Confucian teachings of the heart-mind and human nature (*xin xing* 心性) as substance (*ti* 體), so therefore I cannot carry forward the teachings of Zhu Xi.

23. Translator's note: See also above, in "On Ethics," under "Intuition and Inherent Goodness in Mencius and Xunzi."

232 | Notes to Further Comments on Ethics

24. *Mencius* 7B25, trans. D. C. Lau, *Mencius: A Bilingual Edition*, rev. ed. (Hong Kong: Chinese University of Hong Kong Press, 2003), 321.

25. Translator's note: See *Response*, §2.3, in this volume. There, Li argues that higher pleasures, in contrast to more base and basic pleasures, are unquantifiable, and therefore, "the idea of 'greatest happiness for the greatest number' can only refer to material aspects of life."

26. See *Mencius* 3B3, 6A6, and 6A10.

27. *Mencius* 2A6, 6A6; trans. Van Norden, *Mengzi*, 46, 149.

28. *Analects* 4.3.

29. *Analects* 13.20.

30. Translation follows Chan, *Source Book*, 105.

31. *Mencius* 2A6, 6A6; trans. James Legge. All translations from James Legge are taken from the Chinese Text Project, at ctext.org.

32. Translator's note: Translation of this term follows Sylvia Chan. Li elsewhere writes, "'Storing goodness in beauty' was traditionally advocated by Chinese Confucianism. Confucius discussed becoming established through ritual (*li yu li* 立於禮) and completion through music (*cheng yu yue* 成於樂) (*Analects* 8.8), which refers to cultivation of individual character being completed in aesthetics and not in ethics" (*Lishi bentilun* and *Jimao wu shuo* 歷史本體論 己卯五說 [Historical ontology and Five essays from 1999], expanded edition [Beijing: SDX Joint Publishing, 2008], 267). See also the section on "Yi mei chu shan" 以美儲善 (Storing goodness in beauty) in *Lishi bentilun* and *Jimao wu shuo*, 267.

33. Translator's note: References G. W. F. Hegel. "The cunning of reason" (*die List der Vernunft*) is central to Hegel's philosophy of history, in which reason as the universal is unwittingly realized through particular individual pursuits. As for evil in historical development, Friedrich Engels writes, "In Hegel evil is the form in which the motive force of historical development presents itself. . . . It is precisely the wicked passions of man—greed and lust for power—which, since the emergence of class antagonisms, have become levers of historical development" (Friedrich Engels, *Ludwig Feuerbach and the End of Classical German Philosophy* [London: ElecBook, 2000], 36).

34. Immanuel Kant, *Religion within the Limits of Reason Alone* (*Die Religion innerhalb der Grenzen der bloßen Vernunft*) (1793), translated by Theodore M. Greene and Hoyt H. Hudson (New York: Harper, 1960), 17.

35. Translator's note: See the section "Ge qi gong er bu song qi de" 歌其功而不頌其德 ("Lauding achievements but not extolling virtue") in Li, *Renleixue lishi bentilun* (2016), 592–95. This phrase originally occurs in the "Zhou ben ji" 周本紀 chapter of the *Records of the Grand Scribe*. It recognizes the historically situated "achievements" (*gong* 功, or perhaps most appropriately, "contributions" or "utility") of certain particular moral views to the historical advancement of human flourishing, while also denying the broader (universal, absolute) validity of those moral views.

Notes to History, Ethics, and Metaphysics | 233

History, Ethics, and Metaphysics

1. Professor at the Institute of Philosophy, Chinese Academy of Social Sciences.

2. "Lunlixue zatan: Li Zehou, Liu Yuedi 2018 nian duitan lu" 倫理學雜談——李澤厚、劉悅笛2018年對談錄 (Thought rambling on ethics: A dialogue between Li Zehou and Liu Yuedi), *Hunan shifan daxue shehui kexue xuebao* 2018 (5): 1–17. This dialogue continues that and earlier discussions between Li and Liu: "Cong 'qing benti' fansi zhengzhi zhexue" 從「情本體」反思政治哲學 (Reflecting on political philosophy from "emotion as substance"), *Kaifang shidai* 2014 (4): 194–215; " 'Qing benti' shi shijiede"「情本體」是 世界的 ("Emotion as substance" belongs to the world), *Tansuo yu zhengming* 2014 (4): 4–9; "Guanyu 'qing benti' de Zhongguo zhexue duihua lu" 關於 "情本體" 的中國哲學對話錄 (Dialogue on Chinese philosophy's "emotion as substance"), *Wen shi zhe* 2014 (3): 18–29; "Li Zehou, Liu Yuedi 2017 nian zhexue duitan lu" 李澤厚、劉悅笛 2017 年哲學對談錄 (Li Zehou and Liu Yuedi's 2017 philosophical dialogue), *Shehui kexuejia* 2017 (7): 39–48.

3. Translator's note: The original Chinese word here, "*ru*" 入, is quite literally "entering," and this literal rendering seems the most accurate replication of the idea in English. We may contrast history *entering* metaphysics with it *becoming* or *constituting* metaphysics. Li's contention is (roughly) that metaphysical notions are historically accumulated in the psychology of human subjects through situated practice, including discursive practice. Thus, "history enters metaphysics" (*lishi ru xingshangxue* 歷史入形上學) both in that history continuously shapes our metaphysical ideas and beliefs and in that history is itself continuously shaped by people's metaphysical ideas and beliefs. Herein, history remains history, and metaphysics remains metaphysics (or more accurately regarding Li, it remains our metaphysical belief systems). History infuses itself into and unfolds within the context of people's metaphysical beliefs without itself becoming or constituting metaphysics.

4. Translator's note: Li uses the phrase "experience becomes *a priori*" to denote the idea that what people regard as *a priori*—that is, what is taken as *a priori* by a particular individual or group—is a matter of historically formulated ideas being foundational to human life (including in thought, action, social organization, values, and so forth). The phrase is shorthand for "the empirical for humankind becoming *a priori* for the individual." Li elaborates a bit on this below. See also Li Zehou, *The Origins of Chinese Thought: From Shamanism to Ritual Regulations and Humaneness* (Leiden: Brill, 2018), 229–30. Sometimes Li has discussed this idea as rejecting that there are *a priori* principles at all (as in *Response*, §1.1, §2.1, in this volume); later in this work, he discusses the value of certain "transcendental [or *a priori*] illusions," in the sense of holding beliefs in (supposedly) *a priori* truths despite these not (in fact) being *a priori* truths.

234 | Notes to History, Ethics, and Metaphysics

5. Li Zehou, *Zhexue gangyao* 哲學綱要 (Outline of a philosophy) (Beijing: Peking University Press, 2011), 366; Li Zehou, *Renleixue lishi bentilun* 人類學歷史本體論 (A theory of anthropo-historical ontology) (Qingdao: Qingdao chuban she, 2016), 648; Li, *The Origins of Chinese Thought*, 181, 265; and *Response*, §3.16.

6. Translator's note: Li identifies a distinctively Chinese understanding of the world and ourselves rooted in pre-historic shamanistic ritual, in which humans directly and emotionally engaged with the divine. This developed through forms of pragmatic rational thought that are identified especially with early Confucianism, but which have endured throughout history in Chinese thought generally. He elaborates these views on China's shamanistic-historical tradition in Li, *On the Origins of Chinese Thought*.

7. Translator's note: See the postscript to this dialogue, below, for elaboration on how and why "humans living" is fundamental.

8. Translator's note: This is Li's term for the type of reason characteristic of traditional Chinese thought, which he distinguishes from "practical reason" in Western and especially Kantian moral theory.

9. Translator's note: Li's three elements of morality are ideas (or concepts, as cognitive knowledge generally, which comes from experience), emotions, and the will; he identifies these with the classical Confucian notions of *zhi* 知, *qing* 情, and *yi* 意. He also identifies ideas as the "social content of reason"—the substantive basis of understanding and judgement—and the will as the "formal force of reason," while moral action can be "assisted" by emotions, which are neither sufficient nor necessary to moral action (Li, *The Origins of Chinese Thought*, 236). See also Li Zehou, *Lunlixue gangyao xupian* 倫理學綱要續篇 (Further discussions of ethics) (Beijing: SDX Joint Publishing, 2017), 385, 400.

10. See Steven Pinker, *Enlightenment Now: The Case for Reason, Science, Humanism, and Progress* (New York: Viking, 2018).

11. Translator's note: Li refers to his philosophical theory broadly as "anthropological historical ontology," sometimes shortened as "historical ontology" (*lishi bentilun* 歷史本體論). This emphasizes his historical materialist outlook, in which the material conditions of human existence are formative factors of human psychology and culture. Therein, the uniquely human ability to act on rational principles allows them to shape these conditions. Both the content of human psychology and the material conditions of human existence are accumulatively affected by rational human action and interaction, giving free will a central role in "historical ontology." Herein, emphasis on the concrete actuality of human existence as the origin and grounds of moral-rational principles also serves to assert the importance of historically specific circumstance in moral judgment, since concrete circumstance is, in Li's view, prior to any supposedly "*a priori*" principle, as he explains in the preceding essays.

12. Translator's note: Li's advocacy of "emotion as substance" (*qing benti* 情本體) proposes we take human emotions and relations as "substance" in the sense

Notes to History, Ethics, and Metaphysics | 235

of "what is ultimately real and fundamental in human life." See "On Emotion as Substance," chapter 3 of *Ethics*, in Li, *Zhexue gangyao*, 39–63. This would leave us without "substance" in the sense it is often understood in Western philosophy, as "noumenon" or something that exists independently of (and yet somehow also supports) the contingencies of human life.

13. Translator's note: The "realm of heaven and earth" (*tian-di jingjie* 天地境界) is, for Li, a state of emotional faith in something greater than the human, such as the "Way of heaven" and "heaven and earth." This develops on the use of that term by Feng Youlan 馮友蘭, as the highest realm of moral development or state of human life, in which one overcomes the distinction between oneself and other things. See chapter 7, "Heaven and Earth" (Tiandi 天地), of Feng's *Xin yuanren* 新原人. For Li's characterization of the relation between his and Feng's conceptions of the "realm of heaven and earth," see Li, *Zhexue gangyao*, 383–84. Later in this dialogue he declares an explicit aim of his philosophy to be formulating that faith in a way that aligns its objects with the particular and historically situated interests of concrete humans in society. This seems to be a central point motivating this discussion of a historically grounded metaphysics. See also Li's discussion of "The Realm of Heaven and Earth," in Li, *Zhexue gangyao*, 374–83.

14. Translator's note: These two characters together compose the term *benti* 本體, which has become the standard translation for "noumenon" in Kant and other Western philosophers. Throughout his ethical writings, Li contrasts that with his own use of *benti* in this sense of what is foundational in human life, and he sees his own use as closely aligned with traditional Chinese thought.

15. Translator's note: In Chinese, "heaven" (*tian* 天) is largely understood as part of (and sometimes shorthand for) "heaven and earth" (*tiandi*), or the natural world generally. What is "heavenly" thereby often refers more or less to what is natural; and it often also carries an authority similar to the "natural" in Western traditions. We can understand Li here to be stating, "Chinese tradition describes what is normative for humans in terms of what is heavenly (or natural)." Since Li also affirms history is the source of, and shapes, what is normative for humans, history is therefore also the source of, and shapes, what is considered heavenly and naturally—and metaphysically—correct or true. Thus, "history enters metaphysics."

16. Li Zehou, *Lishi bentilun* 歷史本體論 (Historical ontology) (Beijing: SDX Joint Publishing, 2002).

17. Translator's note: Readers may keep in mind that Li simultaneously understands this notion of "fate" also as possessing "a sense of spiritual belonging" (see note 26, below).

18. For his denunciation of Nietzsche, see Pinker, *Enlightenment Now*, 443–48, as well as the section on "Why were you so mean to Nietzsche?" in Steven Pinker, "Enlightenment Wars: Some Reflections on 'Enlightenment Now,' One Year Later," *Quillette*, January 14, 2019, www.quillette.com/2019/01/14/enlightenment-wars-some-reflections-on-enlightenment-now-one-year-later.

236 | Notes to History, Ethics, and Metaphysics

19. Translator's note: On this point, see also Li, *The Origins of Chinese Thought*, 263.

20. Translator's note: This distinguishes "modern social morals" of Enlightenment humanism and modern liberalism from the "traditional religious morals" of, for example, Confucianism. See "The Theory of Two Morals," chapter 2 of *Ethics*, in Li, *Zhexue gangyao*, 13–38, and above in this volume, chapter 1, note 35.

21. Translator's note: Li distinguishes the external social norms of "ethics," as *lunli* 倫理, from the personal virtue of "morality," as *daode* 道德. It is worth noting that this is almost precisely opposite the distinction drawn between ethics and morality by some modern Anglophone philosophers, such as Ronald Dworkin (see for example *Justice for Hedgehogs* [Cambridge, MA: The Belknap Press of Harvard University Press, 2011], 191). This arises from the semantic and etymological character of *lunli* and *daode* being largely opposite the etymology of their respective standard English translations, as "ethics" and "morality" respectively. See also "The Terminological Distinction between Ethics and Morality" in "On Ethics," above.

22. Translator's note: Li argues that historical, social, relational, sensible, concrete human existence is the fundamental ground and origin of social ("external") reason and norms, and that these are "internalized" in the individual psychology of actual human subjects. External norms are the content of "ethics," and their internalization as the complex emotio-rational structure of human psychology provides the content of "morality."

23. We can distinguish transcendental illusions with positive functions, such as those of God, the soul, and freedom, from transcendental illusions that go wrong, such as where communism transforms into a harmful political religion, causing catastrophe and suffering.

24. Translator's note: See below, *Response*, §2.2.

25. Translator's note: Here and below, "disposition" translates *dingshi* 定勢/定式, which seems to refer to general patterns of human thought, feeling, and action established through human culture ("history") and individual development ("education").

26. Translator's note: Li uses the phrase *an shen li ming* 安身立命 often, and by it (to the best of my understanding) intends to denote a state of moral resolution. "Placing oneself morally at ease" translates *an shen*, as the psychological state of moral comfort in which a subject sees and feels oneself to be in accord with moral and ethical demands; "establishing a sense of spiritual belonging" here translates *li ming*, which seems to denote the formation and affirmation of moral identity and purpose. Li links these with Paul Tillich's notion of "ultimate concern" as the basic constitution of religious faith and perhaps meaningfulness in one's life more broadly. (See, for example, the penultimate section of "On Ethics," above.) Li himself once glosses the phrase *an shen li ming* with the English translation "make one's home, a sense of spiritual belonging" (Li, *Zhexue gangyao*, 125).

Notes to History, Ethics, and Metaphysics | 237

27. Translator's note: Kohlberg's three levels each include two stages. The second level (third and fourth stages) recognize and follow notions of good and bad or right and wrong as shared norms of "convention" necessary to social flourishing. The third "post-conventional" level understands principles of right and wrong more abstractly, and independent of their particular social (i.e., legal) formulations. The fifth understands these largely in terms of principles of communal benefit or justice, while the sixth sees them as intrinsically valuable universal principles.

28. Translator's note: Feng's philosophy fused Anglo-American New Realism with Neo-Confucian moral metaphysics, revising the former's affirmation of the reality of objective logical principles structuring the world into affirmation of a non-logical metaphysics that allows humans to apprehend, although not ultimately define, the principles (*li* 理) that ontologically constitute the world.

29. The conference on "Conscience and Cognition: From Mencius and Xunzi to Zhu Xi and Wang Yangming" (*Liangzhi yu renzhi: Cong Mengxun dao Zhuzi, Wang Yingming* 良知與認知——從孟荀到朱子、王陽明), held at Renmin University, Beijing, October 17, 2019.

30. Translator's note: This is a particularly important point in Li's moral philosophy. It distinguishes forms of moral intuition, as products of long-term edification of the will, from animalistic instincts; and it roots moral intuitions in concrete and historical human ideas and practices, rather than seeing them as heavenly bestowed or transcendent.

31. Translator's note: While Li disagrees with core parts of Mencian moral psychology, he strongly endorses this emphasis on moral resolve and sees it as a crucial part of classical Confucian moral theory. For further discussion of the value and significance of Mencius's exaltation of strong and independent individual moral character, see Li Zehou, *Lunlixue xinshuo shuyao* 倫理學新說述要 (A new sketch of ethics) (Beijing: Shijie tushu, 2019).

32. See "Bian xue" 辨學 (Disputing learning) in the fourth book of Ling Tingkan's *Jiaolitang wenji* 校禮堂文集.

33. Translator's note: Li's point here is assisted by the established translation of "free" into Chinese as *ziyou* 自由, literally "from oneself" or "self-arising"—a rendering that substantively and semantically aligns it closely to self-determination and autonomy and not with being "free from," or the negative dimensions of freedom that seem to be the major challenges for libertarian and even compatibilist affirmation of free will, and which Kant himself may be interpreted as giving up in favor of a positive sense of transcendental freedom. Li above recognizes the relevance of those negative dimensions of freedom and discusses them in terms of "casting off" (*baituo* 擺脫) causality, which in substance if not semantics has equivalence to "being free from." Indeed, "free from" may even be a better translation, but would fail to accurately render Li's original Chinese phrasing, which does not use the term "free" here. Li affirms elsewhere that his conception of free

238 | Notes to History, Ethics, and Metaphysics

will includes freedom in both positive and negative senses (see Li, *Lishi bentilun*, 63). Here those two sides lie in self-determination through moral psychology and in "casting off causality."

34. Translator's note: Seems to reference Isaiah Berlin, who asserts that there are "more than two hundred senses of it [the term freedom] recorded by historians of ideas" (Isaiah Berlin, *Liberty: Incorporating "Four Essays on Liberty,"* ed. Henry Hardy [Oxford: Oxford University Press, 2002], 168).

35. Translator's note: "Learning of the heart-mind" generally refers to the philosophical views of Lu-Wang Neo-Confucianism, that is, to the ideas identified with Lu Xiangshan 陸象山 (1139–1193) and Wang Yangming 王陽明 (1472–1529), which emphasize subjective connection to ontological cosmic good through each person's inherent capacity of moral conscience or intuition.

36. "Conscience and Cognition: From Mencius and Xunzi to Zhu Xi and Wang Yangming," held at Renmin University, October 17, 2019, and "The Second Spiritual Humanism Symposium," held at the Peking University Institute for Advanced Humanistic Studies, October 19–20, 2019.

37. Translator's note: Li asks precisely that question, for example, in Li, *The Origins of Chinese Thought*, 140. He also elaborates on this issue as "The Failure of Song-Ming Neo-Confucianism's Pursuit of Transcendence" (*Song-Ming lixue zhuiqiu chaoyan de shibai* 宋明理學追求超驗的失敗), collected in Li, *Zhexue gangyao*, 43–47.

38. Translator's note: Refers to Mou Zongsan 牟宗三, Xu Fuguan 徐復觀, Zhang Junmai (Carson Chang) 張君勱, and Tang Junyi 唐君毅 as authors of the New Confucian "Manifesto" (*Wei Zhongguo wenhua jinggao shijie renshi xuanyan* 為中國文化敬告世界人士宣言); see "Manifesto for a Reappraisal of Sinology and the Reconstruction of Chinese Culture," in Wm. Theodore De Bary and Richard Lufrano, eds., *Sources of Chinese Tradition*, vol. 2 (Columbia University Press, 2000), 550–55.

39. Translator's note: See Li Zehou, *Shiyong lixing yu legan wenhua* 實用理性與樂感文化 (Pragmatic reason and a culture of optimism) (Bejing: SDX Joint Publishing, 2008), 111; also discussed in Li's selected writings on ontology, in discussing "The Realm of Heaven and Earth," in Li, *Zhexue gangyao*, 376. In the latter he describes this belief in the divine, shared by Kant as well, as a "non-religious yet also quasi-religious aestheticist emotional faith in the divine, in the way of heaven, and in heaven and earth," and defines his version of the "realm of heaven and earth" as precisely this state of emotional faith. See also note 13, above.

40. Translator's note: That is, ethical social norms are prior to the subject's faith in them and their psychological internalization as moral principles. These norms form in society through historical "sedimentation," and are then internalized in individual psychology in ways that subjects may experience as moral intuition.

41. Translator's note: "Culture of optimism" (*legan wenhua* 樂感文化) is Li's characterization of traditional Chinese culture in contrast to guilt cultures (such as those fostered by the Abrahamic notion of original sin) and shame cultures

Notes to History, Ethics, and Metaphysics | 239

(as some have described Japanese society). China's "culture of optimism" finds ultimate meaning in the struggle for human fulfilment and flourishing in this world rather than in heaven or the hereafter. Li writes, "China's 'culture of optimism' bases itself in the notion that humans are most fundamental and believes in the power of humankind itself. Although history proceeds in the midst of tragedy, as long as humans 'strengthen themselves ceaselessly' and persevere in their struggle, we can nevertheless ascend from this. Circumstances can be changed and prospects will improve. This involves inheriting the past and developing the future, carrying forward the work of our predecessors we can successfully forge a better path" (Li, *The Origins of Chinese Thought*, 94). See also Li, *The Origins of Chinese Thought*, 46, 155–57.

42. Translator's note: Li here compares Kantian rationality to Mencius's innate moral heart-mind. Both give metaphysical grounds for the moral psychology in which he identifies "free will" to be the core element. Li criticizes the development of the Mencian moral heart-mind, especially the heart-mind of humaneness rooted in compassion, by certain later Confucians, most notably Wang Yangming, as a form of moral intuition giving humans direct access to knowledge of moral goodness, so to speak. This has roots in the "emotional cosmology" that characterizes traditional Chinese thought generally, and Li embraces the emotional cosmology but sees problems with interpreting compassion as offering direct access to the good. Compassion is good and important, even morally crucial, he argues (see below), but morality is still primarily a matter of rational judgment, not of accessing *a priori* goodness through innate conscience—hence Li's long-established advocacy of the Kantian over Mencian formulation of things. At the risk of oversimplifying, we may say that Li advocates a more rationalist Kantian moral psychology while rejecting the Kantian metaphysic of reason, and rejects a more intuitionist or sentimentalist Mencian moral psychology while embracing the traditionally Chinese emotional cosmology.

43. From the "Commentary on the Images" for the *qian* 乾 hexagram in the *Book of Changes*.

44. See Ruth Benedict, *The Chrysanthemum and the Sword* (Boston: Mariner Books, 1989), 222–23, 251.

45. Translator's note: That is, the form of Confucianism suitable for being developed and adopted today, ushering in a new stage in the history of Confucianism. The four stages of Confucian development are the classical (pre-Qin) period, the Han-through-Tang period, Neo-Confucianism, and contemporary Confucianism. See Li's "Shuo Ruxue si qi" 說儒學四期 (On the four stages of Confucianism), in *Jimao wu shuo*; reprinted in *Lishi bentilun* and *Jimao wu shuo* 歷史本體論 己卯五說 (Historical ontology and Five essays from 1999), expanded edition (Beijing: SDX Joint Publishing, 2008), 130–55.

46. Translator's note: Liu here uses Lu Xun's term *nalai zhuyi* 拿來主義, the title of an influential essay advocating, literally, "an ideology of taking," that is, appropriating useful elements of other cultures.

240 | Notes to History, Ethics, and Metaphysics

47. Translator's note: "Subjectality-based" translates *zhutixing* 主體性. Li differentiates between two Chinese terms for subjectivity: *zhutixing* and *zhuguanxing* 主觀性. Semantically, the former emphasizes embodiment rather than mere consciousness, and to emphasize this, Li translates it back into English as a distinct term, "subjectality." This differentiates "subjectivity" (*zhuguanxing* 主觀性), primarily epistemological, from "subjectality" (*zhutixing* 主體性), principally ontological. See Li Zehou, "Subjectivity and 'Subjectality': A Response," *Philosophy East and West* 49, no. 2 (1999): 174–83; "A Supplementary Explanation of Subjectivity," *Contemporary Chinese Thought* 31, no. 2 (1999): 26–31; "Guanyu zhutixing de buchong shuoming" 關於主體性的補充說明 (Additional explication of subjectality) (1983), in *Wode zhexue tigang* 我的哲學題綱 (An outline of my philosophy), sec. ed. (Taipei: Sanmin shuju, 2020), 131–48. Li adds a discussion of "The Epistemology of the Philosophy of 'Subjectality'" to the most recent and comprehensive presentations of his overall philosophy, *Renleixue lishi bentilun* (2016), 333–73; (2019), 2.3–56.

48. Or alternatively, "simulates," depending on how one reads the character *gu* 鼓; this line comes from the "Appended Commentaries I" (*Xici shang* 繫辭上) of the *Book of Changes*.

49. See chapter 1, note 42, in this volume.

50. See Li, *The Origins of Chinese Thought*, 266.

51. Translator's note: Even on these points of agreement, Li finds himself importantly different from Marx. Marx focuses on the implications of tools, technologies, and forces of production for external relations of production and social structures, so as to criticize capitalism and promote proletarian revolution and the communist ideal. Li in contrast looks at how the manufacture of tools has produced the uniquely human dimensions of reason that shape collective and individual psychology—what he calls the cultural-psychological formation and the emotio-rational structure, respectively. Where Marx moves outward toward external relations, Li moves inward toward human psychology.

52. *Cong meixue liangchongxing dao qing benti* 從美感兩重性到情本體 (From the duality of aesthetic sensibility to emotion as substance) (Jinan: Shandong wenyi chubanshe, 2019).

53. This is discussed in *A New Approach to Kant*, *Historical Ontology*, and other works.

54. Translator's note: In this essay, Li considers Cai Yuanpei's 蔡元培 proposal that "aesthetic education replace religion" and proposes that the aesthetic realm of traditional Confucianism is on par with the religious dimensions of other traditions in terms of grounding human existence and morals.

55. "Wei shengmin li ming" 為生民立命, the second of Zhang Zai's famous four statements recorded in *Hengqu yulu* 橫渠語錄.

56. The Chinese version of this text was originally published in *Tansuo yu zhengming* 探索與爭鳴, January 2020. Alterations, and additions, and omissions

Notes to Appendix | 241

have been made to the translated version of this text following specific requests of the author and the editorial judgment of the translator.

57. Li Zehou, *Za zhu ji* 雜著集 (Miscellaneous writings) (Beijing: SDX Joint Publishing, 2008), 323–25.

Appendix

1. Translator's note: This Appendix was co-translated with Paul J. D'Ambrosio. *Response* was written in 2013 and originally published in 2014 in two editions, by Oxford University Press (Hong Kong) in traditional characters and by SDX Joint Publishing (Beijing) in simplified characters. (The content did not vary between the editions.) It first appeared in English as Li Zehou, "A Response to Michael Sandel and Other Matters," trans. Paul J. D'Ambrosio and Robert A. Carleo III, *Philosophy East and West* 66, no. 4 (2016): 1068–1147, and the translation here is revised from that earlier publication. *Response* contextualizes, clarifies, and draws out the implications of the views of Li's *Ethics* (*Lunlixue gangyao* 倫理學綱要), and that project was continued in his comments "On Ethics" and the dialogue on "History, Ethics, and Metaphysics"—the main texts in this volume. The arguments of those later works closely interrelate with the ideas put forth in *Response*.

2. Michael J. Sandel, *Democracy's Discontent: America in Search of a Public Philosophy* (Cambridge, MA: Harvard University Press, 1996).

3. Li Zehou, *Jimao wu shuo* 己卯五說 (Five essays from 1999) (Beijing: Zhongguo dianying chubanshe, 1999); *Lishi bentilun* 歷史本體論 (Historical ontology) (Beijing: SDX Joint Publishing, 2002).

4. Michael J. Sandel, *Justice: What's the Right Thing to Do?* (New York: Farrar, Straus and Giroux, 2009); *What Money Can't Buy: The Moral Limits of Markets* (New York: Farrar, Straus and Giroux, 2012).

5. See "Zhexue tanxun lu" 哲學探尋錄 (A record of philosophical inquiry), reprinted in *Zhexue gangyao* 哲學綱要 (Outline of a philosophy) (Beijing: Peking University Press, 2011), 209–231.

6. Translator's note: In Chinese, *lishi yu lunli de erlü beifan* 歷史與倫理的二律背反, *lishi zai beiju zhong qianxing* 歷史在悲劇中前行, and *hexie gao yu zhengyi* 和諧高於正義, respectively.

7. Li Zehou, *Lunyu jindu* 論語今讀 (Reading the Analects today) (Beijing: SDX Joint Publishing, 2008).

8. Li Zehou, *Zhongguo zhexue ruhe dengchang* 中國哲學如何登場 (How can Chinese philosophy go on stage?) (Shanghai: Shanghai yiwen chubanshe, 2012).

9. As seen in the phrase "Heaven's action is robust" (*tian xing jian* 天行健), in the Commentary to the Qian 乾 hexagram of the *Book of Changes* (*Zhouyi zhengyi* 周易正義, *Shisanjing zhushu zhengli ben* 十三經注疏 整理本 (Beijing: Peking University Press, 2000), vol. 1, 11a).

242 | Notes to Appendix

10. Translator's note: This phrase (*dao shi yu qing* 道始於情), which Li often refers to here and across his ethical writing generally, is found in the pre-Qin bamboo text *Xing zi ming chu* 性自命出 (Natural endowment emerges from heavenly decree). The term here translated as "emotionality," more generally translated as "emotions" (*qing* 情), Li uses sometimes to refer to the felt human experience of social life, in which feelings (*qinggan* 情感) are a constitutive aspect of the shared circumstances (*qingjing* 情境) of human existence. Li relies on these dual aspects of the term of *qing*—emotion and circumstance—in laying out his philosophy; see below §2.1 and §3.5, as well as "The Basic Schema of Li's Ethics" in the introduction. This text sometimes translates *qing* with the term "emotionality" where Li strongly engages the term's sense of shared emotional circumstance—as felt, lived situatedness—rather than merely personal, psychological emotions.

11. Translator's note: This line, which Li also often refers to, comes from the pre-Qin bamboo text "Yu cong er" 語叢二 (Thicket of sayings part II).

12. Translator's note: The fourth stage of Confucianism that Li proposes involves the development and broad adoption of his own philosophical interpretation of Confucian teachings, characterized by the qualities he elaborates here and elsewhere, including the foundational role of "emotion." This intends to usher in a new stage in the history of Confucianism, replacing the third stage, which has run from Song-Ming Neo-Confucianism to the modern New Confucian theories that largely inherit (and modernize) Neo-Confucian philosophy. The first and second stages are classical Confucianism and Han Confucianism, respectively.

13. Translator's note: The two substances are the "techno-social substance" mentioned above and "individual psychological substance" (*geti xinli benti* 個體心理本體), which Li describes in the following paragraph. See also the entries for these in "The Li Zehou Lexicon," in Paul J. D'Ambrosio, Robert A. Carleo III, and Andrew Lambert, "On Li Zehou's Philosophy: An Introduction by Three Translators," *Philosophy East and West* 66, no. 4 (2016): 1062, 1065–66.

14. Translator's note: Translates *liangzhi liangneng* 良知良能; also commonly translated as "innate knowledge" and "innate ability," these terms are primarily identified with the major Neo-Confucian School of Mind philosopher Wang Yangming 王陽明 (1472–1529).

15. Liang Shuming, *Zhongguo wenhua yaoyi* 中國文化要義 (The essence of Chinese culture) (Taipei: Taiwan Commercial Press, [1949] 2013), 102.

16. "Lunlixue dawen bu" 倫理學答問補 (Additional dialogues on ethics), in *Du shu* 讀書 (Reading) (November 2012): 47–60; republished in *Renleixue lishi bentilun* 人類學歷史本體論 (A theory of anthropo-historical ontology) (Qingdao: Qingdao chubanshe, 2016), 158–179, and (Beijing: Renmin wenxue chubanshe, 2019), 183–207.

17. Translator's note: The third phrase, *li yin ren zhi qing er wei zhi* 禮因人之情而為之, is adapted from lines in the "Fang ji" 坊記 chapter of the *Record of Ritual* and in the "Xin shu shang" 心術上 book of the *Guanzi* 管子; the fourth

phrase, *shizhe jin qing, zhongzhe jin yi* 始者近情, 終者近義, is from the first passage of the *Xing zi ming chu*.

18. Li Zehou, "Kongzi zai pingjia" 孔子再評價 (A reevaluation of Confucius), *Zhongguo shehui kexue* 中國社會科學 (Social sciences in China) (1980) 2: 77–96; republished in Li Zehou, *Zhongguo gudai sixiang shilun* 中國古代思想史論 (On traditional Chinese intellectual history) (Beijing: SDX Joint Publishing, 2008 (1985)), 1–49; English translation by Woei Lien Chong (as "A Reevaluation of Confucianism") in *Sources of Chinese Tradition*, ed. Wm. Theodore de Bary and Richard Lufrano, 2nd ed., vol. 2 (New York: Columbia University Press, 1999), 574–80, and translated by Andrew Lambert (as "Reevaluating Confucius") in Li Zehou, *A History of Classical Chinese Thought* (New York: Routledge, 2020), 1–50.

19. Li, *A History of Classical Chinese Thought*, 42 n. 16.

20. See "The Origin of Abstract Ideas," "The Origin of the Idea of Justice," and "The Origin of the Idea of Good" in Paul Lafargue, *Social and Philosophical Studies*, trans. Charles H. Kerr (Chicago: Charles H. Kerr & Company, 1906).

21. Translator's note: Sandel opens *Justice: What's the Right Thing to Do?* describing Hurricane Charley, which hit Florida in 2004, and asking whether it is just for people to inflate prices on goods and services when they are limited and urgently needed.

22. Translator's note: In this section (and sometimes elsewhere) I have added language to bring out the affective dimension of the term "situations" (*qingjing*), which the author has just explicitly connected with emotions through the character *qing*. The term "situations," while a direct literal rendering of *qingjing*, lacks this affective element, and so a literal rendering here loses part of Li's argument, and leaves it sounding like he merely states situational factors are important in figuring out good and bad—not a particularly revolutionary thesis. But the author is clearly up to much more than that here, emphasizing the importance of "*qing*," here rendered "emotional circumstance," to moral reasoning. Hence, I take the liberty of translating some uses of "situation" (*qingjing*) and "circumstance" (*qingkuang*) as "lived and felt" to help voice this dimension of Li's argument.

23. Sandel, *Justice: What's the Right Thing to Do?*, 9.

24. Translator's note: This general diagram of ethics appears in progressively refined formulations in Li Zehou, *Huiying Sangdeer ji qita* 回應桑德爾及其他 (A response to Michael Sandel and other matters) (Hong Kong: Oxford University Press, 2014), 23; Li, "Response," 1079; and Li Zehou, *Renleixue lishi bentilun* 人類學歷史本體論 (The anthropo-historical ontology: An outline of my philosophy) (Beijing: Renmin wenxue chubanshe, 2019), vol. 1 (*Ethics*), 253. See also Jana S. Rošker, *Becoming Human: Li Zehou's Ethics* (Leiden: Brill, 2020), 299. Further discussion of this schema can be found especially in §3.5 below, as well as in the Introduction, under "The Basic Schema of Li's Ethics."

25. Translator's note: The traditional five cardinal relations are those of ruler and minister, husband and wife, parent and child, older and younger sibling, and

244 | Notes to Appendix

friendship. Confucian teachings assign specific duties and virtues to each role in these relationships.

26. Translator's note: The term being translated as "relationism" is *guanxi zhuyi* 關係主義.

27. Liang Shuming, *Zhongguo wenhua yaoyi*, 91; see chapter 5 of that work, "He wei lunli benwei" 何謂倫理本位 (What is taking ethics as fundamental), for extended discussion of the foundational role of interpersonal relations in traditional Chinese morality.

28. These texts appeared as Yao Wenyuan, *Lun Lin Biao fandang jituan de shehui jichu* 論林彪反黨集團的社會基礎, and Zhang Chunqiao, *Lun dui zichan jieji de quanmian zhuanzheng* 論對資產階級的全面專政, in the March and April 1975 issues of *Hong qi*, respectively. They have been digitized at www.marxistphilosophy.org/Hongqi/75/197504-03.htm and www.marxistphilosophy.org/Hongqi/75/197503-20.htm.

29. The first two statements were published by Mao Zedong in *The People's Daily*, February 22, 1975. The third was made by Mao on April 28, 1969, at the first plenary meeting of the ninth session of the Central Committee of the CPC. The fourth is quoted (without specific citation) in Zhang's article.

30. Li, *Zhongguo gudai sixiang shilun*, 186–87; Li, *A History of Classical Chinese Thought*, 184.

31. Li, *Zhongguo zhexue ruhe dengchang*, 107.

32. John Rawls, *A Theory of Justice*, rev. ed. (Cambridge, MA: The Belknap Press of Harvard University Press, 1999).

33. For discussion of the relationship of the concept of regulative and properly constitutive principle or function to Kant's regulative principle, see below in the last paragraphs of §3.14, "The Priority of the Right over the Good."

34. Sandel, *Justice: What's the Right Thing to Do?*, 226.

35. Translator's note: Li's view of morals and human psychology affirms the accumulative gradual development, or "sedimentation," of morals throughout human history. Similarly, the individual's own moral understanding and psychology is an accumulation of experiences in "education." Through these historical processes, we have metaphysics and the *a priori*. (See also chapter 3 notes 3, 4, 11, and 15, above in this volume.) The interrelated ideas of sedimentation, accumulation, experience becoming *a priori*, and history entering metaphysics are major components of Li's ethics and discussed often in the writings collected here. See especially the elaboration on the accumulative quality of history that opens "History, Ethics, and Metaphysics."

36. See "On the Shamanistic-Historical Tradition" ("Shuo wu-shi chuantong" 說巫史 傳統), originally published in Li, *Jimao wu shuo*; English translation in Li, *The Origins of Chinese Thought*, 11–53.

37. "Honor and Disgrace" (Rong ru 榮辱), *Xunzi*; translation adapted from Eric L. Hutton, *Xunzi: The Complete Text* (Princeton: Princeton University Press, 2014), 29, 27.

Notes to Appendix | 245

38. "Discourse on Ritual" (Li lun 禮論), *Xunzi*; translation adapted from Hutton, *Xunzi*, 201.

39. "Discourse on Ritual" (Li lun 禮論), *Xunzi*; translation adapted from Hutton, *Xunzi*, 201.

40. Translator's note: Li here is explicitly declaring an interpretation of the *Zhongyong* that runs counter to the "later Confucians." The Song Neo-Confucians, who canonized the *Zhongyong* as one of the Four Books, explicated this heavenly bestowed human nature (*xing*) as "principle" (*li* 理) and "virtue" (*de* 德) inherent in all persons, which we fail to follow because of our diverse inherent material constitution (*qi* 氣) (Zhu Xi 朱熹, *Si shu zhangju ji zhu* 四書章句集註 [Collected commentaries on the Four Books] (Beijing: Zhonghua shuju, 2012), 17). Li rejects this reading, instead identifying this human nature precisely as our inherent material constitution. See Li, *A History of Classical Chinese Thought*, 137, for an earlier formulation of the link and distinction between the *Zhongyong* itself and later Neo-Confucian interpretations of it; see Li, *Zhexue gangyao*, 45, for a summary philosophical rejection of the "later Confucian" interpretation of human nature.

41. "On the sequence of the hexagrams" (Xu gua 序卦); translation adapted from Richard John Lynn, *The Classic of the Changes: A New Translation of the I Ching as Interpreted by Wang Bi* (New York: Columbia University Press, 1994), 106.

42. Erin M. Cline, *Confucius, Rawls, and the Sense of Justice* (New York: Fordham University Press, 2013).

43. Translator's note: This idea can be traced to the "Record of Music" (Yue ji 樂記) chapter of the *Record of Ritual*, which states, "The way of notes and sounds is connected with government" (*sheng yin zhi dao, yu zheng tong yi* 聲音之道, 與政通矣).

44. Li, *Zhongguo zhexue ruhe dengchang*, 81.

45. Li, *Lunyu jindu*, 46.

46. Fei Xiaotong, *Xiangtu Zhongguo* 鄉土中國 (*From the Soil: The Foundation of Chinese Society*) (Beijing: Renmin chubanshe, 2008), 30.

47. See *Mencius* 4B28 and the "Yi bin" 議兵 (A debate on military affairs) and "Zi dao" 子道 (The way to be a son) chapters of *Xunzi* (Hutton, *Xunzi*, 155, 328); *Analects* 1.6; *Analects* 12.5.

48. Immanuel Kant, *Groundwork for the Metaphysics of Morals*, ed. and trans. Allen W. Wood (New Haven, CT: Yale University Press, 2002), 37, 49 [Ak 4.421; 4.431].

49. Translator's note: "Universal legislation" here renders "*pubian lifa*" 普遍立法, Li's Chinese term for Kant's idea of willing universal laws.

50. Kant, *Groundwork*, 37 [Ak 4:421].

51. Kant, *Groundwork*, 38–42 [Ak 4:421–24].

52. Sandel, *Justice: What's the Right Thing to Do?*, 134–38. Translator's note: Sandel here admits as much: "You may think that I've worked too hard to save Kant from an implausible position. Kant's claim that it's wrong to lie to the murderer may not ultimately be defensible."

246 | Notes to Appendix

53. Translator's note: Quoting Neo-Confucian thinker Zhang Zai 張載, from *Hengqu yu lu* 橫渠語錄 (Recorded statements of Hengqu [Zhang Zai]). These are the first two of Zhang Zai's famous "four statements" (as identified by Feng Youlan), which reflect four principal aims of human life.

54. In Chinese, *haoran zhi qi* 浩然之气; follows D. C. Lau, trans., Mencius: A Bilingual Edition, rev. ed. (Hong Kong: Chinese University of Hong Kong Press, 2003), 61, and Bryan W. Van Norden, trans., *Mengzi* (Indianapolis: Hackett, 2008), 39.

55. Translation follows Van Norden, 78, with alterations.

56. *Pipan zhexue de pipan: Kangde shuping* 批判哲學的批判：康德述評 (Critique of critical philosophy: A new approach to Kant) (Beijing: Renmin chubanshe, 1979); English version published as *A New Approach to Kant: A Confucian-Marxist's Viewpoint*, trans. Christopher Ahn and Jeanne Haizhen Allen (Singapore: Springer, 2018).

57. Immanuel Kant, *Critique of Pure Reason (Kritik der reinen Vernunft)*, trans. Paul Guyer and Allen W. Wood (Cambridge: Cambridge University Press, 1998), A805/B833.

58. From "Jiang gushi de ren" 講故事的人 (Storyteller), Mo Yan's speech in receiving the Nobel Prize.

59. Sandel, *What Money Can't Buy*, chapter 3.

60. Allen W. Wood, *Kant's Ethical Thought* (Cambridge: Cambridge University Press, 1999), 244–49.

61. Wood, *Kant's Ethical Thought*, 244.

62. Roger J. Sullivan, *An Introduction to Kant's Ethics* (New York: Cambridge University Press, 1994), 88.

63. Li Zehou, *Pipan zhexue de pipan: Kangde shuping* 批判哲學的批判：康德述評 (Kant in a new key), rev. 6th ed. (Beijing: SDX Joint Publishing, 2007), 459–60.

64. Translator's note: The case that Sandel discusses involved four crew members stranded at sea. Three of them, Dudley, Stephens, and Brooks, killed and ate their ill compatriot on the twentieth day of their misfortune, only to be rescued a few days later. Sandel uses this famous case from the British courts to comment on moral principles (e.g., utilitarianism versus deontology). See Sandel, *Justice: What's the Right Thing to Do?*, 31–33.

65. Michael J. Sandel, ed., *Justice: A Reader* (Oxford: Oxford University Press, 2007).

66. Originally published in Li, *Jimao wushuo*; English translation in Li, *The Origins of Chinese Thought*, 184–210.

67. Li, *The Origins of Chinese Thought*, 200.

68. Xi ci I; translation follows Lynn, *The Classic of Changes*, 53, with alterations.

69. Translator's note: This is a major theme of Sandel's arguments in *Democracy's Discontent*.

Notes to Appendix | 247

70. Michael J. Sandel, *A Case against Perfection: Ethics in the Age of Genetic Engineering* (Cambridge, MA: The Belknap Press of Harvard University Press, 2007).

71. Translator's note: Li gives a further closely related argument above, in "On Ethics," concluding discussion of Intuition and Inherent Goodness in Mencius and Xunzi. Elsewhere he describes "the mysticality of rationality" as falling within the scope of aesthetics and religion, and as something that cannot be rationally understood or explained but that can be rationally thought about (*Renleixue lishi bentilun* (2016), 569).

72. This little book is for children to learn Confucianism.

73. Sandel, *Justice: What's the Right Thing to Do?*, 73.

74. Li Zehou, "Zhexue tanxun lu" 哲學探尋錄 (A record of philosophical inquiry), *Yuan dao* 原道2 (1994); John Rawls, *Political Liberalism* (New York: Columbia University Press, 1993).

75. "The end of history" is a phrase and theory made famous by Francis Fukuyama, first in his essay "The End of History?" in *The National Interest* 16 (1989): 3–18, and then in his book *The End of History and the Last Man* (New York: Free Press, 1992). With the conclusion of the Cold War, Fukuyama argued that historical social development had, ideologically and politically, reached its "final form" in Western liberal democracy.

76. Sandel, *Justice: What's the Right Thing to Do?*, 261.

77. Li, *Pipan zhexue de pipan* (2007), 457.

78. Li, *Lunyu jindu*, 7–8.

79. Li Zehou, *The Chinese Aesthetic Tradition*. trans. Maija Bell Samei (Honolulu: University of Hawai'i Press, 2010); Marthe Chandler, review of *The Chinese Aesthetic Tradition* by Li Zehou, *Philosophy East and West* 62 (1) (2012): 150.

80. In *Jimao wu shuo*; reprinted in *Lishi bentilun* and *Jimao wu shuo* 歷史本體論 己卯五說 (Historical ontology and Five essays from 1999), expanded edition (Beijing: SDX Joint Publishing, 2008), 130–55.

81. Translator's note: Foxconn is a tech manufacturer that gained international recognition in 2010 for the high rate of suicides by its employees in Chinese factories.

82. "Li Zehou: Zhongguo xianzai xuyaode shi shehui lixiang" 李澤厚：中國現在需要的是社會理想 (Li Zehou: What China needs now is a social ideal), *Zhongguo qiyejia* 中國企業家 (China entrepreneur) 2012 (20).

83. See "Chuni Ruxue de shenceng jiegou shuo" 初擬儒學深層結構說 (Preliminary remarks on the deep structures of Confucianism) in *Huawen wenxue* 華文文學 (Chinese literature) 2010 (5) and *Shiji xin meng* 世紀新夢 (Dream of a new century) (Hefei: Anhui wenyi chubanshe, 1998).

84. In Li, *Shiji xin meng*, and Li Zehou, *Za zhu ji* 雜著集 (Miscellaneous writings) (Beijing: SDX Joint Publishing, 2008).

Bibliography

Ames, Roger T., and Henry Rosemont Jr., trans. 1998. *The Analects of Confucius: A Philosophical Translation*. New York: Ballantine Books.

Ames, Roger T., and Jinhua Jia, eds. 2015. *Li Zehou and Confucian Philosophy*. Honolulu: University of Hawai'i Press.

Benedict, Ruth. 1989. *The Chrysanthemum and the Sword*. Boston: Mariner Books.

Berlin, Isaiah. 2002. *Liberty: Incorporating "Four Essays on Liberty."* Ed. Henry Hardy. Oxford: Oxford University Press.

Boehm, Christopher. 2012. *Moral Origins: The Evolution of Virtue, Altruism, and Shame*. New York: Basic Books.

Carleo, Robert Anthony III. 2020a. "Confucian Post-Liberalism." *Asian Studies* 8 (1): 147–65.

———. 2020b. "Is Free Will Confucian? Li Zehou's Confucian Revision of the Kantian Will." *Philosophy East and West* 70 (1): 63–83.

Chan, Wing-Tsit. 1963. *A Source Book in Chinese Philosophy*. Princeton, NJ: Princeton University Press.

Chandler, Marthe. 2012. Review of *The Chinese Aesthetic Tradition* by Li Zehou. *Philosophy East and West* 62 (1): 147–50.

Chinese Text Project. 2022. ctext.org.

Cline, Erin M. 2013. *Confucius, Rawls, and the Sense of Justice*. New York: Fordham University Press.

Confucius (Kongzi 孔子). 1992. *The Analects*. 2nd ed. Trans. D. C. Lau. Hong Kong: Chinese University of Hong Kong Press.

D'Ambrosio, Paul. 2020. "Li Zehou's 'Harmony Is Higher Than Justice': Context and a Collaborative Future." *Asian Studies* 8 (1): 127–46.

D'Ambrosio, Paul J., Robert A. Carleo III, and Andrew Lambert. 2016. "On Li Zehou's Philosophy: An Introduction by Three Translators." *Philosophy East and West* 66 (4): 1057–67.

de Bary, Wm. Theodore, and Richard Lufrano, eds. 2000. *Sources of Chinese Tradition*. New York: Columbia University Press.

250 | Bibliography

Darwin, Charles. 1982. *The Descent of Man, and Selection in Relation to Sex.* Princeton, NJ: Princeton University Press.

Doris, John M., and the Moral Psychology Research Group. 2010. *The Moral Psychology Handbook.* Oxford: Oxford University Press.

Dworkin, Ronald. 2011. *Justice for Hedgehogs.* Cambridge, MA: The Belknap Press of Harvard University Press.

Einstein, Albert. 1981. *Albert Einstein: The Human Side.* Ed. Helen Dukas and Banesh Hoffman. Princeton: Princeton University Press.

Engels, Friedrich. 2000. *Ludwig Feuerbach and the End of Classical German Philosophy.* London: ElecBook.

Fei Xiaotong. 2008. *Xiangtu Zhongguo* 鄉土中國 (*From the Soil: The Foundation of Chinese Society*). Beijing: Renmin chubanshe.

Feyerabend, Paul. 1987. *Farewell to Reason.* New York: Verso.

Fukuyama, Francis. 1989. "The End of History?" *The National Interest* 16: 3–18.

———. 1992. *The End of History and the Last Man.* New York: Free Press.

Griffiths, James. 2016. "This Is Your Brain on LSD, Literally." *CNN*, updated April 13. edition.cnn.com/2016/04/12/health/lsd-brain-imaging/.

Heidegger, Martin. 1978. *Basic Writings.* Ed. D. F. Krell. London: Routledge.

Kant, Immanuel. 1960. *Religion within the Limits of Reason Alone.* Trans. Theodore M. Greene and Hoyt H. Hudson. New York: Harper.

———. 1998. *Critique of Pure Reason.* Trans. Paul Guyer and Allen W. Wood. Cambridge: Cambridge University Press.

———. 2002. *Groundwork for the Metaphysics of Morals.* Ed. and trans. Allen W. Wood. New Haven, CT: Yale University Press.

Lafargue, Paul. 1906. *Social and Philosophical Studies.* Trans. Charles H. Kerr. Chicago: Charles H. Kerr & Company.

Li Zehou 李泽厚. 1979. *Pipan zhexue de pipan: Kangde shuping* 批判哲學的批判: 康德述評 (Critique of critical philosophy: A new approach to Kant). Beijing: Renmin chubanshe.

———. 1980. "Kongzi zai pingjia" 孔子再評價 (A reevaluation of Confucius). *Zhongguo shehui kexue* 中國社會科學 (2): 77–96.

———. 1990. *Zou wo ziji de lu* 走我自己的路 (Walking my own path). Taipei: Fengyun shidai chubanshe.

———. 1994. "Zhexue tanxun lu" 哲學探尋錄 (A record of philosophical inquiry). *Yuan dao* 原道 2.

———. 1997. "Chuni Ruxue shenceng jiegou shuo" 初擬儒學深層結構說 (Preliminary remarks on the deep structures of Confucianism). In *Rujia sixiang de xiandai quanshi* 儒家思想的現代詮釋, ed. Li Minghui 李明輝, 59–78. Taipei: Zhongyang yanjiuyuan zhongguo wen zhe yanjiusuo.

———. 1998. *Shiji xin meng* 世紀新夢 (Dream of a new century). Hefei: Anhui wenyi chubanshe.

———. 1999a. "Subjectivity and 'Subjectality': A Response." *Philosophy East and West* 49 (2): 174–83.

———. 1999b. "A Supplementary Explanation of Subjectivity." *Contemporary Chinese Thought* 31 (2): 26–31.
———. 1999c. *Jimao wu shuo* 己卯五說 (Five essays from 1999). Beijing: Zhongguo dianying chubanshe.
———. 1999d. "A Reevaluation of Confucianism." Trans. Woei Lien Chong. In *Sources of Chinese Tradition*, ed. Wm. Theodore de Bary, 2nd ed., vol. 2, 574–80. New York: Columbia University Press.
———. 2002. *Lishi bentilun* 歷史本體論 (Historical ontology). Beijing: SDX Joint Publishing.
———. 2007. *Pipan zhexue de pipan: Kangde shuping* 批判哲學的批判: 康德述評 (Kant in a new key), rev. 6th ed. Beijing: SDX Joint Publishing.
———. 2008a. *Zhongguo jindai sixiang shilun* 中國近代思想史論 (On modern Chinese intellectual history). Beijing: SDX Joint Publishing.
———. 2008b. *Zhongguo gudai sixiang shilun* 中國古代思想史論 (On traditional Chinese intellectual history). Beijing: SDX Joint Publishing.
———. 2008c. *Za zhu ji* 雜著集 (Miscellaneous writings). Beijing: SDX Joint Publishing.
———. 2008d. *Shiyong lixing yu legan wenhua* 實用理性與樂感文化 (Pragmatic reason and a culture of optimism). Bejing: SDX Joint Publishing.
———. 2008e. *Lunyu jindu* 論語今讀 (Reading the Analects today). Beijing: SDX Joint Publishing.
———. 2008f. *Lishi bentilun* and *Jimao wu shuo* 歷史本體論 己卯五說 (Historical ontology and Five essays from 1999), expanded edition. Beijing: SDX Joint Publishing.
———. 2008g. *Renleixue lishi bentilun* 人類學歷史本體論 (Anthropological-historical ontology). Tianjin: Tianjin shehui kexue yuan chubanshe.
———. 2010a. *The Chinese Aesthetic Tradition*. Trans. Maija Bell Samei. Honolulu: University of Hawai'i Press.
———. 2010b. *Lunlixue gangyao* 倫理學綱要 (Ethics). Beijing: Renmin Ribao chubanshe.
———. "Chuni Ruxue de shenceng jiegou shuo" 初擬儒學深層結構說 (Preliminary remarks on the deep structures of Confucianism). *Huawen wenxue* 華文文學 (Chinese literature) 2010 (5).
———. 2011. *Zhexue gangyao* 哲學綱要 (Outline of a philosophy). Beijing: Peking University Press.
———. 2012a. *Zhongguo zhexue ruhe dengchang* 中國哲學如何登場 (How can Chinese philosophy go on stage?). Shanghai: Shanghai yiwen chubanshe.
———. 2012b. "Li Zehou: Zhongguo xianzai xuyaode shi shehui lixiang" 李澤厚: 中國現在需要的是社會理想 (Li Zehou: What China needs now is a social ideal). *Zhongguo qiyejia* 中國企業家 (China entrepreneur) 20.
———. 2014. *Huiying Sangdeer ji qita* 回應桑德爾及其他 (A response to Michael Sandel and other matters). Hong Kong: Oxford University Press; Beijing: SDX Joint Publishing.

252 | Bibliography

———. 2015a. *Shenme shi daode? Li Zehou lunlixue taolunban shilu* 什麼是道德?——李澤厚倫理學討論班實錄 (What is morality? A record of discussions of Li Zehou's ethics). Shanghai: Huadong shifan daxue chubanshe.

———. 2015b. "Da Gaogeng sanwen" 答高更三問. *Zhonghua dushu bao* 中华讀書报 (November 4, 2015).

———. 2015c. *Li Zehou and Confucian Philosophy*. Ed. Roger T. Ames and Jinhua Jia. Honolulu: University of Hawai'i Press.

———. 2016a. *Renleixue lishi bentilun* 人類學歷史本體論 (A theory of anthropo-historical ontology). Qingdao: Qingdao chubanshe.

———. 2016b. "A Response to Michael Sandel and Other Matters." Trans. Paul D'Ambrosio and Robert A. Carleo. *Philosophy East and West* 66 (4): 1068–1147.

———. 2017. *Lunlixue gangyao xupian* 倫理學綱要續篇 (Further discussions of ethics). Beijing: SDX Joint Publishing.

———. 2018a. *The Origins of Chinese Thought: From Shamanism to Ritual Regulations and Humaneness*. Trans. Robert A. Carleo III. Leiden: Brill.

———. 2018b. *A New Approach to Kant: A Confucian-Marxist's Viewpoint*. Trans. Christopher Ahn and Jeanne Haizhen Allen. Singapore: Springer.

———. 2019a. *Lunlixue xinshuo shuyao* 倫理學新說述要 (A new sketch of ethics). Beijing: Shijie tushu, 2019.

———. 2019b. *Cong meixue liangchongxing dao qing benti* 從美感兩重性到情本體 (From the dualistic nature of aesthetic sensibility to emotion as substance). Jinan: Shandong wenyi chubanshe.

———. 2019c. *Renleixue lishi bentilun* 人類學歷史本體論 (The anthropo-historical ontology: An outline of my philosophy). Beijing: Renmin wenxue chubanshe.

———. 2020a. *A History of Classical Chinese Thought*. Trans. Andrew Lambert. New York: Routledge.

———. 2020b. *Wode zhexue tigang* 我的哲學題綱 (An outline of my philosophy), 2nd ed., Taipei: Sanmin shuju.

Li Zehou and Liu Yuedi 劉悅笛. 2014a. "Cong 'qing benti' fansi zhengzhi zhexue" 從「情本體」反思政治哲學 (Reflecting on political philosophy from "emotion as substance"). *Kaifang shidai* (4): 194–215.

———. 2014b. " 'Qing benti' shi shijiede" 「情本體」是 世界的 ("Emotion as substance" belongs to the world). *Tansuo yu zhengming* (4): 4–9.

———. 2014c. "Guanyu 'qing benti' de Zhongguo zhexue duihua lu" 關於「情本體」的中國哲學對話錄 (Dialogue on Chinese philosophy's "emotion as substance"). *Wen shi zhe* (3): 18–29.

———. 2017. "Li Zehou, Liu Yuedi 2017 nian zhexue duitan lu" 李澤厚、劉悅笛2017 年哲學對談錄 (Li Zehou and Liu Yuedi's 2017 philosophical dialogue). *Shehui kexuejia* (7): 39–48.

———. 2018. "Lunlixue zatan: Li Zehou, Liu Yuedi 2018 nian duitan lu" 倫理學雜談——李澤厚、劉悅笛2018年對談錄 (Thought rambling on ethics: A dialogue between Li Zehou and Liu Yuedi). *Hunan shifan daxue shehui kexue xuebao* (5): 1–17.

Liang Shuming 梁漱溟. 2013 (1949). *Zhongguo wenhua yaoyi* 中國文化要義 (The essence of Chinese culture). Taipei: Taiwan Commercial Press.

Lynn, Richard John, trans. 1994. *The Classic of the Changes: A New Translation of the I Ching as Interpreted by Wang Bi.* New York: Columbia University Press.

Mencius (Mengzi 孟子). 2003. *Mencius: A Bilingual Edition*, rev. ed. Trans. D. C. Lau. Hong Kong: Chinese University of Hong Kong Press.

———. 2008. *Mengzi: With Selections from Traditional Commentaries.* Trans. Bryan W. Van Norden. Indianapolis: Hackett.

Pinker, Steven. 2018. *Enlightenment Now: The Case for Reason, Science, Humanism, and Progress.* New York: Viking.

———. 2019. "Enlightenment Wars: Some Reflections on 'Enlightenment Now,' One Year Later." *Quillette*, January 14, 2019. quillette.com/2019/01/14/ enlightenment-wars-some-reflections-on-enlightenment-now-one-year-later/ Pinker.

Rošker, Jana S. 2020. *Becoming Human: Li Zehou's Ethics.* Leiden: Brill.

Rawls, John. 1993. *Political Liberalism.* New York: Columbia University Press.

———. 1999. *A Theory of Justice*, rev. ed. Cambridge, MA: The Belknap Press of Harvard University Press.

———. 2000. *Lectures on the History of Moral Philosophy.* Ed. Barbara Herman. Cambridge, MA: Harvard University Press.

Sandel, Michael J. 1996. *Democracy's Discontent: America in Search of a Public Philosophy.* Cambridge, MA: Harvard University Press.

———. 2007a. *A Case against Perfection: Ethics in the Age of Genetic Engineering.* Cambridge, MA: The Belknap Press of Harvard University Press.

———. 2007b, ed. *Justice: A Reader.* Oxford: Oxford University Press.

———. 2009. *Justice: What's the Right Thing to Do?* New York: Farrar, Straus and Giroux.

———. 2012. *What Money Can't Buy: The Moral Limits of Markets.* New York: Farrar, Straus and Giroux.

Sullivan, Roger J. 1994. *An Introduction to Kant's Ethics.* New York: Cambridge University Press.

Tiwald, Justin, and Bryan W. Van Norden, eds. 2014. *Readings in Later Chinese Philosophy: Han Dynasty to the 10th Century.* Indianapolis: Hackett.

Wang Yang-Ming. 1963. *Instructions for Practical Living and Other Confucian Writings.* Trans. Wing-Tsit Chan. New York: Columbia University Press.

Wood, Allen W. 1999. *Kant's Ethical Thought.* Cambridge: Cambridge University Press.

Xunzi 荀子. 2014. *Xunzi: The Complete Text.* Trans. Eric L. Hutton. Princeton, NJ: Princeton University Press.

Yan Fu 嚴復. 1986. *Lun shibian zhi ji* 論世變之亟 (On the speed of world changes). *Yan Fu ji* 嚴復集 (Collected works of Yan Fu), vol. 1. Beijing: Zhonghua shuju.

254 | Bibliography

Yu Zhenhua 郁振華. 2016. "Zai lun daode de nengli zhi zhi: Ping Huang Yong jiaoshou de liangzhi quanshi" 再論道德的能力之知——評黃勇教授的良知詮釋 (Revisiting moral knowing how: An evaluation of Huang Yong's explication of moral conscience). *Xueshu yuekan* 學術月刊 (Academic monthly) (December).

Zhouyi zhengyi 周易正義 (Correct meaning of the Book of Changes). 2000. In *Shisan jing zhushu zhengli ben* 十三經注疏 整理本 (Annotated Thirteen Classics). Beijing: Peking University Press.

Zhu Xi 朱熹. 2012. *Si shu zhangju ji zhu* 四書章句集註 (Collected commentaries on the Four Books). Beijing: Zhonghua shuju.

Index

abortion, 16, 41, 192, 202, 204

absoluteness (absolutism), ethical and rational, 49, 78, 83, 87, 124, 167, 183, 203, 207, 232n35; psychological, 15–17, 27, 39, 71, 84–85, 170, 173, 187–88; of moral norms, 5, 14–17, 70–72, 85, 99, 187–89, 192

aesthetics, 54, 107, 137, 171; as primarily emotional, 6, 73; as "the melting of reason into emotion," 22, 26, 122, 191; aesthetic metaphysics, 80, 104, 114–116; aesthetic intuition, 33, 182

an 安. *See* at ease

an shen li ming 安身立命. *See* placing oneself morally at ease and establishing a sense of spiritual belonging

Analects (*Lunyu* 論語), 45, 47, 63, 88, 91, 101, 153, 159, 177, 180, 217; on learning, 88, 104, 123; on ritual, 29, 31, 155, 170, 187; on humaneness (*ren*), 63, 187, 191

analytic philosophy, 23, 124, 129

antinomy of history and ethics, 15, 66, 72, 78, 99–100, 110, 120, 149

anthropocentrism, 107–109

anthropological historical ontology, 17, 38, 41, 53–54, 56, 61, 104, 107, 109, 117, 192, 234n11

Aristotle, 22, 89, 121, 125, 132; virtue ethics, 135, 157, 165, 202, 212; equality, 89, 133, 159

at ease (*an* 安), 49, 85, 153, 236n26

Barth, Karl, 52

beauty, 33, 70, 95, 232n32

Bentham, Jeremy, 136–38. *See also* utilitarianism

Bernstein, Eduard, 112

Bible, 36, 83, 101–102, 107–108, 156, 196, 200

biotechnology, 194; genetic engineering, 56–57, 67, 73, 194–95; neuro enhancement, 57

Boehm, Christopher, 28–31, 224–25n9. *See also* sociobiology

Book of Changes, 36, 39, 48, 64, 76, 156, 161, 191, 239n43, 240n48, 241n9

Book of Documents (*Shangshu* 尚書), 36

Buddhism, 45, 47, 54, 97, 115, 197; Chan (Zen), 38

categorical imperative, 17, 23, 71, 170, 181, 191, 223n12; Kant's formulations of, 38–41, 168–69

Cai Yuanpei 蔡元培, 190, 240n54

Cassirer, Ernst, 106

255

256 | Index

Christianity, 14, 26, 36–37, 47–53 *passim*, 69, 189, 192; Catholicism, 86, 204; as a two world system, 96; as traditional religious morals, 89; original sin, 37, 53, 105, 177; equality, 90, 133. *See also* God

civic education, 43, 196–97, 200, 206

civic virtue, 86, 192, 197

common good, 55, 151–52, 192, 197–99, 212–13

Communism, 41, 81, 84, 112, 144, 146, 197, 215, 236n23, 240n51

Communitarianism, 3, 22, 42, 67, 89, 119, 135, 142, 157, 198, 201, 213–14

conformance (accordance) with emotions (*heqing* 合情), 44, 150, 187

Confucius (Kongzi 孔子), 35–37, 44–51 *passim*, 54, 61, 70, 162, 170, 180, 187, 191, 217; on learning, 88, 101, 104, 123, 177; rooting ritual regulations in humaneness, 31, 152–53; plus Kant, 212, 214. *See also* happiness of Confucius and Yan Hui

continuous extension of human existence (*renlei de shengcun yanxu* 人類的生存延續), 17–18, 27, 30, 37, 39, 64, 67, 71, 108–109, 111, 115, 130, 138, 152–53, 155, 185, 189–93, 195, 202, 204, 217. *See also* totality of humankind

contractualism, 42–43, 141, 143, 160, 186, 210, 214

Critique of Critical Philosophy (*Pipan zhexue de pipan* 批判哲學的批判), 29, 54, 171, 184–85, 208

cultural-psychological formation (structure) (*wenhua-xinli jiegou* 文化心理結構), 46–47, 95–96, 100, 105, 120, 240n51

culture of guilt, 103, 238n41

culture of optimism (*legan wenhua* 樂感文化), 37, 46, 48, 57, 64, 67–68, 102, 105, 218, 238–39n41

culture of shame, 218, 238–39n41

Darwin, Charles, 31, 182, 225n18

Deleuze, Gilles, 216

difference principle, 150–51, 213

discernment (*quan* 權), 52, 138, 164, 187, 201

Dong Zhongshu 董仲舒, 35–36, 63, 186, 211, 231n13

drawing history into metaphysics. *See* history entering metaphysics

du 度. *See* proper measure

East China Normal University, 21, 23–24, 26, 59, 224n1, n4, n5

Einstein, Albert, 53, 98

equality, 140–48, 156–60, 167–68, 183, 196–201; Christian, 90, 133; liberal, 32, 40, 55, 141–42; gender, 89–90, 148; today, 151, 206; versus relationism, 42–43, 135, 165

emotio-rational structure (*qing-li jiegou* 情理結構), 6, 106, 124, 126–27, 132, 152, 166, 178–80; its importance, 206, 211, 214; components of, 22, 26; historically formed, 34, 95; traditional China's, 43–46, 49–52, 155, 162, 217; emphasized in Confucianism, 56, 65, 101, 120–21, 158, 212; relational, 135, 150, 152, 160–61; and human nature, 73, 123, 170, 182

emotion (*qing* 情): as *qing* 情, 6, 10, 62, 73, 121, 129–31, 173, 228n43, n45, 230n4, 242n10, 243n22; as part of morality, 6–9, 10–12, 26,

41, 59–60, 65, 69–70, 106, 120, 129, 153, 174–75, 234n9

emotion as substance (*qing benti* 情本體), 79–80, 126–29, 234–35n12; emphasis on relations, 12, 135, 206; importance today, 42, 65, 162–63, 203; as distinctively Confucian, 51, 120–21, 210–11, 228n44

emotional cosmology, 3–4, 36, 64–65, 88, 102–105, 161, 165, 192, 209, 239n42

emotionality (emotional situatedness), 10–12, 129–30, 133, 134, 152, 161, 173–74, 178, 190, 192, 214, 242n10, 243n22; the Way begins in emotionality (*dao shi yu qing* 道始於情), 11, 121, 130, 192, 213, 242n10; rituals are generated from emotionality (*li sheng yu qing* 禮生於情), 11, 121, 130, 154, 192, 242n11

emotion and reason, integration of (*qing-li* 情理), 3, 6, 8–9, 22, 44–47, 101, 120–24, 133, 160–61, 174, 179, 186–87; melting of reason into emotion (*lixing ronghua* 理性融化), 22, 26, 122, 191

empiricism, 1, 23, 32, 34, 75–77, 136, 153, 177, 189, 202, 208

empirical (experience) becoming *a priori*, 32, 75, 79, 101, 174, 214, 233n4

Engels, Friedrich, 110, 112, 189, 194, 215, 232n33

Enlightenment, 67, 78, 82–83, 88, 107, 126, 141, 214, 226n35; anti-Enlightenment, 16, 24, 42, 126

establishing oneself through ritual (*li yu li* 立於禮), 29, 65, 123, 177, 232n32

euthanasia, 169, 203, 204

evil, 15–16, 34–37, 171–81 *passim*, 187–91; individual conceptions of, 9–10, 166; punishable, 53; eradication of, 100; radical evil, 72, 103

Feng Youlan 馮友蘭, 86, 116, 157, 235n13, 237n28, 246n53

Feyerabend, Paul, 82

filial piety, 31, 42–43, 50, 61, 63, 87, 99, 152, 162, 181, 202–203

Foucault, Michel, 81, 216

four arrows, model of, 9–12, 173–75, 178, 190, 210

four stages of Confucianism, 106, 121, 213, 239n45, 242n12

Four-Seven debates, 100

freedom (liberty), 54–55, 141–44, 196–201, 206–208; social and economic freedom, 41–43, 66, 193, 204; and modernity, 184; as moral progress, 148; of belief, 197; and equality, 133; and utilitarianism, 137; of choice, 27, 139–40, 180, 201; free individuals, 157–58, 160, 163, 168, 182; free will, 27, 38–39, 60–61, 70–72, 92–95, 103, 167–71, 174–76, 182–91 *passim*, 195–96, 223n12, 234n11, 236n23, 237–38n33, 239n42; and determinism, 114

ganxing de shenmi 感性的神秘. *See* mysticality of sensibility

Gauguin, Paul, 57

gay marriage, 40, 193–94, 204

global warming (climate change), 109, 111

God, 10, 17, 26, 36, 47, 51–53, 83–84, 88–90, 93, 97, 101–109 *passim*, 114, 116–17, 125, 127, 161, 174, 184–85, 216–17, 236n23

258 | Index

greater self (*da wo* 大我), 54, 67, 113
Guan Yu 關羽, 101
Guan Zhong 管仲, 187
Guyer, Paul, 185

Han Yu 韓愈, 103
happiness of Confucius and Yan Hui
   (*Kong-Yan lechu* 孔顏樂處), 37, 114
harmony, 102, 110, 120, 133, 150,
   152–53, 158–60, 163, 165, 210–11,
   215; is higher than justice, 89, 120,
   152, 165, 208–210
Hawking, Stephen, 98, 109
Hayek, Friedrich, 151, 182
heaven, 48, 110, 127, 156, 192,
   195, 210; as *tian* 天, 36, 53, 101,
   235n15; Christian, 105; the Way
   of heaven, 15–16, 76, 78, 80–81,
   84, 88, 96–102, 104, 109–111,
   114–15, 238n39; the will of heaven
   (heavenly decree, *tianming* 天命),
   39, 87, 99, 101; heavenly heart-
   mind (*tianxin* 天心), 36, 211;
   heavenly principle (*tianli* 天理),
   17, 35, 49, 62–63, 72, 85, 121, 155;
   heaven's action is robust (*tian xing
   jian* 天行健), 48, 64, 103, 241n9
Hegel, G. F. W., 76, 183–84, 209;
   criticism of Kant, 72, 168, 198;
   definition of philosophy, 124;
   distinction between ethics and
   morals, 172; historicism, 78, 132,
   213, 232n33
Heidegger, Martin, 21–22, 98, 111,
   125, 127, 216, 227n42
historicism, 4, 24, 67, 85, 130, 132,
   207, 209, 215; Anti-historicism, 42;
   New historicism, 80
history proceeds in the midst of
   tragedy, 15, 66, 72, 120, 141,
   239n41
history entering metaphysics (*lishi ru
   xingershang* 歷史入形而上), 9, 54,

75, 78–79, 100, 104, 115, 229n67,
   233n3, 235n15
human nature, 49–51, 96, 102–104,
   156, 187–90, 231n22, 245n40;
   good or bad, 34–36, 64–66, 177;
   in neo-Confucianism, 62–63; a
   priori, 83, 86–87; animalistic, 88; as
   the emotio-rational structure and
   humanization of nature, 126–27,
   160, 166; as moral psychology, 39,
   41, 73, 169–71, 175
humaneness (*ren* 仁), 62–63, 100, 153,
   161–62; rooting ritual regulations
   in, 31, 129, 153, 191; being internal,
   32–33; as emotional role relation,
   43, 86, 158; and human nature, 49;
   Confucius on, 50, 61, 70, 170, 190;
   and the Way of Heaven, 36, 76, 104
Hume, David, 44, 101, 121, 175,
   181–82; on sympathy, 69, 157,
   166, 177; is-ought separation, 108;
   supplementing Kant, 64, 175
Humeanism, 59, 65

individualism, 2–3, 12–13, 17, 35,
   133–36, 161, 178, 183–84, 203, 210;
   anti-individualism, 89; the atomic
   individual, 54–55, 57, 67, 127, 135,
   140–41, 165, 183–84, 190, 201–202,
   206
individuality, 12, 40, 43, 49, 66, 92, 135
innate goodness, 32–37, 50, 61–66,
   92, 103, 177, 239n42
intellectual intuition (*zhi de zhijue* 智
   的直覺), 37
intuitionism, 7–8, 32–33, 182, 239n42
Islam, 47, 56, 71, 84, 113, 193, 197,
   200, 216

James, William, 37
Judaism, 47, 216
justice, 129–33, 152–53, 163–64,
   199; historical, 76, 141; complexly

situated, 138, 147–48; procedural justice, 197, 200–201, 204; formal justice, 143, 164, 202, 204, 206; sense of justice, *see under* Rawls, John. *See also* harmony is higher than justice

Kang Youwei 康有為, 194, 208
Kant, Immanuel, 38–40, 166–78, 181–85, 195, 212–14; rationalism, 5–7, 92, 101, 223n12; the transcendent(al), 88, 97–98; transcendental illusion, 93, 114, 144; and Hegel, 76, 78, 198, 209; the starry heavens above me, 98, 102; radical evil, 72, 103, 176; humans as ends, 12–13, 17, 24, 38–41, 54, 140, 167–69, 186, 202. *See also* categorical imperative
Kierkegaard, Søren, 83, 87
Kohlberg, Lawrence, 83, 85–88, 172, 237n27
Kongzi 孔子. *See* Confucius
Kong-Yan lechu 孔顏樂處. *See* Happiness of Confucius and Yan Hui
Koran, 196, 200

Lafargue, Paul, 131
Laozi 老子, 76, 125
learning (*xue* 學), 26, 32, 61–62, 88, 102, 104, 123, 177–78; learning to be human, 26, 123
Legalism, 45, 47, 65, 211
Leibniz, G. W., 102
li 理. *See* principle
Li Rui 李銳, 53
Liang Shuming 梁漱溟, 42–44, 128, 135, 157
liberty. *See* freedom
liberalism, 2–3, 12–13, 17, 41–42, 54–55, 67, 62, 89, 135–36, 139–43, 148, 150–52, 157, 167–69, 182–84,

193, 197–203, 209, 212–14; liberal principles, 24, 40, 190; liberal democracy, 199, 211; egalitarian liberalism, 129, 139, 151; anti-liberalism, 42, 142–44; libertarianism, 139, 182, 204
Liji 禮記. See *Record of Ritual*
Liu Shipei 劉師培, 130
Locke, John, 141, 143, 157, 183–84, 214
Lu Xiangshan 陸象山, 7, 238n35
Lunyu 論語. See *Analects*

Ma Zu 媽祖, 101
MacIntyre, Alasdair, 89–90, 135, 161
Marx, Karl, 84, 112, 143–46, 157, 208–209, 215, 240n51; and Kant, 40, 141, 183; and Hegel, 76, 132, 157, 184, 198
Marxism, 4, 24, 84, 112, 143, 151, 183
Mencius (Mengzi 孟子), 32–37, 59–70 *passim*, 153, 190–91; and emotional cosmology, 4, 102–104; on proper measure, 110; on relations, 156, 159; on empathy, 166; moral psychology of, 87–88, 92, 100, 170–71; on human nature, 49–50, 177–78
Mengzi 孟子. *See* Mencius
Mao Zedong 毛澤東 (Chairman Mao), 35, 144–45, 187, 194, 244n29
metaphysics, 4, 75, 98–99, 125, 192, 229n67, 233n3; neo-Confucian, 63, 213; inseparable from the physical, 79–81; as serving human life, 109, 114–15. *See also* history entering metaphysics
melting of reason into emotion (*lixing ronghua* 理性融化). *See under* emotion and reason, integration of
modern social morals, 13, 17, 37, 40–41, 43, 56, 65–66, 88–89, 134, 141–42, 149, 151–52, 160–61, 163,

260 | Index

modern social morals *(continued)*
165, 168, 184, 196–98, 200–216
passim, 226n35
Mou Zongsan 牟宗三, 35, 37, 48, 87,
97, 212–13
mysticality of reason (*lixing de shenmi*
理性的神秘), 38, 98, 195, 227n39,
247n71
mysticality of sensibility (*ganxing de
shenmi* 感性的神秘), 38

Nagel, Thomas, 5
Nazis, 84, 139, 181, 189, 216
Nietzsche, Friedrich Wilhelm, 81–82,
184, 214–16, 235n18
nihilism, 54, 115, 184
noumena, 102, 126, 195, 235n12

one-world outlook, 46–53, 56, 102,
104; versus two-world outlook, 51,
96–97, 101, 121
original sin, 37, 53, 66, 102–105,
238n41
overlapping consensus. *See under*
Rawls

Parfit, Derek, 5
phenomenology, 22
philosophy of mind, 22, 93–94,
124–25, 127, 129, 179
Pinker, Steven, 77–78, 82
placing oneself morally at ease and
establishing a sense of spiritual
belonging (*an shen li ming* 安身
立命), 52–53, 56, 85, 87, 235n17,
229n64, 236n26
Plato, 101, 125, 194
political art, 150, 205–206, 209
postmodernism, 16, 22, 24, 54, 55, 78,
80–82, 89, 126, 184
pragmatic reason (*shiyong lixing* 實用
理性), 46, 48, 65, 72, 76, 133, 214,
218, 234n6

priority of the right over the good,
152, 163, 193, 198, 200–209, 213
proper measure (*du* 度), 22, 30, 72,
75, 78, 110–11, 128, 133, 147–50,
201, 205, 208, 215
public reason, 65, 141, 153, 160,
163–65, 201, 204–206, 214
public virtue, 165, 181, 197, 199,
206–207

quan 權. *See* discernment

rationalism, 4–9, 12, 89, 161, 223n12,
239n42; anti-rationalism, 126, 218;
morphological rationalism, 8
rationality, 50, 218; Enlightenment
rationality, 82, 107; established
through history, 79; integrated with
emotion, 44, 47, 49, 158, 162, 165;
rationalization of shamanism, 49,
133. *See also* mysticality of reason
Rawls, John, 136, 143, 150–51, 173,
176, 182, 184–85, 197–98, 205, 210,
212–13; overlapping consensus,
151, 173, 198, 204–205, 213; sense
of justice, 157–58, 165–66; veil of
ignorance, 140, 143, 184
Reading the Analects Today (*Lunyu jin
du* 論語今讀), 116, 120, 210–11
relationism, 12, 42, 133, 135, 161–66
passim, 202–208 *passim*, 213–14
relativism, 14, 16, 40–41, 78, 83, 173,
188–90
Record of Ritual (*Liji* 禮記), 29, 158,
162, 179, 208, 242n17, 245n43
republicanism, 3, 192, 198
rights (individual), 32, 42, 55–56,
136, 140–42, 167, 169, 183, 193,
196–212 *passim*, 204–205; women's
rights, 148, 189–90, 202, 204
ritual education (lijiao 禮教), 156, 211
Rousseau, Jean-Jacques, 157, 183–84,
215

rule by people, 162–63, 199, 206
rule by virtue, 31, 201
rule of (through) ritual, 31, 162
rule of law, 162–63, 185, 198–99, 201, 206, 211
Russell, Bertrand, 125
Ryle, Gilbert, 59–60

Sanzi jing 三字經. See *Three Character Classic*
Sartre, Jean-Paul, 180–81
Scanlon, T. M., 5
Schmitt, Carl, 214, 216
Searle, John, 82
sedimentation, 22–25, 44–46, 72, 77–78, 86, 92–93, 95, 99–100, 111, 153, 173, 188, 192, 207
shamanism, 26, 30, 39, 48–49, 110, 133, 154, 174, 179, 211, 216, 234n6
shamanistic-historical tradition, 49, 64, 98, 104, 114, 161, 234n6
Shangshu 尚書. See *Book of Documents*
slavery, 13–14, 132, 167; abolition of, 198
Slote, Michael, 8, 90
Smith, Adam, 163, 166, 177
sociobiology, 4, 29–30, 61, 166, 182
solidification of reason (*lixing ningju* 理性凝聚), 122, 170–71, 174, 176, 179, 188, 191, 195
Strauss, Leo, 214
subjectality (*zhutixing* 主體性), 61, 113, 117, 230n5, 240n47
suicide, 16, 142, 169, 202–203, 215
Sunzi 孫子, 139
supreme goodness (highest good) (*zhi shan* 至善), 37, 64, 108, 152, 185, 191–93
surrogate pregnancy, 128, 142, 194

Taliban, 139, 188, 200
Tan Sitong 譚嗣同, 35, 43, 63

techno-social substance, 122, 195, 242n13
theory of two morals, 56, 66, 83–89 *passim*, 112, 119–20, 163, 201–202, 207–208, 212, 226n35. *See also* modern social morals, traditional religious morals
Thing-in-itself, 97–98, 102, 196
Three Character Classic (*Sanzi jing* 三字經), 32, 43, 193, 196, 200, 206
tian 天. *See* heaven
Tillich, Paul, 52, 236n26. *See also* ultimate concern
Tocqueville, Alexis de, 214
totality of humankind, 17–18, 37, 66, 77, 79, 109, 167, 183, 190, 203, 208–209
traditional religious morals, 37, 52, 56, 65–66, 84, 86, 89, 113, 134, 152, 160–61, 163, 192–97 *passim*, 200–201, 205–210, 212, 216, 226n35, 228n44
transcendence, 57, 101, 114, 165, 183, 192, 238n37; transcendent, 10, 50, 52, 65, 75, 83, 85, 87, 96–98, 174, 236n30; immanent transcendence, 96, 213
transcendental, 87, 96, 143, 184–85; transcendental illusions, 84, 96, 114, 144, 233n4, 236n23; transcendental self, 135, 203, 216
transformative creation (*zhuanhuanxing chuangzao* 轉化性創造), 29–30, 42, 210, 212, 218
transforming consciousness to become wisdom (*zhuan shi cheng zhi* 轉識成智), 37
transforming the people through virtue (education) (*yi de hua min* 以德化民), 152, 201
trolley car problem, 3, 24, 136, 138
two-world outlook, 51–52, 96–97, 101, 121

262 | Index

ultimate concern, 52–53, 85, 87, 199, 216, 236n26

utilitarianism, 3, 24, 67, 89, 113, 129, 135–40, 147, 150–51, 176, 178–79, 193, 212

value neutrality, 132, 155, 189, 197–204

veil of ignorance. *See under* Rawls

virtue ethics, 3–4, 42, 44, 52, 67, 89, 95, 113, 135, 152, 157–58, 165, 198, 202, 212

Wang Guowei 王國維, 21, 101

Wang Yangming 王陽明, 7, 35, 61–62, 65, 68–69, 72, 92, 100, 103, 105, 239n42

Wittgenstein, Ludwig, 12, 21–22, 98, 127, 178

xue 學. *See* learning

Xunzi 荀子, 4, 34–37, 49–50, 59, 61–66, 88, 101, 103, 130, 153–57, 159, 177–78, 186

Yan Fu 嚴復, 55

Yijing 易經. See *Book of Changes*

zhi de zhijue 智的直覺. *See* intellectual intuition

Zhongyong 中庸, 36, 70, 156, 227n37, 245n40

Zhu Xi 朱熹, 7, 35, 62–64, 72, 97–98, 100

Zhuangzi 莊子, 194, 215